Leadership from the Margins

Leadership from the Margins

Women and Civil Society Organizations in Argentina, Chile, and El Salvador

SERENA COSGROVE

RUTGERS UNIVERSITY PRESS

NEW BRUNSWICK, NEW JERSEY, AND LONDON

LIBRARY OF CONGRESS CATALOGING-IN-PUBLICATION DATA

Cosgrove, Serena, 1963–
    Leadership from the margins : women and civil society organizations in
Argentina, Chile, and El Salvador / Serena Cosgrove.
        p. cm.
    Includes bibliographical references and index.
    ISBN 978-0-8135-4799-2 (hbk. : alk. paper) — ISBN 978-0-8135-4800-5
(pbk. : alk. paper)
     1. Women—Political activity—Latin America.   2. Leadership in women—
Latin America.   3. Women in development—Latin America.   4. Civil society—
Latin America.   5. Social movements—Latin America.   I. Title.
    HQ1236.5.L37C67 2010
    305.42098—dc22   2009048293

A British Cataloging-in-Publication record for this book is available
from the British Library.

Copyright © 2010 by Serena Cosgrove

Visit our Web site: http://rutgerspress.rutgers.edu

Manufactured in the United States of America

This book is dedicated to the women of Latin America who are transforming their communities, countries, and continent—sometimes under great risk and often at immense sacrifice. Thank you for inspiring with your example. Your contributions are creating a more equitable and sustainable Latin America.

CONTENTS

Acknowledgments   ix

1 Women and Civil Society Leadership in Latin America   1

2 The Emergence of Civil Society in Argentina, Chile,
       and El Salvador   42

3 Argentina   90

4 Chile   117

5 El Salvador   155

6 Policy Implications of Women's Civil Society Leadership
       in Latin America   185

Appendix: Organizations of Interviewees   199

Notes   203

Bibliography   211

Index   227

ACKNOWLEDGMENTS

This book would not have come to fruition if not for the candid feedback, encouragement, and persistence of Adi Hovav and Leslie Mitchner, my editors at Rutgers University Press. Both Adi and Leslie, as well as the entire Rutgers University Press team, were professional and thorough in their commitment to this project. I would also like to express my gratitude to the multiple anonymous reviewers who provided insights and suggestions for improving the text. This unsung assistance has been vital to the project, and I am most grateful for their feedback. I, however, take full responsibility for any errors that may still be found in these pages. All translations from Spanish—including references cited and interviews—are the author's.

Throughout the research and writing of this book, a global community of academics, development practitioners, and activists has provided assistance, including recommending leaders for interview, providing insights into civil society organizing, and sharing materials, articles, and research on women and civil society. In El Salvador, I would especially like to thank Morena Herrera, Blanca Mirna Benavides, and Rosibel Flores, three Salvadoran civil society leaders and feminist scholars who were major contributors to the FUNDE book on the Salvadoran women's movement. In Chile, I would like to extend my appreciation to Rita Moya, Luisa (Ximena) Curín, Pati Jara, Wladimir Painemal, and América Millaray Painemal for their commitment to engaged, scholarly work about the contributions of Mapuche women. In Argentina, I would like to acknowledge María de la Paz Zapiola for her invaluable diligence as my research assistant and for translating the book into Spanish; her hard work, contributions, and research were vital to the completion of this book from start to finish. I also extend my appreciation to María Laura Schiffrin for her friendship, example, and commitment to the empowerment of Argentine women.

And in Bariloche, I will always be grateful for the friendship of Amalia Lemos and Audry and Edward Shaw; together we formed a mutual support group that served each of us to move forward on life goals and projects. Over the course of the months of our weekly meetings, I completed much of the ethnographic chapter about Argentina. I am grateful to Carlota Irina (Lotti) Silber, Victoria Sanford, Kelley Ready, and Julie Shayne for their friendship, support, and research about gender and Latin America. To my readers, I could not be more enthusiastic about the important contributions of these scholars. If you are looking for additional reading, I recommend their research and publications (see the bibliography).

I would also like to thank AVINA for encouraging me to carry out the research for this book as well as showing interest in its conclusions. To the AVINA team, an affectionate thank you for all the conversations about the contributions of women to sustainable development in Latin America. To the mentors and supervisors I had in the course of this research—Peter Cleaves, Germán Castellanos, Sean McKaughan, and Maria Cavalcanti— without your understanding and support, this book would have taken many more years than it did. And I owe a debt of gratitude to the Knowledge Management team at AVINA—María Eugenia Rodríguez and Valeria Freylejer. Not only did you consider this book a valuable contribution, but you also covered for me when I was away carrying out interviews.

Seattle University, my alma mater and current employer, has also played a significant role. An academic community is crucial for the writing endeavor. I am thankful to the following people: historians David Madsen and Marc McLeod for insights about how to write history; Theresa Earenfight for inviting me to give a universitywide presentation about my book (which compelled me to complete drafts of all the ethnographic chapters); Bob Novak at the Lemieux Library for helping me find journal articles, books, and databases for this research; Jodi Kelly for continuing to mentor me years after the statute of limitations ended; and Steve Sundborg SJ who understands that today a university—be it in southern Chile or in the northwest corner of the United States—must be engaged in the world, and Father Steve is making this happen at Seattle University.

My family has provided me with unstinting encouragement for this project. To my *comadre* and best friend, Marlene Kenney, I am grateful for your friendship and how you remind me to keep perspective even in the densest of moments. To my daughters—Meme and Alex—my gratitude for accompanying me on research trips and interviews, as well as for forgiving me certain bouts of distraction as I worked to finish this manuscript. I will always be grateful to my sister, Shady Cosgrove: thank you for your editing skills, generosity with your time, and compassion. While I worked on this book, you wrote three novels. May they become best-sellers. To my sister and brother, parents, and in-laws—Lucas, Grace, Irene, Jim, Bonnie, and Conrad—I am most grateful for your faith that this project would eventually manifest in a published book.

And for your patience and support, I thank my husband, Marty Bosworth. Not only do you share my commitment to getting out the message that women are transforming the world, but you also believe change starts at home: a very important quality in a man whose wife is working full time and writing a book.

This volume builds on twenty years of research in Latin America. Both the Inter-American Foundation and the Fulbright Program provided crucial support for my research in El Salvador in the mid-1990s. Additionally, thank you to all the women and men who have taken time from their commitments to talk to me about the contributions of women civil society leaders in Latin America. After so many years, I am sure that I have failed to include all the names of people who provided much-needed assistance. This is not due to a lack of gratitude but rather to a lack of neurons on my part.

Leadership from the Margins

1

Women and Civil Society Leadership in Latin America

I argue with my *compañeros*, thank God, as one equal to another. If I have to swear, I swear. If I have to act feminine, I do it. And if I have to fight, I fight, never forgetting that I am a woman.

—Magdalena Jamargo, Argentine Printers' Union

I didn't want to accept the position [of community president] because I am a woman and men are screwed up, they are macho . . . But I was always talking to them about the land, that we had to take our land back. Whatever happens, will happen, but we Mapuche have got to make ourselves heard so at least we won't be called sheep.

—Petronila Catrileo, President Lonko Juan Segundo Marileo, Pocuno, Chile

We women see ourselves . . . without political or ideological differences, rather women who come together for a problem that we share: struggling for space for women in politics.

—Virginia Magaña, President National Association of Salvadoran Councilwomen and Women Mayors, Santa Tecla, El Salvador

Traditionally men have benefited from gender hierarchies, occupying leadership positions across Latin American society, but a number of factors—political, economic, and historical—have aligned to expand leadership opportunities throughout the region in civil society organizations (CSOs) for women, especially women who have been marginalized by poverty, be it urban or rural, or by ethnicity. Many of these organizations—a number of which are led by women—are successfully achieving their goals and creating new hope for the disenfranchised and marginalized in Latin America. These women leaders are setting up child care centers, addressing domestic violence in their communities, organizing campaigns for safe neighborhoods, securing access to basic services for their families and communities, working to get children who have dropped out of school back into classes, improving public education in their countries, and calling on the state to implement much-needed environmental laws. Given the challenges the planet Earth and all its peoples face at this present historical juncture—war, terrorism, global warming, and increased exclusion of people for reasons of difference—this focus on women civil society leaders provides concrete examples of social change from margins created by gender discrimination, racism, poverty, and other forms of social exclusion. Women in Latin America are uniquely positioned to contribute solutions to the major problems threatening their societies because their culturally ascribed roles as caretakers in the home and in the community, as well as their activism and volunteerism during periods of economic and political crisis, mean they have often developed skills like networking, cooperation, and listening across difference.

This book brings attention to the power, courage, and commitment of women civil society leaders at the grassroots and national levels in Latin America through a close examination of their leadership experiences, achievements, and challenges in Argentina, Chile, and El Salvador—three countries that share a history of state violence and authoritarianism as well as vibrant civil societies in which women leaders have contributed significantly to democratization. This book shows how the Madres de Plaza de Mayo, a small group of primarily working- and middle-class Argentine mothers, became contributors to ending a dictatorship and achieving a return to democracy for Argentina by demanding that the government return their illegally detained, *disappeared* children alive. For Chile, I describe the successful efforts of a group of rural Mapuche women to create Rayen Voygue,[1] an independent, financially sustainable organization committed to preserving Mapuche crafts and weaving techniques in addition to empowering poor, rural women—Mapuche and Chilean alike—through income-generating strategies and consciousness raising. In the case of El Salvador—a country polarized, almost frozen, by political differences—I illustrate the achievements of one of the only pluralistic civil society organizations in the country, the National Association of

Salvadoran Councilwomen and Women Mayors (ANDRYSAS). ANDRYSAS brings women mayors and municipal council members together across the spectrum of political parties by providing them with technical training and gender empowerment workshops, in addition to promoting the development and implementation of gender policies at the municipal level throughout the country.

Due to gender inequalities throughout Latin America, women experience higher levels of poverty and discrimination than men (Craske 2003, 58). Yet, because of their roles in the family and their communities as mothers and caretakers, empowerment for women translates into improved economic conditions and well-being for them as well as their children and communities (UNICEF 2006).[2] For this reason, the United Nations, bilateral and multilateral aid agencies, international foundations, state agencies, and civil society organizations often focus on women, especially in the areas of education, health, and income generation. As regards these three areas, indicators demonstrate some improvement throughout Latin America for women, but "there is a gap between the expected goal and achievements related to broadening women's rights" (Valdés, Muñoz, and Donoso 2005, 16).

In the area of education, more girls than boys are attending school—primary through secondary—as well as graduating from college in Latin America (World Bank 2007). But these advances are threatened by the fact that in the face of economic crisis, families often encourage girls to drop out of school before boys due to the internalization of gender hierarchies that favor boys' education over girls'.

Regarding women's employment, all three countries experienced economic crises during the democratization processes of the eighties and nineties that had gendered consequences, putting the burden of family survival on the shoulders of women. "The crisis—and the structural adjustment policies that governments adopted to deal with it—hit the urban poor, especially women, very hard" (Jaquette 1994, 3). In Argentina, women remain underemployed due to the continued effects of the economic crisis and the subsequent devaluation of the peso in 2001; in Chile and El Salvador, however, women are entering the workforce in greater numbers (Valdés, Muñoz, and Donoso 2005, 33). Regardless of the country, Latin

American women tend to cluster in the informal and lowest paid sectors of the economy, such as the service sector and assembly work at home or in *maquilas* (assembly plants).

In terms of women's reproductive health, updated figures are not available for Argentina, but both Chile and El Salvador have shown advancement in indicators such as increases in women's access to birth control and live births to mothers over the age of twenty (43 percent and 46 percent, respectively), but this progress lies in stark contrast to the fact that each of these two countries has severe anti-abortion laws that punish women who seek abortions rather than address the conditions that compel women to seek abortions in the first place (Valdés, Muñoz, and Donoso 2005). Though Argentina's abortion laws are also conservative—only permitting abortions when pregnancies threaten the physical life of the mother—women who arrive at hospitals because of botched abortions are not arrested, as has happened in Chile and El Salvador (Hitt 2006).

Women still lag behind men in areas such as income, management opportunities, and political representation even though many Latin American governments have made efforts to tackle inequalities (Valdés, Muñoz, and Donoso 2005). In Greater Buenos Aires, Argentina, women's average income in formal-sector, urban employment is only 59 percent of that earned by men: for every dollar a man earns, a woman earns fifty-nine cents. In Chile and El Salvador, the levels are higher in urban formal sector jobs: 77 percent and 87 percent respectively (Valdés, Muñoz, and Donoso 2005, 32). None of these figures, however, apply to the informal sector— where primarily women generate income as street sellers, market stall vendors, and door-to-door saleswomen—nor to the agricultural sector, where women often perform significant yet underpaid or unpaid work in planting and harvesting. Access to political representation is an absorbing topic given the three countries under study. The president of Chile from 2006 to 2010, Michelle Bachelet, is a woman representing the multiparty coalition the Concertación. In 2007 Cristina Kirschner won the presidential elections in Argentina under the Peronist party. These gains aside, women's participation in elected positions remains woefully lower than men's. Argentina has achieved 32 percent parity, Chile 27 percent, and El Salvador 18 percent. Chile shows declining levels of parity between the genders at the national level, but all three countries have slowly increasing

t the local level (Valdés, Muñoz,
de Sociología y Ciencias Políticas,
on Cañas 2009, 2).

n tangible and intangible ways.
asure, as in the case of wages.
ing inequalities directly through
more broadly through legislation
vancement in these areas can be
reed-upon indicators such as the
itment (see Valdés, Muñoz, and
idden aspects of the discrimina-
tion that women face, such as having to work a double day—income generation and family responsibilities—or a triple day—income generation,
family responsibilities, and community activism. This *triple burden* (Craske
2003, 67) means that women from poor communities are often working
around the clock to guarantee their families' survival.

Women still suffer discrimination in the areas of reproductive health
and their vulnerability to gender-based violence, especially domestic violence. In the past decades, health ministries and women's movements
throughout Latin America have achieved advances in opening access to
birth control and preventative information about women's health, but
estimates indicate that over 3.8 million Latin American women seek
unsafe abortions every year, over 4,000 of whom die (World Health Organization 2007). Poor women suffer disproportionately in comparison to
middle-class or elite women because they cannot afford private clinics or
trips to countries that offer legalized abortion. Because abortion is a divi-
sive political issue, few Latin American governments confront the issue
due to the potential backlash from conservatives. Mala Htun, a political
scientist, summarizes the situation in the region: "Since middle-class
women generally have access to safe abortions in private clinics, many see
little reason to press for liberalization of abortion laws. It is primarily poor
women who suffer the consequences of clandestine abortions" (Htun
2003, 6). Many women face violence at home at the hands of their partners. An estimated 20–50 percent of Latin American women cope with
domestic violence (Morrison, Ellsberg, and Bott 2004, 3), a cross-cutting
phenomenon that affects women irrespective of their social class, race,

ethnicity, or religion. Economic and political crises often create additional stress and can exacerbate levels of violence at home. Many countries do not track incidences of domestic violence, making it difficult to quantify the phenomenon in individual countries. In Argentina, more safe houses are needed, as existing houses for battered women and children are always at full capacity (Ynoub 1998).

Broad-based women's movements and regional meetings throughout Latin America as well as international campaigns—such as the UN-sponsored Women's Decade (1975–1985), the Fourth World Conference on Women in Beijing (1995), and international pressure to fulfill commitments to improving indicators of women's equality—have attained great advances in bringing attention to the importance of addressing women's inequality, but long-term change depends on legislation, its implementation, and the transformation of commonly held stereotypes about women's roles in society. From society to society, members are socialized to expect certain kinds of behavior from men and women. Though these *gendered* expectations differ from group to group, equality between men and women, as well as a celebration of gender differences, remain elusive in many Latin American contexts. Transforming how women are treated, perceived, and included requires an ongoing commitment—by governments, civil society groups, and individual citizens—in order to amend unfair laws, guaranteeing their implementation, and demanding programs and services to address the gender-based discrimination and violence that women face. However, this kind of transformation also requires the deeper work of cultural change—shifting societal perceptions, stereotypes, habits, and customs—which occurs when ample sectors of society see women as proactive citizens gaining equal treatment.

Women's participation in the leadership of civil society organizations is crucial for changing society's views about gender roles: example after example of proactive women making a difference in their communities and countries facilitates the emergence of new social constructions for what it means to be Latin American women. Today Latin American women are challenging gender stereotypes as they cope with more and more responsibility at home and in their communities by taking on leadership roles in civil society organizations, from self-help groups to nationwide nongovernmental organizations (NGOs). Civil society—the wide spectrum of organizations, associations, networks, and social movements outside of direct state control—has been expanding in Latin America in response to economic crisis, authoritarian or undemocratic conditions, discrimination, neoliberal structural adjustments slashing state spending, corruption, environmental degradation, and other issues.[3] Civil society organizations, ranging from informal community associations to formal NGOs, are making significant contributions in determining the direction of development priorities in Latin America.

Civil society is an arena where women's participation equals or surpasses that of men throughout Latin America (see Craske 2003; Jaquette 1994; Jelin 1990; Stephen 1995, 1997; and Waylen 1994). Anthropologist Lynn Stephen summarizes the research on this issue: "Women are the backbone of a wide range of social movements in Latin America, including rural and urban movements for improved living conditions, student movements, feminist movements, and movements for human rights, land reclamations, relatives of the disappeared, labor unions, abortion and reproductive rights, democratization of political systems, and more" (1995, 807). Even at the leadership level, women are achieving greater representation in civil society organizations, taking advantage of leadership opportunities, and making progress toward parity with men.[4] Many of these organizations comprise vital women's movements that also provide women with significant civil society and transnational leadership experiences through participation in Latin American women's and feminist conferences and meetings. A number of factors contribute to this phenomenon. Because caretaking is a culturally ascribed characteristic of women in many Latin American contexts, women able to get an education often choose such professions as social work, nursing, and education, and they choose to work in CSOs providing health services, welfare programming, and technical assistance. Elite women have historically played leadership roles in charitable activities and organizations because these activities were seen as a socially acceptable extension of their caretaking roles in the home. As I describe in depth in the following chapter, documentation of the activism of working-class and poor women in unions, community and ethnic associations, and church-related volunteerism dates back to the 1800s in Chile and Argentina and to the early 1900s in El Salvador. A number of historians, including José Bengoa, Inga Clendinnen,

Donna Guy, Margaret Power, Aldo Lauria-Santiago, Maxine Molyneux, and Gabriel Salazar, depict how women and other disenfranchised groups have formed organizations advocating for social rights and women's equality: access to health and housing, parental rights for mothers, civil rights within the marriage contract, the right to vote, equality in education, and ending domestic violence.

Beyond historical and cultural factors, political and economic crises over the past decades have also propelled women—especially from working-class and marginalized sectors—into leadership positions. The survival of their families and communities depended on their organizing skills when confronted with widespread unemployment and cuts to state spending for housing, health, basic food subsidies, and other services. Authoritarian regimes—characterized by human rights abuses and disregard for basic democratic rights—forced many women to take action by joining organizations demanding the release of illegally detained relatives, respect for human rights, and a return to democracy.

This book focuses on women's leadership experiences in civil society organizations in the two Southern Cone countries of Argentina and Chile and the Central American country of El Salvador. Country selection depended on a number of different yet interrelated factors. First, I wanted to include countries from both Central and South America. I was not able to include the Caribbean in my selection due to lack of resources, but I do include insights about women's leadership from Dame Nita Barrow, a preeminent woman leader from the West Indies, in the discussion about what it means to be a leader. Second, funding for research as well as my professional obligations facilitated frequent travel and even extended stays to the three selected countries. For this kind of research, it is essential to build relationships of trust with civil society networks, experts, and women leaders themselves, and this requires commitment over time. Furthermore, these three countries have similarities and differences that generate compelling comparisons, evoking reflection on the factors that inform women's civil society leadership. They share histories of authoritarian regimes that harshly repressed civil society organizations: the Argentine "dirty war" from 1976 to 1983, the dictatorship of General Augusto Pinochet in Chile from 1973 to 1990, and the Salvadoran civil war from 1980 to 1992. And, in all three countries, civil society leaders, especially women, were major contributors in either returning their countries to more democratic conditions or in democracy building after the conflict. Interviews with these women, as well as with those who have become activists in recent years, facilitate an understanding of just how much women's organizing and participation has contributed to democratization and the ongoing struggle for the expansion of social, cultural, economic, and political rights in Latin America. In all three countries, women have gained increased access to the state, which I examine in greater detail in the Chilean and Salvadoran chapters. Argentina, Chile, and El Salvador have much in common concerning women and civil society organizing, but they also have differences such as a long history of civil society leadership by women in Argentina, the active involvement of indigenous women leaders in Chilean civil society, and the cross-class pollination that informed civil society development in El Salvador.

Of the three countries under study, Chile has the highest standard of living followed by Argentina; El Salvador has the greatest poverty. Argentina is the largest in terms of territory, with over one million square miles; Chile is about a third the size of Argentina; and El Salvador is a small country of roughly 8,000 square miles, making it the smallest yet most densely populated country in continental Latin America. El Salvador has 825 inhabitants per square mile, while Argentina has thirty-seven and Chile fifty-five. Size and population density are important issues for El Salvador, as these factors have aggravated tensions about land tenure, ownership, and use past to present.

Theoretical Framework

This book builds on a vibrant scholarship within Latin American studies, women's studies, and the social sciences that analyzes specific realities from the perspective of those who have been marginalized, those whose voices are often not heard in official discourses. Since the seventies, many feminist anthropologists and sociologists from throughout the Americas have dedicated their research to understanding how women experience particular events differently from men. For instance, if communities expect women will provide drinking water for their families, then a project for building a well close to the community will lessen women's work, but if the opposite occurs, women may find themselves walking additional distances to carry water home. It is essential to analyze women's and men's activities, responsibilities, and roles before implementing development projects. Gender influences how women and men are socialized to perform certain roles in the family and society; these roles generate different points from which they interact with the social forces around them. Women's particular experiences, as well as how politics, economic policies, and civil strife have different repercussions for them than for men, have been the topics of extensive research (see, e.g., Babb 1993; Bose and Acosta-Belen 1995; Jelin 1990; Rodríguez 1996; Safa 1995; Silber 2004; Stephen 1995, 1997). The work of these social scientists has shown that women often play unrecognized but central roles in relation to community development; the health, safety, and welfare of their families; and the generation of income for their families; as well as documenting women's more visible roles in the struggle for more responsive, democratic governments or attention to gender-related issues. Different explanatory models have been developed to describe women's civil society participation and leadership in Latin America, including strategic gender interests versus practical gender interests (Molyneux 1985, 232–233), the triple workload of women (Craske 2003, 67), the feminist/feminine dichotomy between feminist organizations and women's organizing, and the public/private dichotomy in which women's protagonist role at home is highlighted against the backdrop of discrimination in the public sphere (Stephen 1995, 1997). Throughout the ethnographic chapters and conclusion of this book, I build on these models, showing how women's civil society leadership in Argentina, Chile, and El Salvador requires a continual reworking of how we understand women's leadership and activism. The explanatory scope of theoretical frameworks or models is always limited by the gray areas and contradictions they generate when applied to specific groups, communities, or individuals.

Each of the four models mentioned has contributed significantly to understanding the roles of women in Latin America, yet each one has raised new questions that could not be answered by the model itself, requiring new research, analysis, and explanations. Molyneux's (1985) use of the analytical categories of strategic and practical gender interests facilitated a more nuanced understanding of the range of women's activism. Nonetheless, this view comes up short in its analytical power because what may begin as a practical gender need, such as participating in a communal kitchen, can often lead to the emergence of strategic gender issues when women working together on a common practical issue start reflecting together on gender roles, discrimination, domestic violence, or the gendered division of labor. Even the most practical of gender issues can become strategic: "the simplest act of organizing, regardless of its content or intent, often has the result of disrupting domestic routines and divisions of labor" (Stephen 1997, 271). In addition, basic needs are not just informed by survival but also by the social constructions of identity and power relations (Lind 1992, 137), thereby situating them as simultaneously practical and strategic issues. In this book, many of the women leaders interviewed have either integrated strategic and practical interests in their work or started out focusing on a practical interest that ultimately led them to question strategic interests. A prime example of this is how the vision of the Salvadoran organization of mothers of the disappeared, CO-MADRES, "has expanded to embrace a much wider definition of human rights, one that incorporates the rights of women" (Stephen 1995, 817).

Women's triple workday is a useful analytical tool for bringing attention to how hard women are working, although it divides women's activities into separate categories. Many Latin American women carry out their responsibilities simultaneously or in an interspersed manner, such as taking care of children while selling at the market or participating in income-generating activities as part of a community development project. Many of the women interviewed for this book refer to the multilayered, simultaneous, and dense set of activities they carry out on a daily basis.

The debate on whether or not Latin American women activists are feminist (self-identifying as feminists and consciously challenging gender inequalities) or simply working on issues that affect women raised the issue of who gets to apply the definition. Do northern or elite feminists get to determine whether Latin American women are feminists? Or do Latin American women get to make this decision? The supposition that the scholar is able to determine what is a feminist action and what is a women-related action in other women's activism is culturally insensitive if not racist. This reflection did, however, contribute to raising awareness among northern feminists about the importance of not imposing the mind-sets or concepts of U.S., white, middle-class feminism on women from different cultures and places, because ultimately it is up to Latin American women to determine whether or not they want to call themselves feminists and to consider their work as feminist in nature. Furthermore, this whole debate begs the question of whether it is ultimately useful or not to use the feminist category as determinant of whether or not a woman's activism challenges oppressive gender roles. Sometimes a simple action such as attending a workshop may challenge a gender stereotype. The lines are often blurry between resistance and accommodation to gender roles (Stephen 1995, 807); and the outcomes of civil society participation can lead to consciousness-raising around gender issues whether or not the action was feminist from the outset. Some of the women interviewed for this book self-identify as feminists and some do not. Some identify with grassroots forms of women's organizing and eschew the feminist label. Others have long trajectories as feminists in the feminist movement within their countries. Others see themselves as working with men and women on particular issues, not solely with women. This research attempts to allow the voices and commitments of women leaders from a spectrum of civil society organizations to describe their actions, their understandings of the contribution of their work, and how they self-identify themselves—not how the researcher identifies them.

And finally, the private-public dichotomy was initially a useful rubric for recognizing women's contributions in societies where gender hierarchies restrict women's actions outside of the home; it brought attention to the important contribution and power of women as caretakers and leaders within the family and household as compared to the public leadership of men in the community and beyond. At a time when women's contributions were invisible, this model facilitated seeing women. However, as with most dichotomies, the limitations of the public/private model become apparent, especially in the Latin American context where women's activism, contributions, and even domestic roles have appeared in the public sphere from the 1800s to the present day. From the organizing of feminist anarchists in late nineteenth-century Buenos Aires to the mothers and relatives of the disappeared in all three countries under study in the late twentieth century, women's private and public roles and responsibilities have always been present in public settings. Lynn Stephen articulates how women's mothering is not just a private or domestic action: "Women's presence within a political movement or confrontation in what is culturally labeled a public space makes visible the fact that mothering has always been both public and private" (1997, 273).

The work of feminist social scientists in Latin America has generated descriptive ethnographies, broad-based studies, and explanatory models to help describe what they have observed. I frequently refer to these works as I unpack the interviews and research for this project. Nonetheless, the study of women and leadership in civil society organizations in Latin America requires constantly problematizing and updating explanatory models and research categories under investigation because "concepts are crucial . . . they determine the questions one asks and the answers one is likely to get" (Schamis 1991, 207). It is important to orient theoretical frameworks around the realities emerging from the analysis of research participants' stories. Theorizing about how women become leaders in Latin American civil society organizations "ha[s] to grow out of historically and specifically grounded instances of mobilization and must be mediated by the voices and interpretations of those who are doing the acting" (Stephen 1997, 22). For instance, *women*, *leader*, and *civil society* have to be sufficiently defined and located in particular circumstances so as to avoid such pitfalls as conflating very different kinds of people into overly simplified categories (what Stephen calls "homogenizing difference" [21]), obfuscating arguments with poorly defined terms, and using terms whose usage contributes to the maintenance of oppressive stereotypes.

Gender

As the interviews for this research demonstrate, women are challenging gender stereotypes as they cope with increased responsibility at home, in their communities, and in the other spheres where they are active, such as local associations, formal organizations, and social movements. Gender—akin to other social constructs of difference—is defined as the culturally ascribed roles for what it means to be a woman and a man in particular contexts. In many cultures, difference—such as gender, race, or ethnicity—is used to marginalize certain groups, excluding them from opportunities and spaces to exercise power and decision making. Caroline Moser, international development gender expert, defines gender as "the social relationship between men and women, in which women have been systematically subordinated" (1993, 3). Lorber argues that gender "establishes patterns of expectations for individuals, orders the social processes of everyday life, is built into the major social organizations of society, such as the economy, ideology, the family, and politics, and is also an entity in and of itself" (1994, 1). As an analytical tool, a *gender perspective* encourages comprehension of a given social reality by allowing us to look at the situation from different points of view. Since gender defines appropriate masculine and feminine behavior, using a gender perspective facilitates understanding how women and men experience particular realities in different ways, be it at an individual, family, community, or institutional level. In patriarchal cultures, where women are subordinated to men, examining social reality from the female perspective allows the observer to trace how women are affected by this difference, how they accommodate it, and how they resist it. In the case of leadership, men and women are socialized differently regarding how they should use power. Gender hierarchies—defined as "situation[s] where social power and control over labor, resources, and products are associated with masculinity" (Gailey 1988, 32)—and structures of subordination translate into men having more access to formal positions of power than women. Gender hierarchies in patriarchal societies tend to inhibit women's access to public leadership roles and inform the kinds of leaders women will be if they do manage to become leaders (Freeman, Bourque, and Shelton 2001, 8–11).

Obviously, gender is not the sole factor that explains differences between the experiences of certain women and men because their lives—especially their leadership styles, experiences, and opportunities—are not determined just by gender roles. Rather, actions and choices are informed by gender and other factors such as life events and circumstances, race, ethnicity, education, sexual orientation, social class, and political activism. Because the category of "women" refers to so many different kinds of human beings from an immense diversity of cultural, ethnic, religious, and social class backgrounds even within Latin America, researchers need to be cognizant of these differences and not make claims that all women face the same challenges. Attention must be paid to the differences among women. Nonetheless, because discrimination against women remains so pervasive and women's organizing happens across national, cultural, and geographical borders, the conceptual rubric of "women" can still be used as long as the differences between women are identified. This view is corroborated by Chilean feminist Patricia Chuchryk in her discussion of the use of the term: "Despite the fact that women of different social classes experience oppression in different ways, they are all subject to the same structures of patriarchal domination . . . suffer(ing) from domestic violence, economic dependence, sexual aggression, discrimination in the work place, lack of reproductive control, and clandestine abortion" (1994, 82).

Throughout this book women leaders share their challenges, goals, and work, facilitating insight into the complexities of how they negotiate the intersection between their cultural understandings of gender with the world they are trying to transform. Lynn Stephen describes the intersection in the following way: "In many cases women who inhabit these positions have found ways of coping, of redefining marginality, of struggling and resisting, of encountering joy and happiness in human relations" (Stephen 1997, 6). For some women activists, the negotiation translates as "their daily battle to persuade their husbands to allow them to participate in public activities" (Arizpe 1990, xix); it also means simultaneously juggling multiple roles as mothers, income earners, and volunteers/activists in civil society organizations.

Civil Society

Civil society is a multifaceted, historically charged concept referring to a broad range of citizen activities outside of direct state control. The concept has become popular in international development circles, having reemerged after the collapse of communism in Eastern Europe and Russia and the return to democracy in many countries in Latin America (McIlwaine 1998a, 415). Civil society, like other concepts mentioned in this introduction, has to be linked to concrete realities so as not to become a blurry concept with shifting definitions and multiple usages. Civil society "is not separated and ideal; it must exist in the real world. It must be located in time and space" (Alexander 2006, 3); otherwise, it is just a popular term appropriated by different, ideological agendas for contradictory ends. Even though the term "civil society" is used by a variety of interests to justify different actions—from structural adjustment policies to empowerment and democratization discourses—I argue that as long as the concept is defined and located in particular places and times, it remains a useful conceptual rubric because it describes the contributions of an influential sector of society, especially throughout Latin America. As Edwards posits, "recognizing that civil society is contested territory—in both theory and reality—is the first step in rescuing a potentially powerful set of ideas from the conceptual confusion that threatens to submerge them" (2004, vii).

Theorists agree that civil society refers to organizations and social movements outside of direct state control, such as unions, community associations, voluntary associations, NGOs, and self-help groups (Alexander 2006; Edwards 2004; Foley and Edwards 1996; McIlwaine 1998a, 1998b; Mitlin 2000; Salamon 1994; and Salamon et al. 2004). According to most theorists, the sphere of civil action represented by the term has great importance to democratization throughout the world because it creates an associational space in which citizens can build coalitions, collaborate on projects or causes, and organize to achieve change on issues of importance to them. Foley and Edwards (1996, 38) write, "Civil society . . . has come to be seen as an essential ingredient in both democratization and the health of established democracies." It is the purpose, potential, and role of this civil sphere, as Alexander (2006) calls it, that causes so much discussion among politicians, theorists, activists, and development practitioners who frequently use the concept to promote radically different programs, policies, and agendas, from the support of social movements critical of their governments to the withdrawal of support for government spending on social programming. To understand how the term has come to be used to justify a plethora of different agendas, its emergence as a concept must be traced.

The roots of civil society can be found in Aristotle's writings. His "interpretation of the ancient Greek *polis* as the 'association of associations,' founded on bonds of friendship and religious loyalty to the homeland" was a precursor to Enlightenment and Industrial Age philosophers who began to use the term to theorize the role of the citizen and citizen groups in the emergence of different forms of government and economic systems (Hodgkinson and Foley 2003, ix). Enlightenment philosophers took this current of thought in the direction of perceiving civil society as protection against state incursion into the realm of individual rights and freedoms (Edwards 2004, 7). During the industrial revolution, the emerging division of labor, the growing complexity of production processes, and a modern interpretation of justice led Adam Ferguson, Scottish political philosopher, and Thomas Paine, American revolutionary thinker, to write about the responsibility of citizens to keep their governments democratic. Yet there remained a contingent of theorists who worried that civil associations or fractions could manipulate politics to their own ends. James Madison described the important role of government to keep factions and interest groups from determining what was best for the whole polity when he wrote to the people of New York State in 1787: "Among the numerous advantages promised by a well constructed Union, none deserve to be more accurately developed than its tendency to break and control the violence of faction" (Madison 2003, 70).

Karl Marx, on the other hand, proffered a different interpretation of civil society in which civil associations perpetuate unjust capitalist relations; he persuasively argued that the capitalist system depends on the support of the citizenry: "Where the political state has attained to its full development, man leads, not only in thought, in consciousness, but in *reality*, in *life*, a double existence—celestial and terrestrial. He lives in the *political community*, where he regards himself as a *communal being*, and in *civil society* where he acts simply as a private individual, treats other men as means, degrades himself to the role of a mere means, and becomes the plaything of alien powers" (Marx 2003, 103). In this critique of capitalism, Marx described civil society as the social organizations that sustain the status quo. Antonio Gramsci, Italian revolutionary and political thinker, recognized civil society's role in perpetuating the status quo, but his work served to bring attention to the civil society's revolutionary potential: "The massive structures of the modern democracies, both as state organizations, and as complexes of associations in civil society, constitute for the art of politics as it were the 'trenches' and the permanent fortifications of the front in the war of position" (Gramsci 2000, 233). Thus civil society can be interpreted as a site for challenging and maintaining the status quo or, to use Gramscian terms, counterhegemonic and hegemonic action respectively (Hodgkinson and Foley 2003, xix).

The present-day interpretation of civil society as a sector of society that nurtures democratic conditions owes much of its inspiration to Alexis de Tocqueville, who visited the United States in the early part of the nineteenth century and was impressed with its strong culture of voluntary associations and active citizenry (Hodgkinson and Foley 2003, xxi). De Tocqueville's enthusiastic endorsement of associational life described its contributions to a strong and enduring democracy. He wrote, "If men are to remain civilized or become so, the art of associating together must grow and improve in the same ratio in which the equality of condition is increased" (Salamon et al. 2004, 122).

The work of these philosophers and political theorists formed the basis for the two primary interpretations of civil society in usage today. From the writings of de Tocqueville a definition of civil society emerged that focused on the important contribution of citizen groups to democracy. This approach is often referred to as the *liberal approach* to understanding civil society and argues that democratic culture and habits emerge from participation and belonging to associations. "This approach puts special emphasis on the ability of associational life in general and the habits of association in particular to foster patterns of civility in the actions of citizens in a democratic polity" (Edwards and Foley 1996, 39). Often this approach is used to justify citizen groups and organizations assuming increased responsibilities to address inequalities or problems in society as seen in the United States in the wake of cuts to state spending and throughout the developing world in response to structural adjustment policies.

The second approach to civil society has its roots in the work of early American revolutionaries and in Gramscian thought as well. This *revolutionary approach* envisions civil society as separate from the state and able to challenge authoritarian regimes (Foley and Edwards 1996, 39). The purpose of civil society is to resist undemocratic authoritarian regimes, demand fulfillment of state promises, and hold the government accountable to its promises. This interpretation represents much of the action of leftist activists and the organizations and movements in which they participate. "Civil society in this sense means 'people power' writ large," argues Edwards, because "the role of NGOs and social movements in mobilizing opposition to authoritarian rule and supporting progress towards multi-party elections has been well documented in Africa, eastern Europe and Latin America" (2004, 15).

Consideration of both the liberal and the revolutionary approaches are necessary to understanding the roles assigned to civil society organizations, especially in Latin America, by governments, other development stakeholders, and social movements. Both approaches can lead to changes being made in government by civil society through the use of their power or civil forces, though in the case of the liberal approach change means strengthening democratic elements in the government, whereas within the revolutionary approach change can mean complete social transformation and the overthrow of the unjust, authoritarian state. Both approaches can use uncivil forces, leading to the use of power in negative and antidemocratic ways. When death squads and paramilitary groups formed in El Salvador during the 1980s to protect the interests of large landowners or state interests, they violated principles of justice and democracy. Even de Tocqueville warned against the impact that uncivil civil society groups could achieve under certain circumstances. He "worried [that] dissidents can league together to 'form something like a separate nation within the nation and a government within the government'" (Foley and Edwards 1996, 45). In the case of the revolutionary potential of the civil society, when a radical political organization from the left takes up arms, it chooses an uncivil path, using violence to promote its agenda. This raises a difficult question about situations when these forces are used for ends that are not democratic. "If civil society is a beachhead secure enough to be of use in thwarting tyrannical regimes, what prevents it from being used to undermine democratic governments" (or values) (Foley and Edwards 1996, 46)? This final issue is crucial to recovering the use of the term. Interpretations of civil society that fail to acknowledge its more unsavory, violent, or "uncivil" elements or that ignore authoritarian leadership styles within civil society groups oversimplify the relations and complexity of civil society (McIlwaine 1998a, 417). This sphere is made up of different kinds of organizations and associations; it can move in uncivil directions, and this risk means that civil society organizations must continually reflect on their accountability, transparency, and political and ideological agendas.

Both the liberal and revolutionary approaches to understanding the role of civil society stress how civil society is distinct from the state (and the business sector and family), thereby missing a key aspect of the

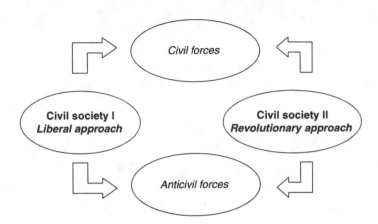

FIGURE I Civil Society Approaches

interconnections between the sectors that comprise society because ultimately the lines are not clear between any of the spheres. As McIlwaine
(1998b, 655) explains, "the separation of the state and civil society is untenable," in grand part because many states throughout Latin America provide
the majority of the funding for local organizations, raising the question,
How independent are these organizations from the state if their budgets
depend on state funding? There is also the issue of political parties. Are
they considered part of civil society or part of the state, especially considering the pervasiveness of clientelistic relationships between political
parties and the electorate in Latin America? Though many civil society
organizations are perceived as social watch organizations monitoring the
state and even the business sector, they are also often involved in supporting, promoting, and creating micro and small enterprises through microcredit funds, technical assistance, and consulting for small businesses.
Hence, the boundary between civil society activities and the business
sector also hides overlapping areas of action. And finally, the assertion that
civil society starts when the individual leaves the home has been challenged for over a hundred years by women's movements around the globe.
Yes, they demand equal pay for equal work; yes, they demand equal treatment in front of the law; but they also demand an end to domestic violence
and a transformation of cultural norms that perpetuate a triple workday
for women. These struggles of civil society movements have led to great
changes within the family making their way into the domestic sphere.

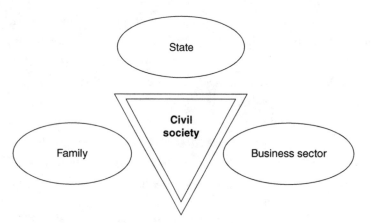

FIGURE 2 Civil Society and Other Sectors of Society

Because it is known for its civil commitment and volunteerism, many practitioners and policy makers idealize civil society organizations and movements as organizations comprised of altruistic citizens incapable of deception, corruption, or authoritarian practices. "With roots very often in religious and moral teachings, [civil society] has acquired a saintly self-perception and persona, and a certain romanticism now surrounds its presumed ability to change people's lives" (Salamon et al. 2004, 119). Just because civil society organizations are committed to civil ends, these organizations should not be reified as the solution to all ills or as paragons of organizational virtue. McIlwaine also cautions against romanticizing these human organizations, because they are not democratic or participatory simply because they are aligned with a noble cause (1998b, 656). The usefulness of the concept of civil society, as well as the recognition of the role of civil society, depends on the inclusion, transparency, and accountability of civil society organizations. The credibility of civil society depends on "emerg[ing] from below, and involv[ing] negotiations among conflicting groups, both within themselves, and with the state and elites . . . Furthermore, discussions and interpretations of civil society should also recognize internal divisions along lines of gender, race, and ethnicity" (McIlwaine 1998a, 419).

For the purpose of this book, I define "civil society" as the organizations outside of direct state control that attempt—locally, nationally, or globally—to make their communities more responsive to the needs of their members. "It is the we-ness of a national, regional, or international community, the feeling of connectedness to 'every member' of that community, that transcends particular commitments, narrow loyalties and sectional interests. Only this kind of solidarity can provide a thread . . . that unites individuals dispersed by class, religion, ethnicity, or race," and gender, I would add (Alexander 2006, 43). This definition includes a wide range of organizations, some of which are described by the women leaders I interviewed, many of whom direct NGOs, formal organizations legally recognized by their governments as not-for-profit organizations. Some women mentioned CSOs, such as community associations and neighborhood committees. Others spoke of social movements. A few of the women considered civil society a preserver of democratic values of the liberal approach, while others identified with the revolutionary approach. Often there is overlap between the two approaches, as pro-democratic actions can be interpreted as revolutionary depending on the historical, political, and economic context and juncture of events.

Discussing the growth of NGOs around the globe, Salamon writes, "the upshot is a global third sector: a massive array of self-governing private organizations, not dedicated to distributing profits to shareholders or directors, pursuing public purposes outside the formal apparatus of the state" (Salamon et al. 2004, 109). However, as much as these organizations are not for-profit businesses or state-run institutions, this sphere obviously does not stand alone; there are areas of overlap between it and other spheres. Given the interconnections, civil society is one of many actors in a complex, globalized world. Civil society organizations, as pure as their intentions may be, can choose to align themselves with uncivil forces and carry out actions that do not forward a democratic set of values or actions. Civil society organizations can demand, act, and work for a strong democratic state, but it is not coterminous with democracy. Edwards (2004, 110) articulates why civil society remains so useful even with its contradictions: "whatever its shortcomings in theory, civil society does offer both a touchstone for social movements and a practical framework for organizing resistance and alternative solutions to social, economic and political problems."

Leadership

A leader is someone who has "the ability to get things done," using status and influence to play a catalytic role motivating others to action (Freeman, Bourque, and Shelton 2001, 10). Sumru Erkut, in her analysis of sixty interviews with women leaders from different sectors of U.S. society—civil society, arts and culture, business, and government—offered a similar definition: "Leadership can be defined as persuading other people to set aside, if only for a period of time, their individual concerns and to pursue a common goal that is important for the responsibilities and welfare of a group" (2001, 2). The concept of followers is decisive to the definition of what it means to be a leader. Gary Wills, in his biographical descriptions of different types of leaders, reminds us that "the leader does not just vaguely affect others. He or she takes others toward the object of their joint quest" (1994, 19). Many theorists agree about how important it is that the leader belong to the group he or she is leading. In the case of many of the women interviewed for this book, they emerge as community leaders or occupy leadership positions within NGOs because they represent their communities, have spent years participating in social movements, or are part of "a 'critical mass'" fighting for a particular goal (Brasileiro 1996, 11).

Many of the women interviewed agree that gender affects leadership because they see different types of leadership styles, specifically feminine and masculine ones; but often women are able to draw upon all styles, whereas men are often sanctioned for using more feminine approaches. There are many ways for a leader to achieve her ends: she can be domineering, authoritative, empowering, and/or consensus-oriented. In civil society movements and organizations, leaders use a variety of approaches, but more democratic models are often pursued due to the social-movement orientation of many civil society organizations. Even though women use a wide range of leadership styles, life experience and gender roles affect how and when women lead. "The exercise of leadership involves power, a concept where research has suggested gender variation" (Freeman and Bourque 2001, 4), which is to say that how a person will use their power is informed by the gender of the user.

As mentioned, in most societies gender hierarchies and structures of subordination translate into men having more access to formal positions of power than women. "Visible leadership still remains a primarily male domain" (Erkut and Winds 2001, 15). These structures inform conceptions about what it means to be a leader. Gender hierarchies in patriarchal societies inhibit women's access to leadership and also inform the kinds of leaders they become if they are able to overcome the barriers to leadership. Often, commonly held understandings of what it means to be a leader are derived from stereotypes. Given the importance of avoiding the reproduction of sexist stereotypes about women and leadership, even by well intentioned researchers, it is of paramount importance to use participant observation and interviews to show the diversity and vibrancy of women's leadership experiences (Martins Costa and Heisler Neves 1996, 57).

The topic of leadership has been troublesome for feminists because they have been wary of leadership either as a research topic or as a goal in and of itself because the concepts of leader and leadership (with notable exceptions) have historically been synonymous with the masculine (Vianello et al. 2000, 6). Freeman, Bourque, and Shelton (2001, 7) describing the intersection of leadership, power, and gender describe a similar phenomenon: "a leader . . . is assumed to be rational, decisive, objective, and strongly motivated to achieve, with a worldview that projects concern well beyond the confines of the domestic sphere . . . [which] still closely corresponds to our stereotyped images of men and the masculine." The women interviewed for this book show that in some cases they do use what poet Audre Lorde refers to as "the Master's tools"—attributes associated with masculine leadership styles—but they also draw on approaches to leadership gained from years of marginalization and struggle on behalf of themselves and their communities.

Another related and knotty issue for many feminists and women activists is their role vis-à-vis the state. If the concept of leadership—especially masculine approaches—generates ambivalence among feminists, then the same can be said about choosing to work from the state, either as elected officials or for state agencies. Since the state is often critiqued by feminists as a patriarchal and sexist set of institutions, working for the state is synonymous with cooptation and selling out. Many of the facets of this debate are revealed in the ethnographic chapters on Chile and El Salvador. In Chile autonomous feminists and other activists are critical of the

National Service for Women (Servicio Nacional de la Mujer—SERNAM), the state agency for women, calling the staff *femocrats* and *institucionalizadas* (Alvarez et al. 2003, 555; Richards 2004), yet many feminists have chosen to work there out of a desire to effect change from within and channel resources to areas of need. In El Salvador, a similar polemic has surfaced over the years regarding the many civil society women activists who have chosen to participate in local and national politics. I argue that the debate about whether or not to participate in politics and state agencies is useful as long as it encourages a critical examination of the motivations, agendas, and real possibilities of change from within. Eloquently reminding us that the litmus test should be addressing the very real inequalities and high levels of violence women face daily, Sharon Capeling-Alakija (1994) of the United Nations Development Fund for Women (UNIFEM) said, "We cannot escape the conclusion that in many parts of the world, even as we speak, women are being 'disappeared' simply because they are women. And those who survive cannot participate fully in development efforts, or benefit from those efforts, as long as they are forced to live with the reality or the threat of violence. . . . But we cannot turn away from these realities. We cannot allow ourselves to be paralyzed by their magnitude. As the poet Audre Lorde said: 'We must never close our eyes to the terror.'" If the debate about participation stymies new approaches, action, or opportunities for women to serve women and address inequalities, then the debate—and its proponents—has become limiting in my view. As the Salvadoran women I interviewed who have chosen to participate in politics indicate, they face institutionalized sexism when working from within the state, but they also describe the results they achieved from their elected posts and the knowledge they have gained from the experience.

The late Dame Nita Barrow, preeminent woman leader from the Caribbean, had a clear understanding of male leadership, its pitfalls, and the potential for social change by women leaders. Because women are socialized differently than men and seldom offered traditional access to leadership, they often develop different styles of leadership. Dame Barrow compared male and female power, calling on women to imagine more inclusive approaches rather than the power-by-domination approach: "The power women generate is different from the popular concepts of what constitutes power from the masculine point of view . . . Do not let us hide behind supposed powerlessness—power by domination is not the only power" (Drayton 2001, 22). Even though gender ideologies and hierarchies often contribute to women's subordination, women receive culturally encoded messages about the importance of caretaking, network building, and relational work that are all extremely useful skills in leadership. Sumru Erkut, in her pioneering research with women leaders in the United States, addressed the relational qualities of women leaders: "women have a much stronger sense of connectedness to others and of being part of the whole. [They] are more gratified by leadership that involves creating a shared purpose, with the leader being part of the whole" (2001, 34). Many women bring certain characteristics to leadership such as inclusiveness, compassion, and sensitivity to others (Wilson 2004, 6). This kind of research corroborates the hypothesis that women can develop horizontal and interconnected forms of leadership through their experience of marginality as members of societies raised to care for others.

Gender is not the only vector that differentiates people, affects how they will lead, and informs their access to positions of leadership; race, ethnicity, class, political identity and militancy, and cultural background also affect access to positions of power. "It seems that hierarchies based on age, class, and education, and *not* simply gender, are just as important in determining the nature of leadership" (Datta and McIlwaine 2000, 42). Obviously a number of factors contribute to help a woman develop and deploy leadership qualities for a particular cause. This is why the study of civil society women leaders in Latin America reveals new insights about the different factors (gender roles, ethnicity, personal histories, social class, kin networks, access to education, and political networks) that facilitate or inhibit women's access to leadership experiences and how they will lead. Experiences of injustice and marginalization affect how people lead; so, for those who experience multiple kinds of discrimination, such as women of color, low-income women, and women with disabilities, they may have an advantage in developing innovative or transformational leadership approaches. Women leaders face a challenging terrain: not only do they face structural barriers to their leadership because of gender, but in some cases they may choose a leadership style that promotes empowerment, includes the voiceless, and uses consensus-building models. This kind of a leadership model brings its own challenges, such as how to use a

leadership model that challenges many of the presuppositions and stereotypes reaffirmed by Western patriarchal, capitalist societies, especially
ones that have experienced periods of authoritarian rule.

Civic Culture in Argentina, Chile, and El Salvador

Before applying concepts of gender and civil society leadership to the concrete experiences of women in the three countries under study, it is important to analyze the civic culture in each country by critically evaluating the
impact of authoritarian rule and the roles such institutions as the military
and the Catholic Church have played during these times. In order to
understand the evolution of civil society organizations in Latin America, it
is necessary to analyze the context in which they emerged, which is to say,
"the historical heritages, the 'rules of the game' and the structure of
opportunities" (Panfichi 1999, 1). All three countries share a set of political
practices known as clientelism, a system in which political parties or state
institutions provide citizens with goods or services with the understanding
that they will vote along the lines of those providing the services. Much has
been written on the topic of clientelism in Latin America (Auyero 2000;
García-Guadilla and Peréz 2002; Sobrado-Chaves and Stoller 2002), and
the definitions coincide describing how clientelistic relations are based on
the idea of buying future votes and political support. "By *political clientelism*
I mean the relations that are established between a *patron* who offers certain services and a *client* who in exchange for those services (or goods) per-
mits the patron to govern and resolve collective issues without the client's
participation" (Sobrado-Chaves and Stoller 2002, 8). Though clientelistic
practices are observable in each country, the political systems of each
country developed along different lines. Each of these three countries
began as a Spanish and Roman Catholic colony gaining its independence
in the early 1800s, but Chile consolidated a series of stable yet contested
democratic governments by 1925, enjoying "one of the most solid democracies in Latin America" until the military coup in 1973 (Schamis 1991, 201).
Argentina and El Salvador, on the other hand, were subject to frequent
periods of authoritarian rule, especially by the military, as well as *caudillos*,
leadership by local strongmen.

In the 1970s Argentina and Chile experienced military coups leading
to periods of brutal authoritarian rule by the military in which civil society

organizations were harshly repressed. These coups and their subsequent authoritarian regimes had "significant gendered components" exemplified by the emphasis placed on traditional feminine roles (read: traditional family values) and the harsh sanctions administered to women who violated them (Htun 2003, 19). In Argentina the military coup of March 24, 1976, started a period now referred to as the "dirty war," or *dictadura* (dictatorship), which lasted until 1983 with the restoration of democracy. During this time, the Argentine army and other state security forces carried out a campaign of terror on the civilian population leading to the disappearance of 30,000 Argentines, including those illegally detained, tortured, and killed, as well as the exile of many more (Feitlowitz 1998, ix). In Chile the military coup of September 11, 1973, overthrew the democratically elected socialist president Salvador Allende and installed General Augusto Pinochet in power. This dictatorship lasted until 1990 with the democratic election of President Patricio Aylwin. Though the repression was the harshest in the first couple of months just after the coup, 28,000 people in total were illegally detained, 94 percent of whom were tortured while detained, and roughly 2,700 people were murdered by security forces (Ministerio del Interior 1991, 2004).[5] In El Salvador, the lack of democratic spaces through the sixties, combined with unmet expectations for land reform and respect for basic rights, contributed to increasing tensions between the government and civilian organizing. In response to state repression and widespread citizen protest, an armed revolutionary movement comprised of different groups under the umbrella organization Farabundo Marti Front for National Liberation (FMLN) was formed and became active across the country. From the escalation of the conflict in 1980 to the signing of the Peace Accords between the government and the FMLN in 1992, 70,000 Salvadorans were killed—an estimated 1 out of every 100—most of them by government security forces (Stephen 1997, 30).

In each of the three countries, the Catholic Church has played a significant yet often contradictory role. From the early 1960s, the Second Vatican Council (1962–1965) encouraged the Church to reach out to impoverished and marginalized sectors of the population; this new framing of the role of the poor led to the dissolution of some of the historical ties between the Church and elites as bishops, priests, nuns, and lay people sought a new relationship with the poor and marginalized of society. No longer the objects of pity or charity, the poor were the privileged children of God and *solidarity* with them—going to live in marginalized communities, sharing their day-to-day situations, and working shoulder to shoulder with them to address the problems they faced—was the path to a deeper relationship with God and humanity. These progressive currents within the Catholic Church led to the emergence of a movement of Church officials and lay people throughout Latin America who worked closely with the marginalized sectors of parishes, organized as Christian Base Communities or Ecclesiastical Base Communities. Because lay women have been so active in their parishes historically, this movement promoted the organization and empowerment of women as citizens (Waylen 1994, 338), providing them with leadership and organizing skills and experience. This revolutionary interpretation of the teachings of Jesus became known as liberation theology based on a new reading of the Bible: "Since liberation theologians argued that the Bible should be read as a living text that spoke to the need to work for social justice in this world, the Church actively organized social activists in general and women in particular" (Kampwirth 2004, xi). Throughout South America and Central America, "the role of the Catholic Church has been essential in the formation and consolidation of civil society organizations" (Panfichi 1999, 8), yet fossilized positions on women's roles and their reproductive and sexual rights has made the Church "an inconsistent ally" (Friedman, forthcoming) for women's movements.

Nonetheless, many people—lay men and women, nuns, priests, and even bishops—were targeted by security forces because of their commitment to the empowerment of the poor. These progressive theological currents greatly influenced the Catholic Church hierarchy in El Salvador and Chile but less so in Argentina. In fact, in Argentina the Church hierarchy actively supported the dirty war, but in the case of El Salvador, Archbishop Oscar Romero and numerous priests, nuns, and laypeople were assassinated by government forces for their solidarity with the poor and marginalized (Feitlowitz 1998, 217–223). In Chile the Catholic Church protected civil society leaders and their organizations. "Under the Pinochet regime, the Church . . . sheltered dissidents, provided services to the poor, and then served as a powerbroker in the democratic transition" (Htun 2003, 102).

There were common elements in the authoritarian regimes of Argentina, Chile, and El Salvador, such as state terrorism against nonmilitary groups seen as subversives, extensive use of the illegal tools of torture and disappearance by state security forces (army, police, national guard, and navy), nationwide publicity campaigns against government critics, and the implementation of conservative economic plans in accordance with U.S. and U.K. policies at the time.[6] Jaquette describes the authoritarian regimes of Latin America as noteworthy in how the military governments "took to [their] self-assigned task of restructuring society and for the terrorist tactics used in pursuing ... opponents, *real and imagined*, on the Left" (1994, 1; emphasis mine). In analyzing these histories, it cannot be forgotten that these tactics were indeed used to eradicate the actual or perceived threat of armed guerrilla groups, but also to install fear throughout society about the price to be paid for civil society organizing: disappearance and torture.

There were important differences between the three countries that deserve to be highlighted. The Salvadoran military apparatus was never able to eradicate the FMLN even with $1 million a day in military aid from the United States during the 1980s. In Argentina incipient armed revolutionary groups were eliminated soon after the coup; this occurrence did not deter the armed forces from continuing their campaign of terror against civilians they perceived as subversive. Though the emergence of armed revolutionary groups was small in Argentina and minimal in Chile, the conflict became so widespread in El Salvador that the Salvadoran security forces were never able to contain the FMLN and ultimately were forced to meet them at the negotiating table.

In the case of Argentina, the Argentine Peronist party—a populist movement under the leadership of General Juan Perón and María Eva "Evita" Duarte de Perón, his charismatic wife—came to power in the 1940s, installing a government whose practices were fraught with clientelism and repressive tactics against critics that led to the military coup of 1955, which forced Perón into exile. However, upon his short-lived—both figuratively and literally—return in 1974, neither he nor his supporters were able to respond effectively to political and economic crisis. The military took advantage of a lack of leadership within the governing Peronist party after Perón's death, staging a coup in 1976 and then instituting economic, social, and political changes while systematically denying rights and actively repressing any dissent.

Chile, on the other hand, did not have such a harsh history of authoritarian regimes. A commitment to democratic practices and governments—testament to effective civil society organizing—marked its history since 1925. From the early decades of the twentieth century, Chile had a vital range of political parties and gradually incorporated basic social and economic rights into state actions, including education, health care, and workers' compensation. This culminated in the 1970 elections in which socialist Salvador Allende, representing a coalition of political parties, won the elections and became president. "[Chile's] open system had even allowed something that would have been routine in western Europe but was unique to Latin America: a socialist coalition intent on implementing structural transformations by means of democratic procedures came to power in 1970" (Schamis 1991, 201).

In each of these countries, women in civil society organizations played a key role in ending authoritarian rule and achieving a return to democratization. In Argentina women "played a central role in bringing about the transition to a democracy" (Feijoó 1994, 109). This was particularly evident in the human rights organizing of the Madres de Plaza de Mayo and other organizations of the relatives of the disappeared demanding the return of their children and other relatives who had been disappeared by government forces. In Chile women across the class spectrum were active in supporting *and* protesting the Allende government; their mobilization both for and against the regime speaks to the extent of Chilean women's activism.[7] During the dictatorship, the women's movement, *pobladores* activists from marginalized urban communities, and the indigenous movement played major roles in achieving the return to democracy (Richards 2004). And in El Salvador, the women's movement and other women leaders from civil society organizations were staunch supporters of the peace process. Women even played a significant role in the FMLN guerrilla forces, making up 30 percent of combatants and support units. "Women were present in both the popular and armed struggle. Within the context of the popular movement . . . women organizing in their feminine capacity as teachers, mothers, and refugees had the potential to achieve certain fundamental alliances with the population that men were not as likely to foster" (Shayne 2004, 43).

There is a current within the social sciences that argues authoritarian regimes create an authoritarian citizenry; this claim has been refuted by two different strands of research in Latin America. One strand of research, led by social scientists such as anthropologist James Scott (1985) and others (Binford 1998, 1999; Molyneux 1986; Roseberry 1994), has depicted how communities manifest a *culture of resistance* in which they continue to struggle for democratic spaces in microways even in very repressive times. The other strand of research carried out by sociologists and political scientists (Booth and Seligson 1984; Tiano 1986) reexamined and adjusted some of the quantitative indicators used to measure authoritarian culture and showed how citizens remain committed, maybe even more so, to democratic values, beliefs, practices, and institutions during periods of authoritarian rule. I find it relevant, nonetheless, to distinguish between the existence of a democratic culture even under authoritarian regimes and the impact of authoritarian regimes on the population. All the women interviewed for this book spoke to how their lives were affected, transformed, or altered irrevocably by living under periods of authoritarian repression. Repressive regimes leave scars on their citizenries that can take years—even generations—to overcome. While most citizens remain committed to democratic practices and institutions—even under or after authoritarian regimes, they know why democracy is important. Many continue to have nightmares or flashbacks about traumatic or frightening experiences that occurred during the repression, and they still catch themselves looking over their shoulders to see if they are being followed.

In the case of these three countries, the women interviewed continue to feel a certain distrust of government in general and state institutions, policies, and political parties in particular. Many Argentineans question the motives of their political parties and institutions, as seen by the growth of civil society organizations and frequent protests against the government in the face of scandal, corruption, and economic crisis. Describing Chile after the return to democracy, Patricia Chuchryk cogently observed that "it would be difficult to overestimate the social, economic, cultural, and psychological destruction wrought by more than sixteen years of military rule" (1994, 67). In Chile, the major decisions about political and economic development still remain in the hands of a few and are seldom negotiable. Gonzalo de la Maza summarizes this situation: "The

democratization reached so far . . . since 1990 has not modified the socioeconomic framework inherited from the dictatorship; it has not recovered
the regulatory role of the state in key areas; it has not achieved citizen
participation; nor has it diminished the existing power inequalities"
(2003, 2). In El Salvador, it is still to be seen if the newly elected, FMLN
president Mauricio Funes will be able to transform the widely held perception that impunity continues to reign. For the time being, levels of violence supersede violence during the civil war period. El Salvador remains
one of the most violent countries in Latin America; it has the highest per
capita homicide rate in Latin America (CDHES 2005b) and police and the
justice system are seldom able to bring perpetrators to justice.

Since the periods of authoritarian rule, all three countries have
experienced unprecedented growth for civil society organizations. In
Argentina, the human rights organizations that emerged before and during the dirty war—the Mothers and Grandmothers of Plaza de Mayo and
the Center for Legal and Social Studies (CELS)—continue their human
rights monitoring and lobbying, but they have been joined by a new generation of human rights organizations—Citizen Power (Poder Ciudadano),
Citizen Participation (Participación Ciudadana), Conscience (Conciencia),
the National Coordinator against Police and Institutional Repression
(CORREPI), and Citizens in Action (Ciudadanos en Accion)—working to
address government corruption, promote citizen participation, and
expand the notion of social, economic, and political citizenship (Peruzzotti
2002). These new actors in the human rights arena are the result of "both
human rights and women's rights organizations expand[ing] the new Latin
American discourse of rights and citizenship" (Jaquette 1994, 4).

In Chile certain sectors of civil society have grown stronger while
others find themselves struggling for limited resources. The professional
associations of teachers and physicians and the environmental movement
are "the politically most important actors" (Panfichi 1999, 19). But it is the
Mapuche movement—composed of indigenous activists representing
about 10 percent of the population of Chile—that continues to challenge
the Chilean state on issues of sovereignty, land rights, and indigenous
rights. De la Maza argues that the Mapuche movement today is more inter-
nally organized and responsive to its members, rather than responding
to outside political interests or pressures, as has happened in the past

(2003, 20). The women's movement is looking for a new direction since their pivotal role in achieving a return to democracy. Marcela Rios Tobar corroborates this: "there is consensus in recognizing that the public presence of the women's movement—including feminist organizations—has gradually dwindled as a political force" since the return to democracy (n.d., 3).

In El Salvador a vital civil society continued to grow after the signing of the Peace Accords in January 1992. During the years directly following the signing of the Peace Accords—a period called the Reconstruction—international aid dollars flowed into the country for reconstruction projects, channeled through state agencies, municipalities, and NGOs. However, by the end of the twentieth century these funds diminished and were eventually redirected to other war-torn and needy parts of the world, and many local organizations were forced to close for lack of funding. Organizations that were able to diversify funding sources, generate some of their own income, and implement transparency and accountability practices are the ones that have survived, including a diverse range of women's organizations, human rights organizations, local development organizations, and research think tanks.

Research Methods and Considerations

Stereotypes and commonly held definitions of what it means to be a leader are informed by structural inequalities that do not preference women, people of color, or those from marginalized backgrounds. The first challenge that confronts the social scientist interested in observing and analyzing leaders and their styles of leadership is the fact that often they themselves suffer from stereotypes about leadership that hinder recognizing different kinds of leadership in action. If Dame Barrow is correct that women do not have to act like men to be leaders, what kinds of leaders are they? Freeman and Bourque note that "a tradition of power as a male preserve has obscured our understanding of women and power" (2001, 11). This is further complicated by the impact of Western, masculinist models of leadership that entail one person heading a group as the spokesperson or leader.

Anthropologist Karen Brodkin Sacks corroborates how easily even feminist researchers get caught using stereotypical definitions of leadership that affect observing women's leadership, let alone analyzing it or theorizing about it or promoting it. Reflecting on her fieldwork with women hospital workers and their attempt to organize a union at Duke University, Sacks could not understand why the women did not take more proactive leadership roles. Ultimately she saw that she had missed seeing women's activism and leadership because of her own stereotypes about leadership. She writes, "As I reexamined the data from my research to try to answer that question, I came to believe that the notion of leadership I had inadvertently promoted was a class-, gender-, and perhaps race-biased one" (1988b, 79). Field notes, interview transcripts, and double-checking conclusions with research participants become very important sources for reexamining what one has been observing, as the researcher must unlearn her own stereotypes of what it means to be a leader. Vigilant attention must remain constant during fieldwork, but also while writing up field notes, transcribing interviews, and analyzing data.

However, the challenge of recognizing women's leadership should not deter research. No matter the leadership model, women are leading. Especially in Chile, Argentina, and El Salvador, women are among the primary catalysts for social change and proponents of gender equity and social justice given their roles in civil society organizations. They are developing new tools, strategies, and visions of transformation. I concur with Dame Barrow: "We need to understand and theorize the processes women use to alter conventional practices, subvert barriers to women's participation, and force societal changes that produce benefits for women as well as a more just society" (Barriteau and Cobley 2001, 7).

Feminist Social Science Methodologies and Dilemmas

Many articulations of feminist methodologies and feminist dilemmas in research proceed from the commitment of the researcher to accompany and support processes of transformations of relations of inequality and of consciousness-raising for the researched (see Bowles and Duelli Klein 1983; Fonow and Cook 1991; Enslin 1990; Geiger 1990; Harding 1987; Reinharz 1992; Wolf 1992, 1996). The danger here, of course, is the assumption that the researcher is already empowered herself (which is often not the case) or that the researcher knows the best path to consciousness-raising for the researched (which is often not the case either). Diane Wolf distinguishes between "consciousness raising that is instigated exogenously by a well meaning outsider" and "when local women initiate the process and learn from each other's experiences" (1996, 26).[8] Though this premise forces the researcher to clarify the power differential between herself and the researched along with her own positionality vis-à-vis the women she is researching, I argue that the question of the power differential between the researcher and research participants—often portrayed as the dichotomy of researcher empowered, researched unempowered—is seldom clear-cut. Furthermore, this dichotomy only serves to perpetuate stereotypes of women from developing countries as unempowered research *objects* as opposed to *subjects or actors or participants*. I propose a more nuanced interpretation in which the power relations between the researched and researcher are complex, many layered, and charged with historical and political tensions. Though many feminist social scientists address the issues of positionality (see Fine 1994; Geiger 1990; John 1989; Williams 1996; Wolf 1992, 1996), the challenge is to deepen the reflection of the complexity and interrelation of positionalities and accountability. Along this vein, Kirin Narayan convincingly recommends that "we might more profitably view each anthropologist in terms of shifting identifications amid a field of interpenetrating communities and power relations" (1993, 671).

In my case, I was born in the United States to a couple of Irish and English descent. My parents divorced when I was ten, and I was raised by a single, working mother. I attended a Jesuit liberal arts college, Seattle University, where I first studied Latin America through a theology course on liberation theology. I have been living and working in Latin America or working on Latin American–related issues from the United States for over twenty years; this has involved two and a half years working as a human rights observer in Nicaragua in 1986–1988, four years monitoring human rights in El Salvador and working with women's organizations there in 1989–1993, graduate school with frequent periods in Central America for fieldwork in 1993–1999, and twelve years with AVINA, a Latin American NGO with offices throughout the region supporting civil society and business sector leadership for sustainable development. My role at AVINA was not programmatic in the traditional sense; rather I led the foundation's knowledge management area promoting knowledge transfer between AVINA staff and partners as well as among partners.

Obviously, my gender, race, nationality, educational background, and work with a Latin American foundation inform how the women I interviewed for this book perceive me when we meet and vice versa. Yes, the risk exists that the women interviewed might be prejudiced or intimidated by me in some way because of these factors, and, yes, these factors also combine to inform how I look at the world. Yet, I believe that people can connect and share their stories honestly with openness, trust, and compassion from each side. I never ask a question I am not willing to answer myself, and I frequently tell parts of my own story to put women at ease in the interview setting. I witnessed extensive domestic violence as a child, and as an adult I have witnessed the disastrous and long-term effects of war and authoritarianism on civilian populations and my own family members. Nonetheless, there are always multiple interpretations of a given reality, and there is always the risk that I have not fully grasped the lives and actions I have been observing. This is why developing long-term relationships with research participants over extended stays is so vital to the research endeavor. As a feminist researcher, I approach the interview setting and the opportunity for participant observation with as much transparency and honesty as possible in an attempt to create a mutually beneficial atmosphere in which participants share from their experiences. The stories these women leaders shared with me come from connections that extend beyond our individual experiences and speak to the challenges and lessons these women have learned in their struggles. In the research endeavor, sometimes the researcher and researched are able to find a place of mutual trust and a conversation emerges whose text can serve to elucidate complex fields of action. "In particular, oral testimony enables us to approach the issue of agency and subjectivity in history" (James 2000, 124).

Research Methodology

In all three countries I carried out numerous interviews with civil society actors, experts, and researchers. I formally interviewed and tape-recorded fifteen to twenty women leaders from each country, choosing in-depth interviews with a smaller sample rather than a more ample but superficial survey. I agree with anthropologist Lynn Stephen's assertion that "by concentrating on a smaller number of in depth exchanges, I am better able to translate the meaning and depth of women's varied experiences onto the page" (1997, 5). I used a snowball sampling technique to identify women leaders to interview, meaning that I gathered recommendations from contacts in each country and from initial interviews with civil society leaders and experts. This participant-driven sampling technique was necessary given the lack of information about the population under study, what is called a "hidden population" (Heckathorn 1997). Few quantitative studies exist about civil society in general for the countries under study, much less quantitative information about women leaders in the sector. The risk of snowball samples is that the sample is biased or limited to the network of the researcher; for this reason, I attempted to get my recommendations from a variety of sources and networks.

Interviews often lasted over two hours and were tape-recorded in the women's homes and offices and then transcribed in their entirety. (See the appendix for a list of the organizations of the women interviewed.) Common elements explored in the interviews with women leaders included the following:

1. Opinion, interpretation, and usage of the term "leader"
2. Evolution and description of leadership experiences together with current work, organizational form of work (NGO, association, social movement), and achievements
3. Views on teamwork, collaborators, and followers
4. Views on the difference between being a manager and being a leader
5. Factors that have facilitated the development of leadership skills
6. Views on differences between women (emphasis on class, political activism, and ethnicity)
7. Challenges or difficulties of being a woman and a leader

Interviewees revised their transcribed interviews and edited them as they saw fit. Letting them decide what parts of their story to share and whether or not to appear with their own names was particularly important given the history of repression in the three countries. Additionally, I facilitated focus groups in each country with the interviewees to get their input on the conclusions from my analysis of their interview texts.

Though I always asked the women leaders the same basic set of questions, I used the semistructured interview format so that I could include additional questions depending on the context and particular experience of the interviewee. For this reason, each of the ethnographic chapters focuses on diverse features of women's leadership experiences. In Chile multiple yet unrelated initial interviews with civil society experts urged me to focus on Mapuche leaders given their exceptional contributions; so a major feature of the Chilean chapter is about gender and ethnicity. In El Salvador the contacts I have developed over the past twenty years insisted I unpack the phenomenon of women civil society leaders and their participation in local and national elected positions. Argentine interviews pointed me in the direction of investigating the intersection of gender and class, and so the research and analysis focused on these issues.

I carried out fieldwork and bibliographic research in each country, assuring that local research and publications about women and civil society organizing informed the analysis of the women's stories. During 2006 and 2007 I lived in southern Argentina, near the Chilean border, for fourteen months, which greatly facilitated the research process in each of these two countries. The Salvadoran part of the research was originally carried out during research and fieldwork stints during 1990–1993, 1994, 1996–1997, as well as visits every year during 2006–2009.

Overview

From the emergence of the first charity organizations in Chile and Argentina in the 1800s to the indigenous and workers unions in El Salvador in the early 1900s, chapter 2 traces how women have led civil society organizations into the late twentieth century. Extensive excerpts from women leaders describe the impact of these events on their lives and their civil society commitments.

Chapter 3 weaves together women leaders' stories of how CSOs and leadership opportunities for women have flourished since Argentina's return to democracy in 1983. Many CSOs reopened their doors after the repression and many new organizations were founded. In the mid-1980s organizations based in the capital city of Buenos Aires began to reach out to marginalized communities, avoiding paternalistic approaches in an attempt to learn from and work more effectively with communities. Women leaders in working-class and marginalized communities were galvanized into action during the economic crises of the late 1990s and the early part of the twenty-first century, building partnerships with other organizations, demanding a response from state agencies, and working together for the survival of their families.

Chapter 4 describes how Mapuche women leaders in Chile are building effective and financially viable NGOs that challenge the class and ethnic barriers that keep rural, poor, or indigenous women relegated to the margins of Chilean society. Their leadership styles draw on indigenous leadership qualities and their cultural authority as respected women in their communities, generating new leadership models for all Chilean women. Though conservative gender stereotypes are particularly entrenched in Chile, the Mapuche women are pressuring state agencies to focus on women's interests and indigenous people's demands. The achievements of these leaders is an invigorating contribution to the women's movement in particular and civil society in general.

In chapter 5 I discuss how the Salvadoran civil war of the 1980s was a class leveler for women that facilitated leadership experiences for working-class and farming women and provided women from more privileged backgrounds the chance to understand the plight of marginalized sectors of society. When the peace accords were signed in January 1992, the country was flooded with international funding for CSOs, creating additional opportunities for women's leadership growth. Women also took the challenge to run for elected offices, increasing their participation in local and national government. These funds eventually evaporated, and financially strapped CSOs were left to cope with a series of monumental societal problems such as increased violence, inflation, unemployment, and environmental degradation in the wake of the war and state spending cuts for social issues. These conditions have lead to a number of successful (and sustainable) CSO-community partnerships in which women's empowerment and local development needs are attended to in an integrated fashion.

Chapter 6 looks for common threads facilitating a regionwide analysis by exploring the trends in women's civil society leadership experiences in Argentina, Chile, and El Salvador and comparing these experiences with those of women in other Latin American countries. Lessons learned from initial collaborations and cross-class projects between women leaders indicate a growing tendency toward cooperation, which may advance these leaders' long-term goals. This chapter proposes policy suggestions for international organizations and national CSOs to recognize and support the important role women play in these organizations' leadership and activities.

2

The Emergence of Civil Society in Argentina, Chile, and El Salvador

> I tell you honestly that the worst thing that can happen in a mother's life happened to me: to have to beg that your daughter die quickly. I pleaded with God that my daughter find death quickly because I knew what had happened in other countries, and I knew about the kind of inhumane torture they carried out against the disappeared here in Argentina.
>
> —Rosa Nair Amuedo, Madres de Plaza de Mayo–Línea Fundadora, Buenos Aires, Argentina

As limited as the historical record is about Latin American civil society organizing in general, and women's organizing in particular, a few committed historians of Latin American history, such as José Bengoa, Inga Clendinnen, Donna Guy, and Aldo Lauria-Santiago, have reconstructed events formerly dedicated to the triumphs of Spanish conquerors and founding fathers to illuminate the protagonism of women, workers, and indigenous people during the periods of conquest, colonialism, early statehood, and the modern era.[1] The work of these historians and scholars is crucial for building a more nuanced understanding of periods that have previously been portrayed from an elitist, male, European perspective. The historical contributions, actions, and achievements of women, workers, slaves, and indigenous peoples are often left out of official, historical discourse. Chilean historian José Bengoa describes this phenomenon: "The history of those who did not accept has been silenced. It would seem that there is a definite tendency to identify human history with the history of the winners. The losers—often perceived as barbarians—don't often have

42

history, or their history has been absorbed into the triumphantism of the winners" (2000, 11). This elision occurs when Spanish conquerors write the history of the local indigenous peoples or when elites write the history of state building, smoothing over the contested nature of events and times. Thus worker strikes get minimized; women's organizing does not get coverage; and indigenous people get left out entirely. As historian Inga Clendinnen wryly observes, "Rescuing the native peoples so casually appropriated to European uses over these last centuries presents essentially the same problems—the necessary dependence on outsider reports, for example—at an even more daunting level of intensity. Alien soldiers rarely make sensitive ethnographers. . . . Therefore the trick is to strip away the cocoon of Spanish interpretation to uncover sequences of Indian actions, and then to try and discern the pattern in those actions, as a way of inferring the shared understanding which sustains them" (1987, 131–132).

The work of historians like Bengoa and Clendinnen to uncover the historical and cultural complexities of indigenous cultures in the Americas provides insight into the struggles of the marginalized and disenfranchised and substantiates claims of their protagonism, contributions, and struggles from the very arrival of Europeans to the Americas.[2] This is how civil society emerges in the three countries under study with the numerous examples of leadership and activism by women, workers, and indigenous people.

In Argentina elite ladies managed charity efforts—such as disaster relief, schools, hospitals, and retirement homes—from the early nineteenth century onward and the working-class feminist anarchists of late nineteenth-century Buenos Aires published *Women's Voice* (*La Voz de la Mujer*), the first documented feminist newspaper in the region. During the dirty war (1976–1983), the mothers of the disappeared were one of the few to challenge the military dictatorship demanding information about their missing children. In Chile, as in Argentina, elite women were active historically in charity efforts, but there are also numerous examples of poor indigenous and *mestizo* women organizing and working together to guarantee themselves and their families sufficient food, clothing, and shelter to survive economic and political crises from the early years of the republic to the present day. In the case of Chile, the twentieth-century women's movement—composed of elite, professional, working-class, and marginal-ized women—was one of the major forces responsible for ending the dicta-torship of General Augusto Pinochet (1973–1990) without resorting to violence. There is less scholarship about the historical role of women in the emergence of civil society organizing in El Salvador than the other two countries, but the recollections of Salvadoran women interviewed by the author about their own lives and those of their mothers and grandmothers provide us with numerous examples of women's activism: indigenous women trying to ensure the survival of their culture and children after *La Matanza* (the Slaughter) by hiding their indigenous identity, women active in the teachers' union, and women activists and leaders from the 1960s to the present who participated in the popular movement comprised of civil society organizations and guerrilla forces. In all three countries, suffrage was an issue that brought women together, but it tended to be an elite and middle class issue rather than a popular demand (see table 1).

Women often choose activism when their livelihoods, family, and/or customs are threatened; the actions they choose to carry out are shaped by social class, race, and gender. These issues also affect the amount of soli-darity or lack thereof that can be found among women activists: the more stratified a society is, the more women are separated by class. Therefore, the less likely it is for cross-cutting movements to form and accomplish significant social change and transformation. Social class and how it has affected women's organizing is a historical tension that has engrossed

TABLE 1

Suffrage by Country

Country	Year	Comments
Argentina	1947	Women's suffrage granted by presidential decree
Chile	1948	Both legislative houses approved law
El Salvador	1950	New constitution granted all women the right to vote
United States of America	1920	Nineteenth Amendment to Constitution

feminist social scientists for the past three decades. In Chile and Argentina, it was primarily elite women who were the first to experience a new consciousness about women's rights due to their access to political ideas from Europe. This consciousness alienated many working-class, poor, and indigenous women who were doubly or triply oppressed. However, feminism did not emerge until the civil war ended in the late 1980s in El Salvador. Because the war had promoted solidarity among women across difference, the women's movement emerged in the 1990s with a much more integrated and diverse constituency: women from the capital, women from the countryside, women from marginalized communities, and educated professionals worked together to build a common platform of demands—such as implementing gender quotas for political candidates, addressing domestic violence, and tackling sexual discrimination in the workplace—for government, public policy, and political parties.

In Latin American history, women have assumed leadership roles in their families, communities, and even countries during periods of economic or political turmoil. The following sections outline events or processes that fomented extensive civil society organizing and women's leadership in each country.

Argentina

In an extension of their domestic and family roles, women have played a significant part in the emergence and scope of civil society in Argentina since the 1800s: "Beyond their distinct and even contradictory ideological positions, from those ladies of charity, including Eva Perón and Amalia Fortabat, as well as the Madres de Plaza de Mayo, women have left a strong imprint on the world of philanthropy and community service in Argentina" (Thompson 1994, 19).[3] Because of women's protagonism, the history of civil society in Argentina is essentially the history of the women's movement in Argentina and reflects the tensions and contradictions that permeate Argentine history, culture, and politics. Even though women performed charitable activities and other actions necessary for the sur-vival of their communities before independence from Spain, they were not able to overcome class divisions and create a broad-based movement to achieve the vote for women; suffrage for women was granted in 1947 by

General Juan Domingo Perón, a charismatic, populist leader who won the allegiance of the Argentine working class—men *and* women. Nonetheless, the actions of women did translate into crucial contributions to the country: women and the organizations they led provided social welfare coverage to the entire country for over one hundred years. Women participated in philanthropic endeavors, led and built political parties, and designed, administered, and taught in an educational system serving the whole country—girls and boys, young women and men.

From Colonial Times to the Early Years of the Republic

From the late 1600s women were essential to the survival of the early European communities in Argentina, though this trend did not translate into equal rights before the law. According to Spanish law, women were classified as children or imbeciles: a curious classification, as the predominant expectation for women of European descent was bearing children and being good mothers. Though the historical record provides more insights into the lives and commitments of elite women, the contributions of working-class, indigenous, and slave women were also important, especially in economic terms (see Carlson 1988; Lavrin 1995; and Molyneux 1986). In the late fifteenth and early sixteenth centuries, much of the reproduction of life—food preparation and preservation, domestic activities, weaving, sewing, child rearing—fell to indigenous and slave women; unions between Spanish men and these local women—often against the will of the local women—were frequent, leading to the first generations of mestizos, or people of mixed ancestry. Once the gold and silver had been plundered in Latin America and the only remaining option was to return to Europe or find new ways to exploit the continent, the conquistadores and their followers sent for their wives or sought Spanish women as brides. Though the percentage of European women remained low until the 1700s, their arrival and presence was key for the "civilization" of the colony, being the holders of European culture, religion, and high society. The labor of working-class, poor, and slave women, on the other hand, produced the bulk of clothing and light manufactured goods necessary for daily life.

For most of Spanish-speaking America—Argentina, Chile, and El Salvador included—colonial law classified women as having the legal status of children, fetuses, and imbeciles. They were not allowed to participate in

politics, own property, or make decisions for their children; they were subject to the rule of their fathers and/or husbands; and when in front of a
judge they were assigned the legal category of minors. "It was taken to be
self-evident that women were not equal to men. Therefore, senior males'
authority derived from their 'natural born' superiority to women" (Dore
and Molyneux 2000, 11). Nonetheless, women did have certain de facto
rights. "It is recognized now that aristocratic women managed large
agricultural haciendas, bought and freed slaves, established entails and
founded convents and charitable institutions and, in fact, were important
and influential in various aspects of colonial life and in the alliances
that transmitted power and money from one family to another" (Carlson
1988, 6), as well as often having power over their dowries once married.
Elite women enjoyed opportunities other women did not; but these
'opportunities' were only allowed as long as they facilitated the expansion
of the colonial, patriarchal project and did not challenge the status quo.
For instance, elite women would hold and wield power when male relatives were absent or deceased, provided they followed the example set for
them" (Carlson 1988, 6).

The options for middle-class women, such as the daughters of book-
keepers or public servants, were also restricted by social mores and gender
hierarchies; one of the few options for a somewhat different life was limited to joining a convent. Nonetheless, nuns' lives were circumscribed by
the Catholic Church and their superiors. Much of the land and wealth
taken from the original inhabitants of Latin America were given to convents, many of which enjoyed large endowments. Colonial convents
offered women freedom from the constraint of fathers and husbands in
addition to opportunities for educational development (Carlson 1988, 8).
In a convent, depending on the order, women were educated and often
worked in the community, though intellectual and theological inquiry
was somewhat limited due to the repressive atmosphere of the Spanish
Inquisition.

Elite women often focused their efforts on philanthropic work, cultural activities, politics, and women's rights, though there was little unified action even among elite women. "There were deep philosophical
divisions between those women dedicated to philanthropic causes . . . and
all of these women were upper class, and did not really reach out to any

other class of women" (Mercer 1998, 4). In the eighteenth century, elite women ran salons, cultural gathering places to discuss new intellectual, artistic, and political ideas from Europe and to perform music and poetry. Women of the upper class frequently involved themselves in politics by supporting different political causes in the salons and social gatherings in addition to raising funds for causes. During the early nineteenth century, women were particularly active in organizing for independence from Spain. They raised money, donated money, and in a number of cases, dressed as men and went to war, as evidenced by Josefa Gabriela Ramos Mejía (1766–1832), who dressed as a male soldier and joined the fight for independence in 1812.

When independence was gained, peace was not attained. Seventy years of civil war followed—a power struggle between the provinces and Buenos Aires. The provinces wanted a federation of provinces, organized around local *caudillos*—local political and military leaders or strongmen— and economic and political autonomy at the provincial level. Buenos Aires wanted a centralized government with control centered in the capital and coastal areas. While men were caught up in the wars or were far from home seeking employment, poor, working-class, and middle-class women kept family, community, and country alive, clothed, and fed. In fact, due to the lack of available labor, many of the provinces created and implemented laws to gain control over the labor of poor or indebted women, creating antivagrancy laws and a system of peonage in which debtors were bound in servitude to their creditors. Police arrested women for vagrancy, debt, and public scandal (read: prostitution or drunken behavior) and put them to work, even if it meant sending them to other parts of the province. Though these laws were not written explicitly for women, they affected women more than men because most men were away fighting or already employed, or their drunken behavior was not considered a public scandal. "The fact that female convicts were put to work in Cordoba as replacements for a scarce male labor force, or forcibly dispatched there and elsewhere in the interior to work as domestic servants, demonstrated the main function of peonage in Argentina: the regulation of a scarce labor supply to secure sufficient numbers of workers for critical areas of the economy . . . only the lower class—the slaves, ex-slaves, and poor of humble birth—were affected by these laws" (Guy 1981, 69).

Women's productive capacity sustained the economies of the provinces throughout the nineteenth century. To survive in the provinces, women produced many necessary products, such as saddles, tack, clothing, sheets, and foodstuffs from the efforts of their tanning, weaving, embroidery, animal husbandry, and gardening. It was a simple step to producing more and selling it as villages, towns, and cities expanded. "On the eve of independence in 1810, women's cottage industries formed a mainstay of the provincial economies in the north, west, and center of the country and became even more important after the outbreak of war. Traders in the interior . . . sold cotton, woolen and fur garments, and foodstuffs, prepared in slave workshops and at home by women of all classes, to workers in the mines of Potosi, Bolivia" (Guy 1981, 66). If the employment and self-employment of women artisans were as significant as the historical record indicates, there had to be a certain level of independence for some women, or at least a curb to machismo in the 1800s, because many of the men were off fighting wars or working on the big farms of the coastal plains called La Pampa. This period, however, could not withstand the political consolidation of the country, and when it ended women lost many of their income-generating opportunities in the provinces. In the capital of Buenos Aires, immigrant women used ethnic and kin networks to find employment in the factories and industries of the modernizing economy but often within sectors of the economy, such as the textile industry and domestic service, deemed appropriate for women and at wages always inferior to men's (Guy 1981, 85).

From Early Republic to Consolidated State

During the century of civil war, political leaders of Argentina made some progress during the nineteenth century to develop a legal framework, an educational system, and a multiparty political system for the new nation. Though some of these developments, such as education, benefited women, the majority of these advances benefited the new elites: the estate owners of the coastal regions and the early industrialists of Buenos Aires. By the end of the nineteenth century, Buenos Aires had emerged as a strong capital, with the provinces accepting their subordination to a centralized national project (Carlson 1988, 1–45). Business interests began to modernize the economy. Major economic activity centered in the capital and coastal areas drawing workers and productivity away from the provinces (Guy 1981, 84–85). This development contributed to the collapse of women's economic prospects in the provinces, though employment opportunities did open up in the capital. Massive European immigration began to arrive in Buenos Aires—people escaping economic depression and political conflict in their own countries and hoping that the Argentine government's propaganda about economic opportunities was genuine.

Bernardino Rivadavia (1780–1845), a liberal president of the fledgling republic, promoted the participation and leadership of elite women in charitable activities. In the early 1800s the first voluntary organizations appeared, though primarily limited to charitable activities. In 1823 Rivadavia founded the Charity Society (La Sociedad de Beneficencia), the organization that was to dominate charity work nationally until the mid-twentieth century. The Charity Society was run by "those ladies of charity," elite women who provided most of the state welfare for women, schooling for girls, hospitals throughout the country, homes for the elderly, and emergency relief for the country for over one hundred years. State monies and elite donations funded this organization, making it in effect the welfare program of the government. The Charity Society was not about transforming gender oppression, but it was about providing a safety net so working-class and poor women could continue to fulfill their roles in society. For the women who staffed it, it must have been a rewarding experience, at least for some, to serve outside the home. From the beginning, gender and class were interlocked factors determining the scope of the institution: "In this institution, as well as in the majority of charitable organizations, women occupied a privileged place in the management/leadership of these organizations. The central role of women in charitable work had little to do with feminism and a lot to do with elitism" (Thompson 1994, 18). Volunteer work with the Charity Society gave elite women the opportunity to be active outside of their homes, but it also fit within their traditional reproductive roles in the family and promoted the status quo guaranteeing elite interests. It moved those roles out into the community, creating opportunities outside the home for elite women while contributing to the installation of a paternalistic approach to the lower classes.

By the late 1800s opportunities for other groups of women appeared in the field of education; Argentina's commitment to education for boys and girls contributed to the integration of middle-class women—active as teachers and administrators within schools and the educational system as a whole—into the public sector as well as establishing Argentina as a country of literate people. Under the leadership of liberal thinker Domingo Sarmiento (1811–1888), minister of education in the mid-1800s, Argentina became known for having the best educational system in Latin America. Much enamored of the U.S. educational system, Sarmiento returned to Argentina after a visit to the United States with many ideas about how to promote progress. For instance, he felt girls deserved education as much as boys. "[He] thought girls should be educated, not just to be better mothers, but to be able to contribute to society by being involved in local politics" (Carlson 1988, 81). Argentine women became teachers and principals of schools for girls, as well as administrators at the highest levels of the educational system. The 1895 census reported that "49% of all men and 41.5% of all women were literate . . . there can be no doubt that there was less discrimination against women in education than in most countries of the world at that time" (Molyneux 1986, 125). Education is a significant factor in indices of women's empowerment (Valdés, Muñoz, and Donoso 2005); not only does it translate as increased opportunities for income generation, but it also facilitates women's knowledge and expectations regarding their own rights.

Argentine working- and middle-class women tended to focus on women's rights to education and the other feminist issues of the socialist and anarchist platforms. Socialism and anarchism expanded in Argentina due to the arrival of militant immigrants who were part of the large wave of European immigrants in the late 1800s.[4] Both of these parties found fertile soil in Argentina for their political organizing (Molyneux 1986, 121): harsh working conditions for the working class, an immigrant population sensitive to progressive European political ideas, and an incipient state apparatus with an ambivalent commitment to democracy. Not until 1912 could all male Argentine citizens vote. Reluctant to offer potentially radical immigrants citizenship, Argentine law made it difficult for immigrants to gain citizenship and the right to vote or have a legal say over state policies (Molyneux 1986, 122).

The socialist and anarchist movements had progressive platforms regarding the rights of women, though discrepancy often existed between principles and actions. "Both socialism and anarchism focused on the working class but also expressed some sympathy for the principle of women's emancipation" (Molyneux 1986, 123). There was an active feminist contingent within the anarchist movement; feminist anarchists believed women "were doubly oppressed—by bourgeois society and by men" (132). As published in the feminist newspaper *Women's Voice*, a group of feminist anarchists declared, "We hate authority because we aspire to be human beings and not machines directed by the will of 'another,' be this authority, religion, or any other name" (129).

Though the anarchist movement supported women's liberation in theory, there was often ambivalence or outright criticism of women who pursued a feminist agenda by militants who felt it was shortsighted to prioritize feminist concerns at the cost of the class struggle. In their minds, women's liberation would automatically occur once the revolution had happened. Molyneux summarizes the lack of solidarity that male anarchists offered the women editing *Women's Voice*: "this apparent sympathy for feminism in principle within the Anarchist ranks was matched by substantial opposition in practice" (127). Anarchist feminism in Argentina was riddled with ambiguities that hampered the efforts of its militants from building a broader base of support for three interlocking reasons: first, male anarchists felt it was more important to focus on worker rather than feminist issues; second, the clandestine nature of anarchist actions made it difficult to communicate the message on a mass level and attain support from less radical sectors of society; and finally, early anarchist feminists could only raise their concerns and propose overthrowing the government due to the radical approach of the anarchist critique in which reform was seen as palliative—the only route was revolution. Even though the organizing efforts of these early feminist anarchists did not build a widespread movement, the revolutionary feminism of early Argentine anarchism differed from other forms of feminist organizing in Argentina and other countries of the time because of its working-class composition: "As one of the first recorded instances in Latin America of the fusion of feminist ideas with a revolutionary and working-class orientation, it differs from the feminism found elsewhere in Latin America . . . which centered on educated middle-class women" (120).

Competing for the hearts of the working class, the Socialist Party eventually eclipsed the anarchist movement. Founded in 1894 by Dr. Justo, who "wanted to cure social ills by improving . . . the existing order" (Guy 1988, 63), the Socialist Party was reformist in nature and committed to working within the guidelines of a democratic society. The Socialist Party surpassed the anarchist movement in the early twentieth century in membership growth and acceptance within Argentine society in general. Though not as outspoken as the feminist anarchists, the Socialists proposed numerous reforms on behalf of women's rights. Early Socialist feminists included Cecilia Grierson, Alicia Moreau de Justo, Juana Rouco, and others who "launched the struggle for equal rights, better educational opportunities and reform of the civil code, and in so doing they radically redefined the politics, strategy, and terrain of feminist struggle" (Molyneux 1986, 141). These women—in great part responsible for reforms to the civil code in 1926—had overturned the law that classified women as minors. With the 1926 reforms, women were legally required to be treated as adults and could request parental rights over their children in the case of death of their husband or separation (Pite 2002, 5; see also Htun 2003). "According to the new law, married and minor women could choose their own professions and did not have to turn their wages over to husbands or fathers" (Guy 1988, 75). Socialist Party members—men and women—also made headway for women in Argentine society by showing that laws, public health policies, and programs had little chance of success if they were flawed by gender and class prejudices (77).

Though women's civil society actions appear divided along class lines—the elite-run Charity Society, the working-class feminism of early anarchists, and the middle-class feminist reformism of socialism—a number of women worked across class boundaries on issues that affected all women: the right to citizenship, the right to inherit property, parental legal rights over minor children (*patria potestad*), and the right to vote. This was not enough, however, to foster a mass movement across boundaries and mobilize women across the class spectrum; working-class women had yet to find a leader they felt represented their interests.

From the Populism of Peronismo to the Dirty War

The next wave of development of civil society occurred because the new pool of immigrants—influenced by progressive European political currents and developments—began to organize themselves, first just to survive and then to flourish as unions and other associations. Class tensions became exacerbated, leading many women activists to dedicate themselves to political parties and unions (See James 2000). From the late 1800s until the 1930s, immigration from Europe brought five million men, women, and children to Argentina, creating a workforce for industrial development. "This massive immigration along with economic development helped to create a large and independent middle class as well as an urban proletariat" (Carlson 1988, 41). Though women made up 20 percent of the labor force in the industrializing capital, these opportunities were somewhat limited: native-born women were less likely to be hired than immigrant women due to effective ethnic networks in the industrial sector; protective legislation for women actually kept employers from hiring women in many cases; and women received less pay than men for a day's work (Guy 1981).

Many of these immigrants brought their political commitments to their new country: "The first generation of immigrants lived the tension between establishing a new home and keeping alive the links and identity associated with the old. For some, strong echoes of political struggles in the 1920s, 1930s, and 1940s intensified these tensions" (James 2000: 14). Union organizing at this time in the meat-packing plants and other industries contributed to the development of a fairly unified working-class identity, the efforts of which met a champion in General Juan Domingo Perón.

General Juan Perón and his wife, Evita Perón, needed working-class women's endorsement to increase popular support for Peronismo. Elected president in 1946, Perón was able to channel civil society agendas toward state interests by modernizing the country; he instituted basic labor rights, advocated for women's right to vote, and established a minimum safety net for the working poor. But when Perón granted suffrage to women in 1947, many women's organizations did not respond positively, indicating that they wanted to earn the vote, not get it as part of populist politicking. Nonetheless, because Evita founded the Peronist Women's Party, which by 1952 had 500,000 members and 3,600 offices throughout the country,

Perón and Evita brought women into politics in a massive way that had never previously occurred in Argentina (Fraser and Navarro 1980, 107).

Because of Evita's populist bent and working-class background, the elite women's groups, especially the Charity Society, scorned the Peróns. However, when the ladies of the Charity Society learned that Perón was considering taking possession of the organization and nationalizing it, they begrudgingly invited Eva to be their honorary president and assist with fund-raising activities. Eva told them the days of charity were over and it was time for social justice (Fraser and Navarro 1980, 116). In 1948 the government took over the Charity Society, renaming it the Eva Perón Foundation and giving Eva full leadership of the new organization. "And it was indeed in Evita's sole hands, for everything that it accomplished had been planned, supervised and carried through by her" (118). Evita and her foundation employed 14,000 workers, distributed 400,000 pairs of shoes, 500,000 sewing machines, and 200,000 cooking pots; the foundation also built schools and housing and ran hospitals (118–130). Though much of the work of the foundation was administering donations, Evita and her staff personally attended many of the people who sought assistance from them. The foundation may not have been quite as elitist as its predecessor, the Charity Society, but the foundation had such a broad mandate, assumed so many social welfare responsibilities, and provided so many direct donations to people that it left little space for other civil society organizations. "Moved by deep personal convictions but simultaneously fulfilling a political mandate for the *Peronista* state, the leadership of Evita transformed the rules of private philanthropy. When the State assumed the monopoly of the public good, it became the only distributor of aid ... From this perspective, one of the central questions is whether the Peronista State granted social citizenship ... or if it instead closed the doors to more autonomous actions by civil society" (Thompson 1994, 49).[5] Thompson's critique here includes the actions of the Eva Perón Foundation but extends to embrace all of Peronist politicking. Clientelistic relations were instituted that co-opted more than they empowered, limiting civil society organizing and citizen participation. Many accounts of Eva's philanthropic endeavors corroborate Thompson's cogent concern that though the aim may have been redistribution, the impact was clientelism, not social justice.

Yet the contradiction remains: as much as Peronismo may have co-opted civil society organizing, it transformed the lives of many working-class men and women, creating the impression of citizenship, something they had never previously enjoyed in Argentina. Early union organizers—especially women—still remember the time of Perón with nostalgia; the Peróns were seen as champions of the working class. María Roldán, one of the first union organizers in the meat packing industry in the working-class city of Berisso, remembers that "in Perón's time Berisso was one of the happiest places on the face of the earth. I have seen the people happy, shopping, going on their vacations because we got paid vacations, too" (James 2000, 70). To this day, Perón is credited for all those advances gained. When asked why she still has such faith in Perón and Peronismo, María Roldán responded, "Because thanks to him we have civil rights for women, pensions so we don't die in a plaza of hunger like an old horse. I cashed my pension check today and that of my husband. I'm not going to be rich, but I can buy a *bife* [piece of beef], a liter of milk, I get by. Perón left me that, because it didn't exist before. They say there were laws before Perón, but they were stuffed in a chest full of cockroaches" (99). If Perón is nostalgically remembered as the father of modern working conditions, Evita Perón was his charismatic equal and is revered as a modern-day saint by many in Argentina. Her working-class roots and early death to uterine cancer in 1952 have only fueled this interpretation of her, substantiated by anecdotes of her goodness, commitment to the poor, and generosity. In the course of the interviews for this book, Evita was frequently referred to with tenderness and respect.

Despite the fact that Perón enjoyed widespread support among the working class, he had many critics among the elites and middle class. Peronist leaders used strong-arm politics, intimidation, and repressive tactics to coerce compliance with populist politics. Dissent began to grow as economic crisis deepened and the Peronist security forces became more repressive in order to maintain power. "To economic collapse and corruption were added the methods of Perón's security forces. They had successfully muzzled his enemies, and this had left them with an appetite for more. . . . Torture had been used in Argentina before Perón, and would be used even more after him. His contribution during the last years of his government was to make it part of police procedure"

(Fraser and Navarro 1980, 172). With the coup of 1955, Perón was forced into exile in Spain, exposing his followers to harsh repression; this set the stage for even more brutal state actions in the years to follow. Magdalena Jamargo, herself a longtime union organizer, witnessed the illegal detention of her father, a Peronista union organizer when she was a child. She recounts:

> I come from a family in which my father was a member of the Peronista party for many years. He was a delegate to the cobblers' union. In the year 1955 under the repression of Aramburu and Rojas, he was illegally detained . . . disappeared for a year . . . obviously because of his militancy as a Peronista. I was eight years old at the time. And we were left scarred by his disappearance, how they took him from our house, and during his disappearance, the ensuing dismemberment of the family. In our case, there was no exile; the family remained in Buenos Aires, in Argentina, but we split up . . . a series of events that changed us all. My papa was held in the Olmos Prison. When they finally acknowledged they were holding him, he still remained imprisoned until 1956 when he was let go on conditional parole. A number of years passed under military rule until Perón returned to Argentina, but soon thereafter, the military took power again.
>
> As I mentioned, when my father was taken, we were left deeply scarred. I believe that there are things that one carries inside that can't be erased, at some point they will reappear, but for quite a long time, we weren't activists, we spoke as little as possible about politics and unionizing. It wasn't until I was an adult and began to think and reason . . . well, first off because I was a Peronista and secondly because I had that desire within me to help society, to help people; we need a better society.[6]

This period affected Magdalena and her family in severe financial, emotional, and psychological terms; her father was blacklisted after his imprisonment; and she and her brother had to go to work to support the family. She was twelve and had to abandon her studies. Her father never recovered his previous courage and commitment after imprisonment; he was disillusioned politically, weakened emotionally, and broken physically. He died of tuberculosis soon thereafter. In 1987 Magdalena joined the Argentine Printers Union and ultimately rose up to hold a position of power within it, but the years following her father's disappearance continued to be filled with fear.[7] As evidenced by what happened to Magdalena's father and her family, the period following Perón's exile was marked by the persecution of Peronistas, martial law, disappearances, torture and extrajudicial executions.

By the time conditions permitted the return of Perón in 1973, there was much expectation on behalf of civil society organizations about the new political opening, but Perón's chance to make good on his promises began to dim immediately and was extinguished with his death in 1974. Cata Jiménez, a young community activist at the time, was encouraged to go to the airport to welcome Perón home from exile. She still remembers that event even today:

> I remember when I was thirteen or fourteen years old and I was very involved in the community, not in politics, but there were people here who were militant activists. I would go out with them but I did not know that they were . . . I don't know if I should say the word [*looks inquiringly at her neighbor to see if she can tell me the word, neighbor nods yes*] . . . they were the *Montoneros*. Anyway, I was hanging out with them, they were good people, trying to help out in the neighborhood, they built a little room and brought vaccines, they helped kids study, they helped out, all these kinds of things. But I was just a kid and didn't know. The last time I hung out with them was when Perón returned. I went to the International Airport with the different Peronist factions . . . And in the midst of it all, a battle started between the different factions, from the far left to the far right. I was in the midst of the shooting. . . . They say that at that moment Perón wanted to leave, asking himself "Why have I returned to this?" I was there. I remember all of this; I remember we ran from the airport into the surrounding countryside. Everyone was running in different directions. We had to run because the shooting was something impressive; we had to flee from those who had come to meet Perón. I remember that I found a place to hide, full of other people escaping the shooting.[8]

Cata's memory of Perón's return to Argentina after his exile reveals how Peronista supporters had divided during his absence, splintered so much that the only thing they held in common was violence, which they directed against each other. These tensions did not bode well for a successful long-term government, as ensuing events revealed. Isabelita de Perón, Perón's third wife and vice president, assumed the presidency when her husband died in 1974. Unable to control hyperinflation and growing civil unrest, her presidency was cut short by an army coup, and she was replaced by the first of three military juntas in 1976. The next eight years became known as the dictatorship, also referred to as the *dirty war* in academic literature; the authors of the coup called it the Process for National Reorganization, or simply el *proceso*.[9] This time is described as "brutal, sadistic and rapacious" (Feitlowitz 1998, ix) because the army and security forces implemented a eerily efficient plan to quell dissent. In a tactic witnessed under other Latin American authoritarian regimes, the army and other government security forces closed democratic spaces and took control of schools, universities, and the means of communication in order to instill a new political, economic, social order. The threat of subversives was used to eradicate the Peronist Montoneros and non-Peronist guerrilla movements (which could not have numbered more than 15,000 combatants in the early to mid-1970s).[10] The security forces then turned their attention to anyone remotely progressive in their political thought. In this fashion, the armed forces and other state security forces systematically eradicated the civilian left through exile or disappearance, which meant taking prisoners to secret concentration camps, torturing them, and then killing them. The generals of the dirty war and their collaborators attempted to eliminate activism through the disappearance of over thirty thousand people; this silenced most civil society organizations. "The repression suffered by the Argentine people during the military government had been the most severe in the country's history" (Htun 2003, 99). This attack on basic human rights by the Argentine armed forces and government security forces led to the exile, imprisonment, and death of women and men civilians.

During this period (1976–1983), most civil society groups, including women's groups, had to cease their activities. One of the few civil society organizations that had a public face, even under the weight of the repression, was the Madres de Plaza de Mayo, formed by mothers of the disappeared in early 1977. These primarily working- and middle-class mothers with disappeared children began to meet and walk around the plaza in front of the presidential palace, sharing information and strategizing about how to locate their children. "The original group was made up of some 14 women between the ages of 40 and 62 who crossed paths in their endless, frustrating search for their sons and daughters" (Feijoó 1994, 112). Rosa Nair Amuedo was a housewife and mother of three adult children when Patricia—her youngest daughter, recently married, and mother of two—was disappeared. Tato, Patricia's husband, was killed by the security forces who kidnapped her.

> I don't know if it would console me to have her bones or to have a place where I could take flowers. There is nothing that consoles me. A child can die but not this way. One never imagines that her child could die this way. This is what happened to the children of every mother of the Plaza de Mayo, never knowing how or where or what the reasons may have been. My daughter was taken because she was married to a Marxist, a man with ideals who was not a guerrilla.[11]

Rosa had just finished raising her own children, but with the assassination of her son-in-law and disappearance of her daughter, she became mother to her two grandchildren—a newborn and a toddler. Under government auspices, many of the children of the disappeared were stolen from their mothers and given away in adoption to military families, but with Rosa this did not happen. She continued to search for Patricia, joining the Madres in 1977.

> We would meet and walk around the statue of Belgrano. There we would walk and talk; every time it was with someone new. Who was taken from you? From where? Trying to see if anyone had news or had seen your son or daughter. It was the only place where you could talk because at home no one spoke about what had happened . . . but in the plaza, yes, we talked . . . we never thought that we would become what we are today. The only thing we wanted was that they tell us where our children were, how long they would be there, and when we could see them. We never thought we would never see them again.[12]

When Rosa joined the Madres de Plaza de Mayo, it was a small group of mothers desperately looking for their children. As the repression grew, the group became an organization that refused to let repression and fear quell their questions, demanding the return of their children and ultimately a return to democracy. When no one else was protesting publicly, this group of mothers began to circle the Plaza de Mayo, desperate for information about the whereabouts of their children. During the dictatorship, the Madres demanded the release of their disappeared children; after the return to democracy, disagreements over their role in society led to a split in the organization. Madres de Plaza de Mayo–Línea Fundadora (the Founding Line) focused on legislation on behalf of the disappeared and their families, while the Grandmothers of the Plaza de Mayo worked for the recovery of children and babies stolen from disappeared parents. The Association of the Madres de Plaza de Mayo, on the other hand, turned its efforts in a more radical direction, fighting for more systemic social change. Both groups demanded those responsible for the repression be tried in court; and in the nineties and early twentieth-first century, both organizations protested the impact of structural adjustment policies on the poor. The Madres was "the only group who challenged the political boundaries imposed by a government that banned all political activities and political issues" (Mercer 1998, 5). They used the respect given to mothers as protection from state repression, asking, "Wouldn't you do the same if your children had disappeared?" They hoped the generals would not directly attack them due to the cultural value attached to motherhood and the fact that the regime itself used traditional notions of motherhood and nation to justify the supportive role women were expected to play in society. A return to traditional gender roles for women was a common goal of authoritarian regimes: "Military discourse had a significant gendered discourse ... Latin American military governments similarly expressed their right and reason to rule in gendered terms, and appealed to traditional virtues of feminine care and devotion" (Htun 2003, 19).

The dirty war, which forced civil society organizations to close their doors or operate clandestinely, had a profound impact on activists, organizers, and especially the women leaders interviewed, who were all affected by the repression—either imprisoned themselves or threatened with imprisonment, distraught searching for disappeared loved ones and family members, forced to choose between death threats or exile, and living in constant fear of the repression. Many young activists were forced to choose exile over the threat of being disappeared. Victoria Matamoro had to go into exile with her three young children due to her organizing of university students against the repression:

> The uprooting of exile is not something you choose. You have to leave because someone else decides you have to go; if not, they will kill you. Or if you do decide to stay, they will mistreat you, kill you. You live with that constant fear that makes you begin to lose pieces of yourself, your sanity, and balance. Even today, I do not pardon the people who did this or people who still keep committing atrocities in the world. I do not forgive them. And I don't understand them either. But I do manage to put them in a place of indifference within myself. And this is what helps you keep believing that a different system of living, of co-existence, of sharing is possible. And you leave everything, leave your ability to make choices. The choice. You chose to come here, chose to be sitting across from me with your file folder, with those clothes on, you chose which perfume you want to wear, which bed to lay down on. You chose all this. And [in exile] you have to leave it all behind so you can save your life. And this becomes part of your life, and it follows you all the days of your life.[13]

Argentina lost a generation during the dirty war, but to this day the scars from the repression and the fear can be found right on the surface, *a flor de piel*. For many activists, memories of the dictatorship remain vivid and they still struggle to make sense of the brutality. For others, their actions today stem from a commitment to assuring this never happens to Argentina again. Understanding civil society organizing and leaders requires taking into account the history of repression and how it has affected Argentine society.

Chile

From the outset of the 1540 campaign to claim the southeastern part of South America for the Spanish Crown, and through the years of ongoing hostilities with the indigenous people of the region, Spanish conqueror Pedro de Valdivia and his followers relied on indigenous women to build a society strong enough to survive the early years of Chile's colonization. Though only a few Spanish women, such as doña Inés Suárez and doña Mencia de los Nidos, actively participated in these campaigns on the side of the Spanish, local indigenous women were raped and coerced to serve as concubines and servants for the Spanish men, most of whom came to the region without their female relatives or wives. This is corroborated by the Chilean historian Gabriel Salazar (1992), who describes the Spanish Conquest in Chile as worse for indigenous women than in other parts of the Americas, because in Chile it took the Spanish and then the Chilean government two hundred years to subjugate the local indigenous peoples. This ongoing violence was often directed against native women, who were treated as "spoils of war" (Salazar 1992, 67). The unions—more often coerced than chosen—between Mapuche women and Spanish men engendered a Chilean family prototype: the indigenous mother gives birth alone, outside of the bounds of Western marriage, to interracial, illegitimate children, *mestizo* consequences of the Spanish conquest (Montesino 1992, 17). From 1540 on, women were used to build the new colony, either through the social restrictions placed on elite women who arrived from Spain or through the exploitation of indigenous women and the new generations of mestizo women, born of indigenous women from unions with Spanish men.

In Chile, the protagonism and solidarity of women—economically as well as civically—were extensive and widespread, and this phenomenon occurred more frequently among poor women than elite women.

> The history of the women of the *bajo pueblo* is different [than the history of elite women]. When faced with the extremes of patriarchy, women of the *bajo pueblo* showed more creative strength rather than simple rebellion: more productive work, more reproduction of life, and more affection and community solidarity. And throughout history, more daring to overcome popular machismo to the extent that they achieved an inversion of roles and created an alternative leadership developing a popular culture that was uninhibited, matriarchal, community-oriented. (Salazar 1992, 67)[14]

From the eighteenth century to the mid-nineteenth century, the mestizo population—previously limited to servitude on the haciendas—began to acquire small pieces of land, leading to the creation of a peasant or *campesino* sector of small farms in the countryside. Women were responsible for the home, small animal husbandry, and the crafts of weaving, sewing, ceramics, baking, and putting up preserves, cordials, and wine making. This time of relative prosperity revolved around women, their production, and their hospitality. From the early 1800s on, this golden epoch began to decline as wheat prices plummeted and the wars for independence began, completely disrupting family life for the Spanish and mestizos in Chile, as well as for the indigenous families who occupied the territory south of the Bio Bio River in south central Chile.

The Mapuche, the Spanish Colonizers, and the Chilean Nation

The indigenous people of the region—known as the Reche people and then by the late 1800s as the Mapuche—numbered about a million at the time of the arrival of the Spaniards (Bengoa 2000, 21; Boccara 1999, 426; Foerster 2001). Since repulsing Pedro de Valdivia's attempts to subdue them in 1580—having adapted Spanish horsemanship and military prowess to their own ends—they had maintained their own nation from the Bio Bio River south to where continental Chile ends and the fjords and islands of the Chilean Patagonia begin. As of 1599 all Spanish had been expelled to north of the Bio Bio where the present-day city of Concepción lies. From 1580 on the Spanish and the Reche people signed a series of treaties in which the Reche and their territory were recognized as an independent nation. This agreement lasted until the late nineteenth century and the final phase of Chileanization (the consolidation of the Chilean state).

At the time of the conquest Reche culture consisted of an economy based on hunting, gathering, and subsistence agriculture; because the Reche had not evolved into a socially stratified, advanced agricultural society like other Latin American cultures at the time of contact with Europeans, local communities were geographically dispersed and mobile, often picking up and moving according to the seasons, game, and availability of wild fruits and vegetables (Bengoa 2000, 23–27). Family lineages or *lofs* were the primary social and economic unit of society; more simply,

"The family was the center of this society" (31). Every lineage or extended family was ruled by a *lonko* (chief) who had the responsibility of providing for his extended family of warriors, their families, as well as his own wives and children. Marriage was patrilocal; and for powerful lonkos, it was polygamous, with wives moving to live with husbands in order to extend kinship and keep peace among the lineages. Polygamy became more widely practiced during times of conflict with the Spaniards because it was "used as a wartime strategy to increase the Mapuche population" (Richards 2004, 126). Indigenous religious beliefs were animist and based on the inherent interconnection of humans, spirits, and nature.

Contact with the Spaniards and the ensuing war led to many brutal transformations for the Reche, the least of which was losing 300,000 people to typhoid fever by 1554 (Richards 2004, 35). Nonetheless, their adaptability was indispensable to their survival, as demonstrated by their openness to new ideas such as cattle-raising, horseback riding, and agricultural practices. Some constants always remain as exemplified by their commitment to family, land, and ritual, thereby maintaining certain common threads and preserving their culture over the centuries (Bengoa 2000, 367). Their continued independence from Spain allowed them to maintain control over their own land and economy, and thus they began to dedicate themselves to raising cattle, horses, and sheep, which they had learned from the Spaniards. The hunter-gatherer became a mounted cowboy. Religious beliefs also changed;, and the Mapuche came to believe in a central god figure named *Nguechen* rather than a pantheon of spirits and deities. It was to this god that the *machi*—healers and spiritual intercessors—communicated in order to safeguard beliefs and practices and heal community members from physical and spiritual illnesses. A machi is "a person [man or woman but generally a woman] who serves as an intermediary between the world of the spirits and the human plane; she also is a healer using medicinal herbs" (Bengoa 1992, 116). Though there were regional dialects, the common language used was Mapudungun. This period ushered in a time of prosperity—economic and demographic—for the indigenous people living south of the Bio Bio through the late seventeenth century (Foerster 2001), but it was to end due to war, civil war, and land pressures. By the late seventeenth and early eighteenth centuries, the Mapuche people were experiencing growing conflict with Europeans encroaching on Mapuche lands crossing the Bio Bio and starting farms in Mapuche territory.

In 1810 conflict erupted as Chile fought for independence from Spain, beginning thirty years of war: first the war for independence from Spain, then internal conflicts, followed by the war against the Peru/Bolivia Confederation, which lasted until 1839. For the Mapuches and many poor mestizo families, the 1800s were times of war, hunger, and displacement. Because the men were off fighting, women were left to safeguard their families. Many women left the countryside, erecting homes on the outskirts of cities (Salazar 1992, 71). These bands of communities became known as places of hospitality, good food, and celebration. However, when men from the cities began to frequent these *ranchos*, the censure of the Church and local authorities was brought to bear. The women—having been accused of "prostitution, maintaining enclaves of men, and cohabitating shamelessly with men"—were evicted and either expelled from the country or made servants in the homes of judges or military men (Salazar 1992, 72).

By the time the Chilean army returned from fighting in Peru in 1839, they had gained modern military strategies, experience, and arms technology, especially relevant were the Spencer repeating rifles, which did not need to be reloaded after each shot (Bengoa 2000, 248).[15] This military knowledge and technology combined with a state project of Chilenization under the leadership of Colonel Cornelio Saavedra led to the subjugation of the Mapuche by the Chilean armed forces, a process that de la Maza described as "using the same army for internal colonization" (2003, 5). Beginning in 1869 the Chilean military campaign against the Mapuche took the form of pillage and scorched earth, in which Chilean soldiers and paramilitary groups "burnt houses, rucas, and crops. They imprisoned whoever they found, killing women and children. They took all animals they found and treated them as spoils of war" (Bengoa 2000, 210). By the time it was over in 1881, the Mapuche had suffered much more than just the direct impact of the oppression: they had also experienced famine and the spread of smallpox that accompanies times of war. The Chilean state promptly claimed most of Mapuche land as belonging to Chile and available for distribution to European settlers. "Mapuche lands were reduced to just 510,000 hectares, or 6.4 percent of their original territory" (Richards 2004, 127). The Mapuche were assigned to *reducciones* (reservations), where they were expected to farm small parcels of land (Bengoa 2000, 329). Lineages were disbanded, families separated, and 70 percent of the reservations were located in the IX Region, isolating the Mapuche from Chilean culture in general and in many cases from each other (Foerster 2001).[16] In 1884 a cholera epidemic swept through the region killing 15 percent of the Mapuche population (Bengoa 2000, 335). What the Spaniards had been unable to attain during the conquest, the Chilean government accomplished over a period of a couple of years: the dismemberment of the Mapuche nation and the permanent subjugation of the Mapuche people. At this same time, many poor mestizo women, forced to flee the fighting of the preceding decades—along with Mapuche women seeking better prospects—left their homes and moved to the tenements of Santiago to work as seamstresses in the economic boom of the textile industry and clothing manufacturing. Even though this meant salaried work, living conditions in the tenements that had replaced the *ranchos* of the preceding era were harsh and salaries were low in the face of growing inflation.

Organizational Efforts for Justice

In the early 1900s women textile workers and women in saltpeter mining areas participated in a movement for social justice and political inclusion in which unions and leftist political parties, including the Socialist Party, also participated. Because many of the economic opportunities were in the cities, migration increased from the countryside to the cities. "This generated a noticeable social polarization and a great agglomeration of the popular classes in the cities, with precarious housing and sanitary conditions" (Irarrázaval et al. 2006, 44). It was at this time that women workers began to create community organizations to address the deplorable living and working conditions they faced. This type of organizing has existed vibrantly in working-class communities since the late 1800s.

In Chile, women across the class spectrum founded organizations. Inspired by the feminism of doña Belén de Zarraga, a Spanish anarchist who traveled throughout Chile in 1913 speaking on behalf of women's rights, working-class women founded women's centers in the mining towns of Iquique and Antofagasta as well as anticlerical centers (Correa and Ruiz 2001; Pardo 1995). Elite women organized charity events, similar to Argentine elites of the time, as well as forming women's groups to reflect on how society limited women's options (Salazar 1992, 65). Also around this time, Mapuche social organizations began to form. The first Mapuche women's organization, the Yafluayin Women's Association, was founded in 1937 to bring together Mapuche women and learn more about their culture (Painemal 2005).

The protests of 1905 demanding a state response to inflation and the hunger marches in 1914, in which men and women alike participated, showed how dissatisfied the working class was with the intolerable conditions of the time. These protests culminated in the National Food Workers Assembly presenting to lawmakers a thorough plan of economic and social reforms. The government called a state of emergency and implemented repressive measures called "the process against the subversives" (Salazar 1992, 75) in which government forces actively suppressed civil society attempts to propose measures that would ameliorate the dearth of social, economic, and political rights. This approach did not deter the activists. And in 1925 the Constituent Assembly of Workers and Intellectuals wrote a new constitution for the country based on equality between the sexes.[17] The first speech of the meeting to ratify the new constitution was made by a woman who received a standing ovation from all present (75). Again, this proposal was not even considered by lawmakers, and the 1925 constitution for Chile that was approved by lawmakers contained no explicit reference to women, their equality, or their rights. Though these civil society efforts, which were cross-class and mixed gender, were repressed by government forces, the potential for a strong civil society capable of generating substantive proposals for addressing social inequalities was emerging. Although their efforts were met with repression, they retrenched. Salazar describes the process: "It may be that the people lost these political-military battles but they won many socio-cultural battles; it's just that the official record does not take these wins into account. Social history shows that in these cases, the people and the *rotos* fell back. But to where? To the private sphere and communal space . . . associative networks of a communal character" (Salazar n.d., 6).[18]

The initial organizing efforts of the early twentieth century were not in vain, as they created a base of organized, progressive men and women. With the emergence of a small middle class and a strong working class by the 1920s, the left began to coalesce into different political parties and coalitions. These parties proposed reforms and increased state services for the working class and marginalized sectors of the mestizo population. For most of 1932 to 1952, the Popular-Front leftist coalitions governed the country and fulfilled promises to expand the role of government and implement policies to afford full citizenship to the working class and urban proletariat of the country. "Constituted by the Radical, Socialist, and Communist Parties, the coalitions triumphed in the 1938, 1942, and 1946 presidential elections and won control of the executive branch of the state" (Rosenblatt 2000, 262). During these governments, Salvador Allende, medical doctor by training and socialist politician, emerged as a political leader from cofounding the Chilean Socialist Party in 1933 to taking various different political posts with the Popular-Front governments. The policy work of these governments—attempting to institute popular reforms while currying to elite, liberal economic interests— affected women's roles and organizing in numerous (and sometimes contradictory) ways. Access to education created new opportunities for women, but traditional stereotypes—such as the sole male provider per family—engendered the idea that a woman's role was to stay at home. Though these governments aggressively promoted a male activism that avoided alcohol and other vices, which decreased domestic violence and levels of alcoholism, these campaigns strengthened the idea of the male breadwinner and the stay-at-home mother, which contrasted with the gender roles of the poor and working-class that had emerged historically in previous epochs (268). Nonetheless, women did take advantage of the progressive political climate and increasing role of the state to gain better health care and more access to education, not to mention full suffrage in 1949.

Socialist Elections, Authoritarian Dictatorship, and a Return to Democracy for Chile

In 1970 Salvador Allende won the presidential election of Chile; Allende was a socialist who represented the coalition party the Unión Popular (UP-Popular Union), which included people from the following parties: Socialists, Communists, Radicals, Social Democrats, and Christian Democrats. Allende's government was committed to building a socialist project that included the masses—the urban and rural poor and the indigenous peoples of Chile—as well as economic progress for elites. "The Allende government attempted to pave a 'peaceful road to socialism,' implementing Marxist reforms within a democratic framework. Allende nationalized industries, accelerated the process of agrarian reform, and incorporated peasants and workers into the political system on a massive scale" (Baldez 2002, 1). Similar to the preceding period, the inclusion and equality of women was a stated goal of the Socialist Party, but state rhetoric on gender roles served to effectuate few actual changes for women, continuing to envision women as supportive mates and good mothers. "Despite the view, typical of socialist movements, that all people, regardless of sex, would benefit from a move toward class equality, and despite his own belief that the integration of women at all levels would be essential for the success of the movement, Allende did little to incorporate women, who often ended up in supportive roles" (Richards 2004, 33–34).

For three years, Allende and his government struggled to implement the economic and political goals they had set. Some of the new policies—along with sabotage by producers and resistance by elites—produced hardships for the general population, such as electricity shortages, food shortages, and long lines for basic food stuffs. Allende detractors—including many women and the elites—played on these shortages as well as on some peoples' fears of communism to amplify the atmosphere of hardship and insecurity. Women on the right—upset at food rationing, Allende's socialist agenda, and the threat to traditional gender roles by leftist rhetoric—organized protest marches against the government demanding their concerns be addressed.[19] These demonstrations contributed to the government's increasing loss of credibility.

Allende's perceived loyalty to the Communist Party in the Soviet Union, along with his friendship with Fidel Castro, served to alarm cold war proponents in the United States. Little attention was paid to the fact that he condemned the use of violence to achieve political ends and was strongly critical of the Soviet Union's invasion of Hungary in 1956 and Czechoslovakia in 1968. The U.S. government and the Central Intelligence Agency (CIA) attempted to influence the presidential elections in favor of Allende's opponents, and, having failed at that, worked actively to destabilize the economy and create dissent, providing funding to opposition parties, sectors of the Chilean Army, and CIA operatives in the hopes of encouraging a coup. Henry Kissinger, national security advisor to President Richard Nixon, warned the president in 1970 that the Allende election created "one of the most serious challenges ever faced in the hemisphere" and that the president's "decision as to what to do about it may be the most historic and difficult foreign affairs decision you will have to make this year" (National Security Archive 2004).

When General Pinochet and much of the Chilean army carried out a coup on September 11, 1973, the U.S. government was not adverse to the fact that events had finally conspired to overthrow Allende. Sadly, though, the coup not only led to much bloodshed—including the death of President Allende—it ushered in one of the darkest, most frightening, least democratic times of Chilean history. Similar in intent to the subjugation of the Mapuche in the 1870s and 1880s, General Pinochet implemented a plan of terror to subdue subversive elements of society into acquiescence, as well as an overarching political and economic plan to position Chile as a neoliberal country with extensive opportunities for foreign investment. "Under Pinochet's dictatorship, Chile experienced the imposition of what was perhaps the most extreme model of neoliberal socioeconomic reform of all Latin American states" (Richards 2004, 3).[20] Pinochet's campaign of terror frightened people into not questioning human rights abuses or a larger neoliberal economic plan. Though the repression was the harshest in the six months following the coup, 35,000 to 40,000 people were illegally detained, the grand majority of whom were tortured while in detention, and roughly 2,700 people were murdered by government security forces.[21] "The democratic institutional breakdown led to a breakdown of the organization of the political, economic and social system that had been in force for the past 50 years" (Irarrázaval et al. 2006, 47). The government carried out information campaigns actively promoting an individualistic spirit, propagating the message that individuals should meet their own needs and not rely on a welfare state to provide services. If someone could not meet their needs, they were told they needed job training, not citizen participation.

Laura (who prefers not to use her real name when talking about the dictatorship), codirects an NGO serving marginalized sectors of the population south of Santiago. She witnessed the terror firsthand when she was a teenager living at home and then as a university student. She and her family were supportive of the Allende government:

> I come from a leftist family . . . So, of course, my family experienced the arrival of Allende as a major win, the commitment of my family was great, and this meant that when the coup happened and the dictatorship started in 1973, a wave of persecution hit my family. I was a direct witness to what was going on. I was twelve or thirteen years old at the time. Imagine a child that old being completely aware of what was going on. Uncles and aunts were exiled. A number of cousins were killed. And the police came to my house looking for my mother. I spent my time searching, trying to get my cousins out of prison and having to keep my mom safe.[22]

Many people—formerly active in the Allende administration—were either disappeared or forced into exile, seeking political asylum in Canada and Europe. In addition to targeting individual people, the dictatorship forced civil society organizations to close. "During this period various civil society organizations were intervened and under surveillance" (Irarrázaval 2006, 47). But under the protection of the Catholic Church, a number of organizations began organizing against the dictatorship, and women were leaders as well as activists in them all. Relatives of the disappeared demanded the return of their relatives. After the first couple of years of repression the terror lessened, and people cautiously began to oppose the dictatorship. In the marginalized communities ringing the major cities (called *poblaciones*), *pobladoras* (the women of these communities) worked together for mutual support, economic survival, self-help, and mobilization against the regime. They worked closely with feminist organizations to discuss the role of women in society and the need to return to democracy. Women led the way in creating a pro-democracy movement that included workers, women community leaders, intellectuals, and the Mapuche (see Richards 2004).

During the dictatorship, women protested the repression of the government, and they demanded the reappearance of loved ones who had been disappeared or jailed. Under the auspices of the Catholic Church, social service organizations thrived. Many of today's feminist nongovernmental organizations and human rights NGOs first formed as self-help groups in the social outreach offices of the Catholic Church. The Solidarity Vicarage of the Catholic Church hosted the first meetings of the *arpilleristas*, craftswomen who used embroidery and appliqué to depict the political oppression they, their families, and communities were experiencing. These evocative and colorful pieces of folk art were smuggled out of the country and sold abroad to raise money to support families torn apart by the repression. The following description of an arpillerista shows how women used folk art to protest the dictatorship and generate much needed income: "[The arpillerista] does not use words because words have been denied her. But she can speak through a skill traditionally considered feminine, the use of thread and needle. Her needlework becomes testimony, based on the daily happenings of the inner history of a people . . . thread and needle are now at the service of images representing a collective memory and the almost epic testimony of a suffering people" (Moya-Raggio 1984, 279). Arpilleristas were often from the urban, working-class neighborhoods or poblaciones, but they were not the only women who benefited from the Church's protection. Pobladoras, or the women inhabitants of the poblaciones, also used Church protection to form self-help groups to feed their communities and generate income, gaining leadership skills and challenging the dictatorship. Because of the cuts to food subsidies and a reduction in state services to the underprivileged by the Pinochet regime, many former working-class families fell into poverty. "Poverty, expressed as lack of goods and services which fulfill the basic cultural and material necessities for existence, force women into a space of survival which they must resolve every day. In this way, their social participation is motivated in great part by the immediate and the urgent: the reproduction of life" (Ruiz, Solano, and Zapata 1998, 3). The poverty resulting from the political and economic policies of the neoliberal government of Pinochet—not to mention the political repression that affected these communities—forced many women to become activists just to provide food for their families.

In a negotiated transition to democracy, Patricio Alwyn, the head of Concertación, a coalition of center to left political parties, won the 1990 presidential elections; but Pinochet and the Chilean army continued to retain control over political and economic policy in the new era. "The armed forces retained substantial ideological and financial autonomy. Pinochet continued as commander in chief and enjoyed exclusive rights to nominate candidates for top army positions" (Htun 2003, 133). Pinochet's continued power notwithstanding, the Concertación government created new state agencies that attempted to address discrimination against women and the indigenous peoples of Chile. The National Women's Service (Servicio Nacional de la Mujer—SERNAM), an executive-level agency—was founded in 1990 "to promote women's equality" (Franceschet 2003, 12), and the National Corporation for Indigenous Development (Corporación Nacional de Desarollo Indígena—CONADI) was founded in 1993 "for indigenous affairs" (Richards 2004, 129). These agencies have demonstrated some success in incorporating women's and indigenous peoples' perspectives into some state programs, but they also created fissures concerning the risks of cooptation and dependence on state funds for civil society organizing.

El Salvador

The history of the emergence of civil society organizations in El Salvador provides an interesting contrast to both Argentina and Chile. El Salvador is an extremely small country, roughly the size of the U.S. state of Connecticut, and this facilitates communication and travel within the country, whereas parts of Argentina and Chile—especially in the south—remain very isolated to this day. El Salvador did not experience a period of more progressive government such as the Peronist movement in Argentina and the coalition governments in early twentieth-century Chile. What differentiates El Salvador the most from Argentina is how class and gender have served as cross-cutting factors that unified the popular movement rather than weakening it. Salvadoran women and men, farmers, city dwellers, workers, professionals, academics, feminists, and Christians (Catholics, Protestants, and Evangelicals) were all targets for the repression of the government security forces as they attempted to eradicate guerrilla forces in the late twentieth-century civil war that racked the country for well over a decade. As a result of their participation in civil society organizing efforts, activists came in contact with all kinds of Salvadorans, expanding their very notions of what it means to be Salvadoran. Certain similarities exist between El Salvador and Chile as both countries made the transition from authoritarian forms of government to more open democratic conditions in which the left in general and the women's movements in particular were able to achieve significant levels of participation and presence within the state apparatus. This meant not only getting jobs in newly formed state agencies for women, but also winning legislative posts at the national level, not to mention municipal governments. The differences between Chile and El Salvador may lie in how the women's movement in each country has evolved since the return to democracy. In Chile the women's movement has lost a lot of its momentum; according to many analysts, the movement has not been able to find a common issue that unites women as effectively as overthrowing the dictatorship. On the contrary, the Salvadoran women's movement remains a strong voice in civil society, and the advocacy efforts, mobilization of women, and many development projects implemented by a wide range of women's organizations provide services to all kinds of women throughout the country.

From Spanish Conquest to Worker and Peasant Insurrection

El Salvador received its first European visitors in the early 1500s. The Spaniards met with fierce antagonism by the local indigenous peoples of the area (the Lencas and the Pipils) and had to retreat to Guatemala. It was not until 1528, under a second expedition, that the Spaniards took control of the area now known as El Salvador, dividing most of the arable land into large estates among themselves. The rest of the land was left to the indigenous peoples who owned and farmed their land communally. Santos Zetino is thirty years old, and she lives in a small, rural community of indigenous people in the western province of Sonsonate. Following is her description of the encounter between the two cultures:

> Before the Spaniards arrived five hundred years ago, we had religious freedom within our culture. We had the right to worship what we wanted. We worshiped the water goddess, the sun, mother earth, mother moon, and our plants. We had deep freedom. The arrival of the Spaniards was by no means a meeting of two cultures for us. The word meeting implies mutual respect. The arrival of the Spaniards meant rape and discrimination for our women. 500 years ago our women didn't cover their legs with clothing. We were considered provocative and free game to whatever Spaniard. The Spaniards also

brought the Catholic faith, but for us, the cross is a sword. This is how they were ultimately able to conquer us, with the cross. Supposedly, we were saved when we were baptized and our sins were pardoned, but now we know that this was a lie. Christianity was the sword that the Spaniards used to subdue us.[23]

The hacienda system faced a number of challenges, such as not having enough land or labor to work the fields. To gain more land and create a landless peasantry to work hacienda lands, the Salvadoran government abolished the communal lands the indigenous farmers had farmed collectively. According "to a government survey from 1879 . . . over 25 percent of Salvadoran territory was held in communal village lands" (Ready 1994, 188). The communal lands of the local campesinos and indigenous people were legally disbanded, ostensibly to be redistributed individually to the poor and indigenous, but in most cases, the land was usurped by Spanish-descended elites for the production of basic grains and other agricultural products for the world market. "Between 1880 and 1912, the communal lands of the villages were disentailed, expropriated, and sold to wealthy families at give-away prices" (Beverly 1982, 57).

Thus began an ongoing mono-crop pattern of agricultural production that has greatly influenced the economy of El Salvador. Elites dominated the production of different mono-crops, which went through boom-and-bust cycles, only to be followed by the introduction of a new mono-crop. This cyclical process has happened with cacao, indigo, coffee, cotton, sugar, and soy. Following cacao and indigo, coffee was the agricultural product that further extended the process of consolidating large tracts of land in the hands of a few. The indigenous people were forced to be migrant laborers, working the coffee harvests of the elites. The few small landowners or indigenous people who had been able to retain or gain land seldom planted coffee themselves because of the amount of time needed to get coffee trees to maturity. Also, the volatility of the coffee market required that the producer have enough savings or income to survive a year of low prices.

El Salvador, along with the other Central American nations, declared their independence from Spain in 1810. In 1838 the region separated into individual countries, and El Salvador and the other Central American countries became independent republics. Until recently most of El Salvador's presidents have come from the military and have not hesitated to resort to repression to stop social unrest and protect the interests of the landed oligarchy. The transition from the Spanish hacienda model to the coffee plantation model was finalized by the late 1800s and experienced its golden age from 1912 to 1932 (Beverly 1982, 58). During this time, conditions continued to worsen for poor, landless, and indigenous farmers. With the disbandment of the communal lands, there existed a tendency toward *mestizaje*, in which indigenous culture simultaneously permeated the entire population and became less visibly distinct. Though there remain communities of people primarily identifying themselves as indigenous in the country to this day, many indigenous people slowly began to lose their cultural identities and assume a *ladino* one, creating a peasant population that was poor, disenfranchised, and indigenous. This process only intensified in the ensuing years.

A democratic opening in the 1920s gave communists and other leftist groups the political space to organize. In 1928 the El Salvador chapter of the Inter-American Women's Commission was founded by activists committed to gaining the vote for women. Presidential elections in March 1931 were a milestone in Salvadoran history. Prudencia Ayala, a feminist activist, sought to have her name included in the list of presidential candidates in an attempt to bring attention to women's right to vote (Herrera et al. 2008, 63). Though Prudencia was not allowed to run, the elections brought Arturo Araujo, a centrist candidate favored by the left, into the presidential office, and in the following legislative and municipal elections in December of that year, a number of communists won local municipal elections.

Araujo's tenure was extremely short. In December he lost his presidency to a military coup. Up until this time, the oligarchy had governed the country relying on the National Guard to keep order in the countryside. This coup marked a change: under a coup carried out with orders from General Maximiliano Hernández Martínez, the army took over running the country and, as part of the arrangement, committed itself to guaranteeing oligarchic interests. Martínez, who ruled El Salvador from 1931 until 1944, was responsible for "creat[ing] the characteristic institution of modern Salvadorean politics, the military-civilian junta in which the Army upper echelon controls the state security apparatus, and the oligarchy the

economic ministries . . . [from 1932 until 1992], periods of formal democratic rule in El Salvador total only nine months" (Beverly 1982, 59). Claiming that communist subversion had to be thwarted, General Martínez led a
successful army coup in late 1931, taking over the government.

In response to the coup, there was widespread protest and threats of a
general strike across the country. Hoping to channel the dissent, the Communist Party, under the leadership of Agustín Farabundo Martí, voted the
night of January 7 to lead a nationwide insurrection against the government and army on January 16 (Dalton 2007, 245–246). State security forces
detected the plan for the insurrection, arresting and killing Agustín
Farabundo Martí and two other communist leaders soon thereafter (250).
The remaining communist leadership postponed the insurrection until
January 22 but was unable to carry out the necessary preparations in the
face of army repression and losses to their ranks. Undeterred, peasants and
indigenous peoples took up arms throughout the countryside. Strongest in
the western part of the country where indigenous presence was more
extensive, the rebellion managed to capture a few cities in the interior. In
his testimony, recounted to Roque Dalton, Miguel Mármol, a Salvadoran
communist leader who survived these events, described why the insurrection failed: "Until the last moment, the [Communist] Party simply treated
the insurrection like a political event of the masses without developing a
specific military conception of the problem. The Party never realized that
military issues become fundamental once it's been decided there's going
to be an insurrection, and that military problems are solved with military
science and know-how that have their own rules, etc." (252). The insurrec-
tional forces, as disorganized as they were, held a number of western towns
and positions for a couple of days until the army overran them. In a
response calculated to silence the unrest, the army and the National Guard
killed, exiled, or disappeared 10,000–30,000 Salvadorans, mostly peasants
and indigenous people over the next six months; this period is known as
La Matanza (the Slaughter) in Salvadoran history (Ready 1994, 191; Stephen
1995, 809).

There are different analyses of the impact of the repression of La
Matanza. For communist organizers, it was a defeat that took years to
recover from. For rural communities, it was devastating and led to widespread displacement as families fled persecution. For indigenous culture,

many claim that the events of La Matanza decimated indigenous culture because of the killing during the massacre and the fear afterward that pervaded the local population. Indigenous people stopped wearing their traditional garb and ceased to speak Nahuatl with their children. This interpretation is articulately summarized by Santos Zetino:

> In 1932 we stopped wearing our native costumes because so many indigenous men and women were killed for being suspected communists, union organizers or supporters of Augusto Cesar Sandino in Nicaragua. Our women buried their red skirts (*cortes*) and blouses (*huipiles*) in the earth and began to wear clothes that would not distinguish them from the rest of the population. Whoever wore native dress was seen as subversives and killed. The problem now is that there is no one left who remembers how to weave the fabric for our native dress. My mother, for instance, buys her corte in Guatemala, but they are expensive and who has the money to dress their family? Three members of our community are going to Guatemala to study weaving so that they can teach other women in the community to weave. After the 1930s, indigenous people stopped speaking our native language, Nauhatl, because it, like our native dress, was seen as subversive. Today there are few people who speak the language. We want to relearn our language, but there is still much fear. For instance, a woman in our community speaks Nauhatl but doesn't join our group because she is afraid that we'll face persecution from the military for organizing ourselves.[24]

Many Salvadorans—as Santos pointed out—attribute the fact that indigenous people stopped wearing their native dress and ceased speaking Nahuatl in public due to the repression of the period. There is some debate over the extent to which the repression targeted indigenous people per se. Authors Ching and Tilley have analyzed newspaper articles and state and church documents from the time, and they argue that the target of army repression was not solely indigenous people, rather any people of the Salvadoran population suspected of communist or union sympathies. Ching and Tilley indicate that demographic records continued to show that parents inscribed their children with indigenous last names and said their racial background was indigenous at similar or even higher rates after La Matanza. The authors claim that indigenous culture not only survived but continues to make up 10 percent of the present-day population. "The Salvadorean Indians ... are an invisible or ghostly presence in the country: cautious in their public appearance as an ethnic community, officially non-existent—yet still recognized by neighbors, local municipal governments and, most importantly, by themselves as 'indios'" (Ching and Tilley 1998, 125–126). Nonetheless, given that many indigenous people as well as people of indigenous descent were killed during La Matanza, fear of being different or appearing to have progressive political beliefs left scars on much of the rural population for generations to follow.

The Civil War's Impact

From the 1930s on, military governments were the norm for El Salvador, and the U.S. Army emerged as a strong ally supporting the Salvadoran military. After Martínez stepped down in 1944, military governments continued to govern, guaranteeing the expansion of coffee and then cotton production while repressing dissent. Women's activism during this time was not just dedicated to gaining the vote, which they finally achieved in 1950; they were also active in the Salvadoran Communist Party in a group called the Fraternity of Salvadoran Women (Herrera et al. 2008, 63) as well as in other political parties. In 1959 the Cuban Revolution proffered an alternative model to activists, unionists, and intellectuals throughout Latin America. During the 1960s civil society organizing took to the streets again demanding an end to social injustice and a more equitable distribution of land and income. Ironically, the U.S. government played a significant role in igniting social unrest and the appearance of guerrilla groups. The roots of the Salvadoran civil war lie in unmet expectations about social, economic, political, and agrarian reforms. Many of these expectations were created and nurtured by the U.S. government and the Catholic Church. These institutions are not generally known to be proponents of revolutionary politics; therefore, an unpacking of U.S. foreign policy in El Salvador in the 1970s and 1980s, along with an analysis of the deepening commitment of the Salvadoran Catholic Church to social justice, are necessary before proceeding. Poverty alone does not drive people into organized political movements that take up arms. The revolutionary spirit in El Salvador was born from the combination of unfulfilled promises about the implementation of U.S.-sponsored agrarian reforms, the new message of liberation theology, and growing state repression.

The events that heralded the civil war period began in Washington, D.C. When John F. Kennedy came to the oval office in 1960, he immediately went to work on implementing campaign promises to promote development and democracy throughout Latin America. As LaFeber wryly mentions, "Using characteristic Kennedy rhetoric, the president declared, 'Let us again transform the (hemisphere) into a vast crucible of revolutionary ideas and efforts.' The key—and highly misleading—word turned out to be 'revolutionary'" (1984, 148). So Kennedy founded the Alliance for Progress and it was implemented by the U.S. Agency for International Development (USAID). However, with Castro's continued presence and the ongoing cold war, the Alliance for Progress quickly became a strategy for arresting further mobilization of the masses. Trying to prevent social unrest in El Salvador, Alliance for Progress advisors recommended that the Salvadoran government redistribute land to landless campesinos. According to Lynn Stephen, "Land distribution mirrored the distribution of wealth" (1997, 33). In 1976 USAID and others championed "the most far-reaching attempt at agrarian reform . . . [with plans] to expropriate some 56,000 hectares of land" (Simon and Stephens 1982, 5). This attempt was shelved due to major opposition from the oligarchy. However, by 1979 a new Salvadoran government, composed of a civilian-military junta, designed a three-phase agrarian reform that began implementation in 1980. With extensive technical assistance from USAID, the program quickly foundered in the face of continued opposition from the oligarchy and the Salvadoran army. LaFeber argues that the policies of Alliance for Progress actually promoted a revolutionary spirit, but not the revolutionary spirit U.S. political analysts wanted. Kennedy had envisioned something along the lines of the industrial revolution; a different kind of revolution emerged. LaFeber writes, "Ironically, it became the pivotal, perhaps even the essential, step on Central America's journey to the revolutions of the seventies and eighties" (1984, 145); the fact that the agrarian reforms were never fully implemented created civil unrest as expectations for land remained unfulfilled.

On an institutional level, the Catholic Church had generally supported oligarchic interests since the conquest of the Americas in the late 1500s. Generations of poor Salvadoran peasants had been raised believing that just as Jesus embraced his fate on the cross, so should they blindly accept hardships and injustice. The "groundbreaking" Vatican II (Second Ecumenical Council) pronouncements from Rome in the early 1960s described the church as a community of people of God, not a hierarchy (Lernoux 1980, 11). This message had truly revolutionary repercussions because it was interpreted by the Salvadoran Church as calling the faithful to build the Kingdom of God here on earth and not wait until heaven to have their suffering eased. Citizen unrest demanding higher wages, land, and basic services continued to grow in the late seventies, and the Salvadoran Armed Forces responded with repression. Not only were they *disappearing*, massacring, and torturing lay people, but they were also killing Roman Catholic priests and nuns.

Named Archbishop of San Salvador in 1977, Archbishop Oscar A. Romero was known as a timid and studious priest. However, upon the assassination of the priest Rutilio Grande in early 1977, Archbishop Romero began to speak out against the violence. Jon Sobrino, Jesuit and liberation theologian, claims that the repression against the people and the Church served to open the new archbishop's eyes to the plight of the Salvadoran people and inspired him to stand in solidarity with the Salvadoran people, "becoming the symbolic leader of the Salvadoran people" (Sobrino 1989, 36). During the homily of his Sunday mass on March 23, 1980, Archbishop Romero called upon the government security forces to stop the violence. He preached, "In the name of God, and in the name of this suffering people whose tumultuous cries reach heaven, I beg you, I order you in the name of God: Cease the repression." The next day Archbishop Romero was machine gunned to death while performing mass at a small Catholic hospital in San Salvador; by this time six priests had been killed by government security forces (48).

Many activists and those who had suffered army repression in the late seventies were forced to cease their activism in civil society organizations. Many chose to take up arms and fight the government. The conformation of the Farabundo Martí National Liberation Front (FMLN) led to a loose confederation of five armed *tendencias* (groups). From the beginning of armed conflict between the FMLN and the Salvadoran Armed Forces in 1980 until the signing of the peace accords in 1992, roughly a third of the country was held by the FMLN. As state repression increased and civilian opposition grew in El Salvador, U.S. assistance became more military in nature. By the early 1980s, the FMLN was active throughout the country and was regrouping after a failed 1981 national offensive. Civil society organizations began to reemerge—albeit timidly at first—in the mid-1980s due in great part to the international hue and cry on their behalf. Michael Foley describes this process: "Only the international spotlight, plus considerable financial support from abroad, allowed organizations associ- ated with the churches and the Left to begin building anew after 1984" (1996, 71).

George Bush Sr. visited El Salvador in 1984, cautioning the government to decrease human rights abuses. The following year Napoleon Duarte, a Christian Democrat, was elected in what Leigh Binford calls "demon- stration elections" (1998, 11). Elections—regardless of whether additional aspects of democracy were present—were all the U.S. Congress required to continue the assistance to the Salvadoran government. According to Binford, "Military and economic assistance increased from $25 million in 1980 to $500–600 million annually in the mid-1980s" (11–12). By this time the Salvadoran Armed Forces were implementing scorched earth policies à la Vietnam in attempts to "drain the sea of civilians" (10) and thus erad- icate local support for the guerrilla forces. With a population around five million inhabitants at the start of the conflict, these policies forced thou- sands of women, men, and children to flee their homes. Figures estimate that one million Salvadorans were displaced during the war (1980–1992), eighty thousand were killed, and at least seventy thousand were injured or disabled during the war (Murray 1997, 14).[25] "A further seven thousand had disappeared," according to Stephen (1997, 30). During this twelve-year period of civil war, overt U.S. foreign aid to the Salvadoran Armed Forces and Salvadoran government amounted to $6 billion (Murray 1997, 15).

Women and their children suffered disproportionately during the war. While many men fled their homes in fear of forced recruitment, army repression, or joined the army or the guerrillas, their families—wives, mothers, aunts, and children—were often left with the responsibility of ensuring the survival of the family. Ready describes this phenomenon: "This drain on the male population . . . affected family structures. While female heads of household were not a new development in El Salvador, the war forced women to bear an even heavier burden within the family"

(1994, 196). In cases where men left and women and their families stayed at home, women had to provide for their families; and when the situation at home became untenable due to army repression, they had to leave their homes with their children and survive as best they could, on the run in the mountains. Across northern and eastern El Salvador from 1980 to 1986, the Salvadoran Army forced 1,655,572 Salvadorans to flee their homes as part of their scorched earth campaign to eradicate the FMLN (Schrading 1990). Lt. Col. Domingo Monterrosa, field commander of the Salvadoran Army in Morazán, said, "There are times when you have to make war to gain peace" (Danner 1993). Groups of women and children often had to flee army campaigns by going on long *guindas*, or hikes, hiding from the army during the day and walking at night seeking refuge. In the cities women and children sought safety in marginalized communities or joined refugee camps within El Salvador. By the mid-1980s, 20,000 women and children filled refugee camps in Honduras, having walked across the border to seek safety (Fagen and Yudelman 2001, 79).

In December of 1981, El Mozote, a small town in the mountains of eastern El Salvador, had become a gathering place for locals and farming families from more isolated hamlets who knew little of the FMLN and felt safer together. Rufina Amaya lost many relatives, including her husband and their four children in the massacre. She describes the El Mozote massacre that occurred on December 11 and 12, 1981:

> The army had come early in the morning. They separated the men, the women, and the children. Over there, near the side entrance to the church is where they killed the men. They blindfolded them and tied their hands behind their backs. They shot them all on our church's doorstep. When they came to get us women, I managed to slip away. This tree saved my life. I hid behind it and heard the cries of my children, "Mommy, they're killing us . . . Mommy. . ." I had two choices: stay and die with my children or escape to tell what the Army had done. As they killed my children, I had to find spirit and strength. "God," I pleaded, "give me resistance and courage. My children have been killed but give me strength to speak the truth about what has happened here." During that time, I remembered Mary, who watched them crucify her son, Jesus. I thought to myself,

"These are the pains of Mary that I am experiencing right now as
I hear them killing my children and I have to face certain death too
or flee."[26]

In response to the army repression they had witnessed, many women
chose to join the ranks of the FMLN. According to Kelley Ready, "the FMLN
is estimated to have had between 10,000 and 20,000 troops during the
course of the war" (1994, 196). Thirty percent of the FMLN forces were comprised of women. Binford, as do other scholars (see Silber 2004), considers
that the percentage of women participants in the guerrilla is "quite possibly the highest percentage in Latin American history" (Binford 1998, 38).
As combatants, runners, communications specialists, cooks, health per-
sonnel, and rear guard, women played a key role in both the military suc-
cesses and the creation of the broad base of civilian support for the FMLN.
However, they also had to do this under a burden of gender discrimination
and subordination.[27] Binford points out, "Although FMLN propaganda
emphasized the equality of life in the organization and especially in the
campamentos [guerrilla encampments] . . . they made only limited and
feeble efforts to alter pre-war gender ideologies" (37). Frequently the target
of sexual harassment and outright discrimination, women seldom moved
up in FMLN ranks as easily as men. Morena Herrera, a feminist and former
FMLN *comandante*, remembers that her common-law husband, the official
comandante, had to die in combat before she was named interim comandante. As in the case of Morena's experiences, many Salvadoran women
began to develop a feminist consciousness during the war as they faced
institutionalized sexism within the FMLN. And if they fell into the hands of
the army, women—whether catechists, community organizers, or FMLN
combatants—were targets for brutal repressive tactics implemented by the
Salvadoran security forces and the armed forces because these women
were seen as subverting the conservative paradigm envisioned for the
Salvadoran woman as patriotic and maternal. As Stephen describes,
"Women prisoners [were] then punished uniformly with rape, sexual
brutality, and often death" (1997, 37).

The final phase of the war occurred with the FMLN offensive on the
capital in early November 1989. On November 16, the Atlactl Battalion
of the Salvadoran Army—having just received urban counterinsurgency

training from U.S. military advisors—killed six Jesuit priests, all professors and administrators at the University of Central America on the outskirts of San Salvador, along with their housekeeper and her sixteen-year-old daughter. After this tragic event, the voices of Salvadorans and concerned citizens around the world could finally be heard after years of U.S. support for the Salvadoran Armed Forces. The United Nations brokered peace accords that were signed between the Salvadoran government and the FMLN on January 16, 1992, in Chapultepec, Mexico. Though the civil war (1980–1992) led to the deaths of over seventy thousand people, the majority of the deaths are attributed to the army, security forces, and far-right death squads. Summarizing the 1993 final report of the United Nations Truth Commission, Stephen writes that the military—the recipient of millions of dollars in military aid from the United States—and the far-right death squads with ties to the army were responsible for 85 percent of the twenty-five thousand civilian deaths that the commission investigated (Stephen 1995, 808). The peace accords ended the war but did not resolve the myriad social problems confronting El Salvador, including gender discrimination.

The fact that so many Salvadoran women—either as civil society activists or combatants—participated in protests before the civil war and continued working in civil society organizations or joined the FMLN during the war meant that they had become aware of injustice and were willing to take risks to assure change. Blanca Mirna Benavides, long-term activist and civil society leader, was shot in the head during a campaign march in 1991. She describes how she lost her eye: "In 1991 the Communist Party decided to participate in the elections with the UDN [National Democratic Union] that was the legal side of the Communist Party. And a number of us were asked to participate. So I put forward my candidacy and during the closing campaign march, we were shot at. I was hit. The bullet hit my eye. I was hospitalized and then spent months in recovery. Later I underwent eight different operations to rebuild my face. The last one was in 1994."[28]

Because activists like Blanca Mirna in El Salvador had been caught up in the conflict through the sixties, seventies, and eighties, they missed the second wave of feminism, which had a strong impact on the women's movement in the United States and Europe during this time.[29] However, as a gender consciousness began to emerge in the reflections of women and men who had been active in the FMLN and civil society organizations, an autochthonous yet pluralized version of feminism emerged in El Salvador. It was not until the war entered its final stages that Salvadoran women began to reflect on how their experiences were different than men's. They began to talk together in groups about the fact that even in civil society organizations and guerrilla movements they had not been treated as equals. Rosibel Flores, feminist and former guerrilla leader, recounts what it was like during the war: "There were certain things that I saw happening [within the guerrillas] that I did not like. The control that your superiors wanted to have over you as a woman. It got to be obsessive, a bit sick, at times. 'You can't go here or there. You can't do that.' Later I understood that there was sexual harassment and that I could have responded by saying, 'Look, you have a partner and you have no reason to be coming on to me.' But these weren't times when one could report these kinds of things."[30]

They also looked out at society and saw a government and international organizations that provided more aid to men than women. This reflection led to the appearance of a new generation of women's organizations—many of them feminist—which included a diversity of women from the city and the countryside, from professional, working-class, and marginalized communities.[31] As these activist women formed women's organizations, they received extensive censure and critique from male activists and party members. Some were expelled from their former organizations or political groupings. Many were accused of usurping much-needed moneys for reconstruction for other agendas. Many women today are rebuilding their communities, running organizations, and lobbying the government on behalf of the needs of women and children.

Finding Common Threads

Historically, conservative oligarchic interests and the predominant Catholic Church teachings had a dual standard for women. There were the elite women, bound to uphold social mores and European standards, and there were peasant and Indian women who were expected to do most of the social, economic, and sexual reproduction during the early years of the colonies, as well as most of the light manufacturing and crafting once European women joined their men in the Americas. Women's production sustained families during hard times. During economic depression and political turmoil, women's labor force participation kept the countries afloat, exemplified by Argentine and Chilean women during the 1800s and Salvadoran women during the civil war. During the war, Salvadoran women carried the triple load of caring for their families, performing community service, and carrying out productive activities for income generation. Many mothers, sisters, aunts, and grandmothers had to handle household tasks and child care in addition to spending long hours on income-generating activities. Even in the face of such hardship, women volunteered their time as community leaders, educators, health care providers, and participated in development projects. To this day, women provide leadership in the key areas that relate to informal-sector, income-generating projects and local community development projects. In many communities men have lost their provider roles, as economic crisis and the long-term effects of structural adjustment policies have transformed economies. In all three countries, this has led to efforts to address the demasculinization of unemployed men, many of whom are facing self-esteem crises and often turning to increased alcohol consumption because they are no longer able to provide for their families.

In each country under study, women and women's organizations were instrumental in ending the social conflict and rebuilding after the regimes. In Chile the women's movement—involving women from across the country and from different class backgrounds in protests, outreach work, and lobbying—was an unwavering force in getting Pinochet and his government to comply with promises for free elections. In Argentina the Madres de Plaza de Mayo transformed individual loss into collective loss and publicly held the government accountable and demanded respect for human rights, even during the worst years of the repression (Cook 2006, 15). By the end of the dirty war, the Madres and other human rights organizations had been joined by new CSOs, emboldened by the Malvinas debacle, in which the Argentine army lost to England in a fight for the Malvinas Islands. Salvadoran women's participation and leadership were a major force within the popular movement and the FMLN. To this day, Salvadoran women—and the organizations they run—play an increasingly important role in charting the country's development priorities. In contrast to Chile and Argentina, the Salvadoran women's movement that emerged after the civil war has remained a protagonist in determining development priorities for the entire country. The women's movement in Chile lost sight of its goal once democracy was reestablished. In Argentina the women's movement remains active but not a predominant force that affects public policy and governmental agendas. It will be interesting to see if Michelle Bachelet, president of Chile, and Cristina Kirschner, president of Argentina, are able to encourage participation of the women's movement, open up opportunities for women, and address gender discrimination.

Another common theme that emerges from this historical review is the impact of the authoritarian regimes on their respective populations—civil society organizers in general and women activists in particular. All three authoritarian regimes included gendered messages for women and their expected role in supporting the goals of the security forces in charge in each country. Patriotic women were expected to be good mothers but not to play active roles in society or the workplace. Many women activists in all three countries carry scars today from the times of state violence. Whether looking over one's shoulder while walking down the street, flinching when a helicopter flies overhead, or hesitating momentarily before providing one's full name, many of the women interviewed continue to contemplate the times of fear and repression that have marked their lives so indelibly.

3

Argentina

I believe that in the leadership styles of women, the entire person appears, never just a fragmented person fulfilling the function of the role. Women's leadership demonstrates that they act integrally, holistically. They don't treat it like work; ours was not work; it was a life choice, a commitment to a different kind of life.

—María Rosa Martínez, Foundation SES and Save the Children,
Buenos Aires

In Argentina the return to democracy in 1983 created conditions for rapid civil society growth, which has continued into the twenty-first century—expanding notions of human rights to include social, economic, and political rights; alleviating the effects of the economic crisis; ending domestic violence; keeping children in school; strengthening Christian base communities; and promoting community development. Women's participation in civil society organizations is extensive, as is their leadership, which is drawing close to parity with men in many sectors of civil society.[1] In 1983 civil society organizations reemerged and women's organizations were at the forefront. However, they soon had to contend with economic crisis as neoliberal structural readjustment policies and the resulting hardships began to be felt in the 1990s and well into this century. Poverty has intensified to the extent that 23 percent of Argentines live on less that two dollars a day compared to 9.6 percent of Chileans across the border (Heinrich 2007, 15, 45). Argentine CSOs began lobbying the state and assuming some of the responsibilities left in the wake of the privatization of state-owned industries and severe budget cuts to state spending. Today CSOs play a double role in Argentina as intermediaries with the public sector and cultural/historical repositories. "On one hand they are collective systems of societal recognition expressing old and new identities, with important cultural and symbolic meaning. On the other hand, they are non-partisan political intermediaries bringing the needs and demands of those who do not have a voice in the public sphere and linking them up with state agencies" (Altamirano and Caballero 2004, 1).

From within the women's movement and civil society in general, many women leaders are attempting to address differences among women by beginning the process of transforming the class barriers that have kept women divided historically. The vectors of gender and class still inform access to the leadership of civil society organizations in the twenty-first century, but two factors have contributed to new developments in this arena: participation of working-class/marginalized women and outreach by middle-class women to their working-class counterparts. Community associations—and the low-income women they comprise—are the main motors of community development and are beginning to be treated as important development stakeholders by national and international development organizations. According to the women I interviewed, NGO leaders—often from middle-class backgrounds—demonstrate increased class-consciousness, working determinedly to build bridges as NGO open programs in marginalized communities, collaborating closely with community organizations and local women organizers. Today, women's organizations play central roles in community development, the antiviolence movement, and citizen participation movements for a more responsive democracy. Though they have different foci, many of the women from these organizations—ranging from self-help groups to NGOs with nationwide programs—have gathered together once a year since 1986 for the National Women's Meeting (Encuentro Nacional de Mujeres) to learn from each other and reaffirm shared goals. These efforts often transcend class and race boundaries, showing a gradual transformation from division to common ground.

Argentine women civil society leaders draw their motivation and inspiration from a number of sources. Repression and social exclusion have directly impacted the lives of the interviewees and these remain important issues. Some women come to their activism through the Catholic Church, liberation theology, and participation in Christian base communities. Others come to their activism from working with neighbors to get access to such basic services as housing, water, sewers, and gas for their communities. Others have experienced family violence and decided to help other women escape the cycle of abuse.

Civil Society Today

Any conversation about civil society today in Argentina has to start with an acknowledgment of the impact of the dictatorship. Though the dirty war ended in 1983, all the civil society leaders interviewed here—whether active politically during that period or not—still carry vestiges of fear and trauma from that period. Rosa Nair Amuedo, a vital seventy-five-year-old human rights activist and founding member of the Madres de Plaza de Mayo, remains critical of how the different democratic governments have not addressed what happened during the dirty war. She recounts, "I tell you sincerely that I originally had so much faith in democracy . . . but first there was the price Alfonsín had to pay so that there wouldn't be more blood shed. And ultimately it led to the pardons under Menem. . . . All the people that were in the Proceso [Process for National Reorganization] were pardoned under Menem along with those that had already been sentenced."[2]

In a focus group session the following comments elicited nods and agreement from all of the women present: "Even today when I go to marches, I am scared"; "I still cannot understand how one human being could do that to another"; "The fear doesn't go away; it's always there on the surface [es de piel]"; "We're still scared because the bad guys are still there"; "In 2000 I wanted to go and give classes in a marginalized community; my father was scared for me"; "I always sit in a restaurant with my back to the wall facing the door so I know who is coming in"; and "I am always aware of who is walking ahead of me and behind me." Not only does fear install itself in people's minds during periods of authoritarian regimes, but it remains, appearing without warning as a brief flashback or a sudden chill. The long-term psycho-social-emotional effects of living under this kind of fear necessitates more research, but as these comments—and the resounding agreement among all the women present—indicate, fear lingers long after repressive regimes have been replaced by more democratic governments.

It is difficult to quantify Argentine civil society in itself, let alone find statistics on women's leadership within the sector. Statistics have to be reviewed carefully as many put forward wildly different numbers using diverse definitions to justify the inclusion or exclusion of different categories of civil society organizations. For instance, there are thousands of communal associations throughout Argentina that are seldom included in statistics that solely count legally inscribed NGOs. The most recent study carried out by the National Center of Community Organizations (Centro Nacional de Organizaciones de la Comunidad—CENOC), based on self-reporting by member organizations, contends that as of 2005 there were 13,545 organizations listed in their database (CENOC 2005, 1). According to the study, almost 40 percent of organizations are located in the greater Buenos Aires area, which corresponds with the percentage of the country's population that lives there in comparison to the other provinces.[3] The organizations cater to a range of social concerns from social/humanitarian aid (57 percent) to gender-related issues (1.5 percent). Only 7 percent of their funding comes from international foundations, and the rest is divided between funding generated by the organizations themselves (membership dues or direct fund-raising events) and the rest from the state, be it national, provincial, or municipal. On average, each organization has a staff of thirty-five people, seven of whom are paid and twenty-two of whom are volunteers. Almost 60 percent of paid staff is women, and 50 percent of the volunteers are women.

These figures can be used to develop an overall idea about community organizations but should not be taken as a complete description of all civil society organizations in Argentina. Numerous scholars claim it is practically impossible to quantify the sector due to the following issues: the diversity of organizations in the sector, for which estimates vary dramatically from year to year and from source to source; the range of groups, from legally inscribed organizations to informal community associations and self-help groups; and the informality of many of the organizations (Altamirano and Caballero 2004; Roitter, List, and Salomon 1999; Tallarico 1998; Thompson 1994). Due to how they were categorized, the number of women's organizations or organizations that address gender-related issues is also probably much more extensive than CENOC statistics indicate. For example, CENOC's 2005 statistics refer to 203 organizations addressing gender-related issues, whereas statistics from the National Women's Council from as early as 1994 indicate that there were over three hundred women's organizations active in the country (Tallarico 1998).

In 1999 the Johns Hopkins Center for Civil Society Studies published a report prepared by a team led by Mario Roitter that was one of the first studies to use quantitative research to describe Argentine civil society. Though dated, the figures confirm the significant role the sector plays in Argentine society. With operating expenditures at $12 billion per year, civil society comprises 4.7 percent of the country's gross domestic product. Argentina civil society is a major employer in the country, generating over 400,000 full-time jobs. Twenty percent of Argentines volunteer with civil society groups, not as high as Chile but higher than many other Latin American countries. Similar to the CENOC data, the Johns Hopkins study indicates that the smallest of the revenue sources of civil society organizations comes from philanthropy (7.5 percent), whereas the major source comes from membership dues (73.1 percent) compared to 19.5 percent from the public sector (Roitter, List, and Salomon 1999, 374–376, 383).

There are no disaggregated national statistics for the gender of managers and directors of civil society organizations, yet in an informal survey of eighty-nine NGOs based primarily in Buenos Aires, 45 percent were run by women.[4] Additionally, much has been written about the protagonist role of women in civil society, which is also corroborated by interviews with women leaders. Thompson (1995) describes how crucial the role of women has been throughout the history of Argentine civil society. Feijoó (1994, 109) writes how in Argentina "women . . . played a central role in bringing about the transition to a democracy." In her 1990 chapter in *Women and Social Change in Latin America*, Feijoó describes the diversity of women's action in shaping the feminist movement, the human rights movement, and the housewives' movement for urban services and subsidies for basic food necessities. And the case of the Madres de Plaza de Mayo shows how this group "erected the principle of life against a government that dismissed the value of human life" (112) when no other organizations were willing to risk the repression by protesting the dictatorship. Since the return to democracy, women have played a major role in several different movements, such as communal associations for basic services and gender-related issues (Consejo Nacional de la Mujer 1994).

The extent of women's participation and leadership in civil society organizations is supported by many of the interviews I conducted with women leaders. Carmen Olaechea, representative for an international foundation promoting leadership and citizenship participation, discussed women's leadership in Argentine NGOs, saying, "And we women are beginning to occupy leadership positions on a massive level."[5] Gilda Quiles, a longtime community organizer from Malaver, a former *villa miseria* in Buenos Aires, whose organizing and struggle led to gaining state assistance for the construction of adequate housing, confirmed that women participate more in community organizing than men.[6] She said, "I find that there are six women to every man. Women participate a lot more."[7] Victoria Matamoro, veteran community organizer, spoke about her work in villas miseria: "In the villas, community-oriented work is all in the hands of women."[8] Describing the leadership of women in the Christian base communities of greater Buenos Aires, where she works, Marta Manterola said, "In general, the group coordinators are women . . . the number of women coordinators is a lot higher than the number of men."[9] Victoria Matamoro added that indigenous women's leadership is noticeable within the Tobas and Wichis communities in the northern part of the country, though not officially: "In each case, they have male chiefs. . . . But the woman occupies a space of power with her gaze (*mirada*), her silence, and her physical presence, which is impressive. I will give you an example: we were in a meeting in which the men, the chief included, were seated around the table with the members of a health program that we had just started. The women were grouped around us standing, but when the men had to give an opinion, they waited to see if the women approved or not, just by their gaze, before giving an opinion."[10]

Since the return to democracy in 1983, the growth of civil society has been encouraged by the following factors: (1) the new democratic spaces encouraged civil society organizing along a number of different lines, including the expansion of notions of human rights to include political, economic, and social citizenship rights; and (2) a series of political and economic crises have forced the emergence of new organizations attempting to address the massive unemployment and poverty in the face of layoffs and cuts to state subsidies. Since the 1990s a social and economic crisis created by neoliberal, state-sponsored reforms has led to the complete marginalization of the working class and portions of the middle class (Pozzi 2000, 74). This has caused inflation and high levels of unemployment affecting large segments of the middle class and sending workers and their families deeper into poverty. These events have inspired new social movements such as neighborhood assemblies and the *cacerolazos* (waves of civic engagement and protests during 2001 against economic policies of the government), the *piqueteros* (picketers who stop traffic on major highways in protest of government spending cuts that have stopped their lives and livelihoods), and the *cartoneros* (recyclers), with new leadership opportunities for men and women; aside from these opportunities, the crises and challenge just to survive have been very grueling on Argentines, especially women and low-income and working-class families and communities.

Gender and Leadership

Whether or not a woman considers herself a leader depends on what the term means to her and her team or followers. Victoria Matamoro shared her thoughts on the issue:

> I have always rejected the term *leader* for its politico-ideological association with the idea of *fürer* . . . I think that I had to situate the term with the role. Now the issue no longer bothers me. I re-defined the term by examining its contents. And I am not just talking about my leadership but the leadership of Mercedes or Margarita [community leaders with whom she works]. Maybe it's because I gave it meaning and content. I believe that a leader needs to have the attitude of a teacher so he or she can form other leaders. This was a big moment for me. Because with the prior definition, the leader dies with the leader. However, according to my interpretation, no. There have to be many leaders because we have to learn how to lead these processes, to promote them, to accompany them, to coordinate them.[11]

As Victoria's words indicate, her initial discomfort with what it means to be a leader came from having a definition of leader tied to authoritarian and patriarchal leadership styles, but when she located the term within a worldview committed to social transformation, she began to use the word and even to want to promote its usage. Other women leaders interviewed disagreed with the concept of leaders as teachers, given a long history of rather pedantic teaching styles in Argentina. However, they agreed with the concept of a leadership that "shares more, gives to others"; leaders who are "conducting, transforming, and inviting people to participate"; and leaders who believe in "teamwork." They unanimously supported "collective examples of leadership like the Madres de Plaza de Mayo." For these women, the definition of what it means to be a leader is closely tied to the kind of change a leader is trying to bring about and how she is going about achieving it.

Today Argentine women are challenging gender stereotypes as they cope with more and more responsibility at home and in their communities. Since gender refers to what is culturally appropriate masculine and feminine behavior in particular situations, using a gender perspective facilitates understanding how women and men experience particular realities differently. The gendered messages girls and boys receive from their families, schools, and communities explain some of the internal ambivalence and external challenges women face when they exercise their leadership skills. When I interviewed Carmen Olaechea, she was the Buenos Aires Representative for an international foundation; I was surprised that such a dynamic, passionate woman had spent many years denying her own voice and potential. She told me:

> Even though my family is a matriarchy where intelligence is valued, I was educated in the first place to be a mother and wife and to support my man. From an early age, I received messages like the following: if you are more intelligent than the man, don't let him notice. I followed the family mandate, but inside I rebelled. Looking back, I believe that the strongest manifestation of the family mandate consisted in the fact that up until I was 30 years old, I didn't even have a vision for myself as a person apart from my role as mother, wife, and daughter. Simply, it never occurred to me. Later, a diffuse sense of dissatisfaction that I had been feeling continued to grow. It is interesting that when I finally could express this dissatisfaction, I found myself saying: I am not capable of maintaining

my family if something happened to my husband. From this minimal vision, I began the path towards greater self-knowledge. I have
changed my manner of being in the world. This work in the foundation world has been key because it has given me the context and the
stage on which to live my leadership.[12]

Not all boys and girls respond in the same fashion to the gendered messages
they receive because there are intervening life circumstances—such as birth
order, educational opportunities, political events, etc.—that influence how
messages get internalized. This interstitial encounter between cultural messages and what people actually do with them is the place many feminist
social scientists chose to locate their research. Nonetheless, gendered
messages about how girls are supposed to become caretakers often translate
into women who have internalized these characteristics. Susy Casaurang,
psychologist and community educator, explained the contradiction for
Argentine women: "I would say that we women are trained to take care of
others. Caretaking. I do think this is evolving and changing. Absolutely. Even
though I think this, I also know that even with the changes, we are pierced
through and compelled to maintain these images and representations. So,
maybe it wasn't your mother; maybe you come with a different history having overcome this model. But the model still exists."[13]

These internalized characteristics inform how women will lead. Many
of the women interviewed agree that gender does affect leadership
because they see different types of leadership styles, specifically feminine
and masculine styles. The feminine and masculine leadership styles follow
fairly stereotypical gender lines. Feminine leadership styles are inclusive
(integradora), flexible, able to take on multiple fronts at the same time,
maternal, and consensus-oriented.[14] Women tend to promote relational
work, bringing people together and demonstrating sensitivity to the needs
of the group. Many of these characteristics are instilled in girls as part of
their socialization for becoming mothers. Speaking about what a mother
will do for her children, Rosa Nair Amuedo of the Madres de Plaza de Mayo
said, "A mother acts from her guts. To save her children she will face death.
My fear that something would happen to me wasn't for myself, rather for
my children and grandchildren."[15] Victoria Matamoro summarized her
views on the matter in the following way:

But what I notice in women who have leadership skills—and keep in mind I am talking about leadership across different fields—is that women who are achieving social impact . . . have a multifaceted approach. It has to do with the fact that reality is composed of many facets, colors, and sounds. For us women all these colors, sounds, and ways of knowing function simultaneously. Everything at once in the same moment. And one chooses and applies what is appropriate in given circumstances . . . I am Victoria, educator, psychologist, mother, and now grandmother, neighbor, niece of an aunt who now I take care of. Do you see? I will go to the south to work on issues of citizenship, but I will also take advantage of the trip to work with Margarita Green and the farmers. It's this thing of being able to jump from the academic world to the tulip field, to raising rabbits . . . that has to do with feminine approaches.[16]

Other women interviewed described female leadership attributes. María Rosa Martínez, who consults with Save the Children and Foundation SES, still volunteers her time with a women's health collective she cofounded during the dictatorship. She mused, "[Women leaders are] promoters, animators, all that has to do with the role of linking people together."[17] Viviana Fridman, director of Save the Children, said, "feminine leadership has to do with incorporating everything," from work in the organization, to how one's children, parents, and partners are doing.[18] Susy Casaurang agreed with these insights, adding, "I believe that as women we arrive whole to the struggle because we have a logic in which we always include the affective, the bonds with others."[19] Feminine leadership styles include traits that facilitate network building, working across difference, and collaboration.

Masculine leadership styles were described by the women interviewed in the following ways: rigorous, practical, firm, decisive, and linear. Men are perceived as able to compartmentalize, to focus on the issue at hand. Interestingly, almost all of the women agreed that men and women can and do use a variety of leadership styles. In fact, the women often described their leadership as including masculine and feminine styles. They indicated that at times they have to be decisive, firm, keep the issues separated, and at other times use a more inclusive approach. These women are flexible and adjust the response to the situation. Magdalena Jamargo, union leader, described how she can be gentle or tough depending on the circumstances. Men, on the other hand, do not tend to draw on all possible styles available to them, due to societal sanctions or censure for acting "feminine." María Rosa Martínez, who has worked for years in the area of community health education, noticed a difference between organizations led by women and those led by men: "There's another issue about closeness in organizations that are led by men. It would seem that in those organizations people who work there just work there. They don't have a personal life that has a role in the task they are carrying out. I think it is different in organizations led by women."[20] Reflecting on women leaders with whom she has contact, María Laura Schiffrin, who works in the field of youth leadership and education, shared the following insight: "There is a part [of women's leadership style] which requires a certain kind of blindness without which they couldn't lead. There's a part which is stubbornness, like, 'I am going to do what I am going to do no matter what.' They have to have these qualities to resist all the challenges and frustrations they are confronted with. If they didn't have a lot of love for themselves, or digging deeper, a certain hatred or anger, they wouldn't be able to believe in themselves and face the barriers, unexpected events, and boycotts. I see this in these spectacular leaders."[21]

This particular description of women's leadership styles raised quite a lot of comment among the women during the focus group session. All the women offered terms other than "blindness" to describe their focus: "Clarity, not blindness. The leader has to be clear on the decisions to make, the objectives to achieve when faced with obstacles." Nelly Borquez, who works with survivors of domestic violence and their batterers in the working-class city of La Matanza, clarified, "blindness, no . . . indignation is an important value. And it's not hatred, rather indignation. The leader is stubborn and when confronted with adversity, remains standing." Claudia Laub, director of El Agora from Córdoba, clarified that "being strategic is not equal to being blind." Viviana Fridman proffered, "Focused. And perseverance instead of blindness, remain focused on the objective, have the conviction about what is just in the cause beyond the obstacles." Gilda Quiles clarified, "Conviction about the cause. Sometimes it is necessary to face into the challenge even if that means knocking up against a wall."

Though women are making great advances by claiming integrated leadership styles and finding new places to exercise their leadership, they are still not treated equally in the workforce, politics, and other types of organizations; furthermore women still face vulnerability to gender-related violence throughout the Americas (Ruiz Abril 2003). The contradictions between women's abilities and their treatment do not just happen in the public sphere or civil society organizations. They also happen at home and within the family. In Argentina official statistics reflect only the number of individuals who have sought help from governmental agencies; they do not reflect the true extent of domestic violence in general. However, all these organizations consistently work at maximum capacity, and as the word spreads more women and families seek assistance every year. There are no statistics about other forms of abuse at the domestic level, such as psychological abuse. María Laura Schiffrin, who was active in Christian base communities before her first marriage, described how she dropped out of her community work and activism when she married: "I never participated politically because my daughter was a baby and [my husband] was the activist. I didn't attend any meetings or demonstrations. I stayed home alone. It was a couple thing: he took the active militant role in the party, and this meant that I couldn't participate in that space, I had to stay home . . . there is a threat. If you try to free yourself or leave the subjugation . . . you will be left alone."[22]

Even though María Laura had been an active catechist before her marriage, both she and her husband accepted the traditional role assigned to women in marriage: taking care of family and raising children. Denying women the chance to participate, creating a hostile domestic environment, and keeping good women down: all of these actions limit women's contributions to society. A number of the women I interviewed had to leave abusive husbands to be able to continue serving their communities. Cata Jiménez—who along with Gilda and other community members had won the fight to build houses on the land they occupied—married very young, choosing a violent partner who ultimately forced her to respond with violence:

> When one is young, one does stupid things, but life teaches you
> with hard knocks [los golpes de la vida]. I was young and made

> decisions without really thinking. I got married to him to leave
> home and then I had my son. [My husband] treated me very bad for
> six years. I would leave, come back, leave, and come back. I would be
> gone a few months, but then I came back ... I think that you
> shouldn't have to stay if your husband is hitting you. It happened to
> me a lot until one day I said no more, *ciao*. I confronted him and
> I defended myself. I acted like an animal, but I defended myself. He
> had grabbed me that time, and I said this is it, this is over. I almost
> killed him. In fact, afterwards, I thought I had killed him.[23]

Cata and her husband separated for good after this episode, but she
learned from firsthand experience how hard it can be to leave even with
the abuse. After her experience, she befriended Gilda Quiles, an active
community member, and tried to be supportive as Gilda faced an abusive
relationship with the father of her children. Gilda reflected on how difficult it was to leave the situation:

> At first it took me a long time to say that I was going to do some-
> thing about the situation. Because at first, I couldn't even leave the
> house. "Where was I thinking I was going at 7 P.M. out on the street
> with men around?" [he would ask me.] Until the moment arrived
> and I said, "this is what I like to do and this is what I am going to
> do." I paid a heavy price (*buenos palos me costó*) . . . but I did it. Cata
> would say to me: "What are you going to do now? You will go home
> and then what will happen to you?" And I would say: "I'm going to
> put the key in the door and go in." But yes, when I got home, I always
> knew what was going to happen. I think I was more persistent than
> him because he finally got tired and let me do what I wanted.[24]

Even though Gilda was working on issues important to gaining decent
housing for the community, every time she came home from a meeting
she had to face her husband's ire and abuse. He eventually stopped beating her for this, but he continued the abuse for other reasons he invented.
Though it took her a few tries to leave her husband, she finally did:

> Shift into first and step on the gas. Know that things can't continue
> like this. Take the decision, knowing you have to do something. As
> much as you may not know what to do, know that things have to

change. That this is not normal, it hurts your children, and he will continue doing it tomorrow if you don't take control. That my daughter might become a battered woman and that my son might become a batterer. This is what I saw in my future. At first it was hard for me to ask for help in organizations and even here in the community. Because I was so ashamed and in reality, who should feel shame was him, not me . . . until I found people here in the community who helped me see this reality that I was living, that life did not have to be this way.[25]

To get away from her husband, Gilda had to move out. She no longer lives in the community; her husband kept the house and the custody of their two teenage children. Gilda continues to visit the community on a regular basis, participating in the building of the community center and helping to run the community board. Though she sees her children frequently, they are being raised by a violent man, and she worries about how this will affect them as adults. Gilda remains active in the community, and it helps that her new partner is supportive of her community organizing efforts. Gilda is building a more peaceful life for herself and has begun the journey of learning to relate to a partner in a more open and healthy fashion.

Be it through their own experiences at home, in the community, or within their organizations, the women interviewed agreed that the levels of violence affecting home and community life are growing and have to be addressed. Throughout Latin America, many women's organizations are focusing on addressing domestic violence because an estimated 50 percent of families experience violence in the home (Morrison, Ellsberg, and Bott 2004, ii). Economic hardship and increased crime have made many communities sites of violence, as corroborated by Claudia Laub, who directs El Agora, an NGO based in Córdoba, Argentina, that promotes increased citizen participation of communities in decisions that affect their security and development. She has found that women are more vulnerable to violence than men:

The issue of security is totally cross-cutting. A woman will feel secure when she has a house, when her children can go to school, when she has electricity, and can afford to go to the dentist. This is security. And has a lot to do with gender because a woman will

always feel insecure; when she takes a bus, she will be scared. She
has different fears than men. She has a lot more fear that her children will die of hunger and she doesn't have as much false pride as
a man. If a town is safe for women and children, it will be a safe
place for everyone because women don't like violence.[26]

Claudia's outreach to women community leaders in Córdoba encourages
more women to demand that resources get channeled for education, after-
school sports programming, and income-generating projects, all of which
are major contributors to decreasing high levels of insecurity and violence.
Lina Amat, community organizer and catechist, reflected on how insecurity affects her, "Today I am here in the city more frightened by the psychological devaluation than by the physical. At least physical violence
leaves a mark."[27] Current levels of crime and violence in Argentina translate into fear and insecurity for many women, generating yet one more
challenge to be faced when taking on leadership or activist roles in their
communities.

Difference and Leadership

Not all women have the same opportunities to develop their leadership
abilities; some come to leadership through making sure their families
have the basic necessities for survival while others have access to
resources to build nationwide organizations. Elite women have had
the benefits of education, money, and connections, whereas women in
working-class neighborhoods and the villas have become leaders by necessity. "We organize and band together or we will be turned out of our
houses," agreed Cata and Gilda. Both community organizers, they fought
long and hard beside other community members to get the necessary per-
missions for building decent housing. These leadership opportunities are
quite different in nature from those of elite women and raise questions
about the commonalities and, therefore the potential solidarity, between
women leaders.

Though upper-class women play a role in NGO leadership in Buenos
Aires, the vast majority of women NGO directors and managers come from
the middle class. In response to the question, "What is the profile of

women NGO leaders?" Carmen Olaechea responded, "Middle class professionals. There is a small group from the upper class but they aren't the majority of the female directors of NGOs."[28] Many of these professional women have worked hard to make their organizations sustainable and effective in meeting the needs of the people they serve. This often requires developing strategies to establish relationships of trust in marginalized communities where they work. Reflecting on conversations with women NGO directors, Carmen spoke to the importance of maintaining good relations with their community counterparts: "All of them will tell you the story of how they entered the *barrio*. All of them had to gain an ally in the *barrio* who would legitimate them."[29]

The first time I interviewed Carmen, we discussed the strategies many women use to reach out to counterparts in the communities where they work. I asked her if she had a specific example she could share with me about building relationships with women in the communities where she works. She told me a rather superficial anecdote about how she and Luz, an indigenous woman leader, first met and connected: "I remember the time I first met her up in the north. I could tell she saw my white skin and *porteña* ways,[30] but when we had been on the road for a while, she pulled over and we had a barbeque. There were no forks or napkins. I could tell she was watching to see what I would do. When she saw me dig into my food, she told me I was different from other *porteñas*."[31]

The second time I interviewed Carmen, I brought up the story she had told me about how the barbeque helped the two of them get to know each other, but she told me that there was something else, something deeper, that had happened first to facilitate finding common ground:

> Regarding Luz, I want to clarify something. I feel that what connected me to her was not my behavior at the barbeque. That happened later. Something happened beforehand that, yes, made the connection. We sat in the back of the car not speaking a word. Up front, Jorge was talking to Pedro, the two men in the front seat, us two women in the back. Jorge was talking a lot about the IUD [interuterine device] and what was happening to the women . . . uterine cancer, 18 pregnancies and only 8 living children. What it means to lose a child. When he said he didn't know if he could even imagine

what it must be like for a mother to lose a child, I looked at Luz and
I asked her: "Have you lost a child?" "Yes, I have," she said. I said I
had too. We looked each other in the eyes. This is what brought us
together. It doesn't matter where you live or what your social class
is. If you have had to live through losing a child, you are the same.
I felt it and I believe Luz did too. It had put us on the same side. And
it is true that women leaders talk more about their children than
men. I know all of the names of the children of the women leaders
but none of the men's children's names.[32]

The fact that both Carmen and Luz had an experience of deep suffering
in common opened a space of connection between the two. Carmen
went on to say that the fundamental issue for connection between women
is the commitment to finding common ground, "*el espacio de conexión
instantánea*," which can spring from having major life experiences in common.[33] It is not enough to be committed to the same cause, be it citizen
participation or fighting environmental degradation, for instance. Common
life experience opens women to the possibility of connection; whether
they are able to develop a relationship of mutual trust depends on if they
can continue to deepen the connection after sharing the sense of common
experience.

Feminist social scientists have been reflecting on these issues for
many years as they analyze the complexities of their relationships with
their research participants. Writing on familial and political ties to the
women she works with in Nepal, Enslin warns against equating life experiences with equality: "Common life experience does not give us a natural
and mutual understanding rather it brings us into a creative conversation
and opens up possibilities for critical discussion" (1994, 549). Common
ground can set the stage for the possibility of collaboration; issues of
power differentials—class, ethnicity, or other factors—have to be taken
into account if a relationship between equals is to be built.

Many middle-class women leaders have developed strategies to reach
out to women of marginalized communities, but often their counterparts
in the communities do not have reciprocal access to more elite spaces.
Carmen laments that this is often not a two-way process. Women in the
communities do not have the opportunities or strategies to access more

privileged spaces: "The opposite process does not happen [that people from the barrios have access to more elite spaces]. . . . They still have the attitude that what they are doing and creating is small, and doesn't have a lot of value at other levels. Many are designing new approaches to community development, but they aren't aware of this."[34] Although they are creating new and innovative approaches and carrying out pioneering activities—the knowledge of which could help others in similar situations—community leaders are not always aware of the value of their experiences and the need to proactively communicate what they are doing. When Nelly Borquez described her work against domestic violence in the working-class satellite city of La Matanza, she mentioned initial interactions with well-meaning but unaware and naive feminists from the capital. The breakdown in communication lay in the fact that the women in Buenos Aires just did not understand the reality Nelly and her neighbors were facing:

> We began to put names, you may not believe me, on all the things we women do. And that's how we decided to start meeting as women. So we began to work on learning more [about gender] . . . taking advantage of everything that was available, the workshops feminists offered us. And this is how we had our first fights with our friends the feminists. Because they said they were feminists and they didn't understand how meeting after meeting, we returned to our marriages and organizations. "You all were born with hot water," we said to them. "We don't have hot water. We have to struggle for hot water," which the feminists did not understand. What they would try to teach us in the city didn't work for the local conditions and context of La Matanza. . . . There was the time we decided to take on the issue of domestic violence . . . and we began to go to self-help groups in the capital and we began to get trained in prevention. But there we crashed into a wall again because there they said that a woman should go running to call on the telephone, to call the police. And here there were no telephones, not one damn telephone . . . what they tried to teach us in the capital did not apply to the context here. And that's when we said, "Let's do it." And we began to start our own self-help groups.[35]

There is no doubt in my mind about the commitment of professional *porteña* women leaders to the communities where they work. However, if the women in the barrios and villas are to be recognized as their equals, then strategies need to be intensified to make the relationships mutual. Women from the communities must gain access to and utilize more privileged spaces. Victoria Matamoro—through her work with marginalized communities in Batán, a working-class community near the beach city Mar de Plata—encouraged community organizers to reach out to more privileged sectors, and she targeted a nearby public university: "This project provided Mercedes and four other people from the community with the possibility of giving classes in the university once a year to students majoring in occupational therapy. They taught about how to get to know the community, how to work in the community . . . there is nothing better than having people who are actually doing community development work in their communities to be the teachers, to the extent that a methodology for elaborating projects, that Mercedes and I designed, is being used by the students in their field work."[36]

Victoria's work is inspirational because not only has she recognized the power differential between herself and the women she is serving, but she has worked to develop empowering options for the women to play a leadership role in the university setting. Experiencing the value others attach to their hard-earned knowledge is an important external validation for community leaders. As Victoria is doing in Batán, more NGO-to-community projects need to incorporate these kinds of strategies, empowering low-income and working-class women to teach professionals or directly approach governmental agencies on behalf of their communities. National Women's Meetings bring Argentinean women together across a variety of differences—class, ethnicity, sexual orientation, feminist, and nonfeminist.[37] In a paper written after a 1994 meeting, historian Graciela Alonso (2000) argued that the feminist/working-class dichotomy in which middle-class feminists are pitted against working-class women activists is a power play used to divide the women's movement. For her the women's movement and the National Women's Meetings are the genuine expression of multiple identities. In these annual meetings, women from across the country come together to reflect, share, and open a space for solidarity, knowledge transfer, and mutual recognition. Each year at the end of the meeting, the participants vote about where to have the next year's meeting, and the organizing committee is formed by local women from that site. Eight hundred women participated in the first annual meeting in 1986; in 1994 the number jumped to 7,000; and in 2000 there were 13,000 attendees (Consejo Nacional de la Mujer 1994; Diaz and Pizzorno 2000). In 2004 the meeting was held in Mendoza, and over fifty-one different workshops addressed a wide range of issues, including identity, domestic violence, reproductive rights, feminism, and ecology and the environment (Comisión Organizadora ENM 2004).

Given the history of class division within Argentine society, and within civil society in particular, this issue elicited many responses with interviewees. Nelly Borquez acknowledged that there had ultimately been mutual learning and growth between the women's groups of La Matanza and feminists in the capital: "With the academic feminists from the capital, we took advantage of all their knowledge and they learned from our work." I was surprised to learn that the perceptions of difference by class were superseded by concerns about political and ideological differences. Claudia Laub immediately responded, saying, "I couldn't work with the wife of Videla (one of the authors of the 1976 coup) . . . there have to be issues in common such as justice." And Nelly drew an example from her work with male batterers: "It's just like a violent man. To work with him, he has to recognize his guilt. If not, you can't move forward. If he doesn't acknowledge the damage he has done, he hasn't taken responsibility for his actions. If he does acknowledge this, only then can you begin to work with him. The same with the wife of a torturer." The women agreed that when it comes to differences of ideology and worldview, it is important to have some common agreements from which to work, otherwise it is too difficult.

Crisis and Leadership

By the late 1990s spontaneous responses to the economic crisis began to appear as women and their family members began to organize and demand jobs (Dillon 2004). Unemployed people formed a mass movement composed of many different kinds of organizations demanding employment using the tactic of the *piquete*, or picket (Laudano and Chejter 2002).

The piqueteros stop traffic to bring attention to their demands. Economic policies have brought their lives to a halt; therefore, they will bring the flow of traffic and commercial movement to a stop by building barricades across highways. Norma Galeano, long-term organizer in La Matanza, joined one of the newly forming organizations of piqueteros during the crisis: "And we women were participating, sustaining the decision to stop traffic. Each *barrio* organizes itself and builds their own *rancho* where they take their tents and pots . . . everything is shared and then money is raised among the group to buy a piece of meat . . . a small group never goes alone because we know it is weakness to be a few. So, a lot of people participate or we don't go. Thousands at a time. If just a few went, we would face repression. We would be a lot, children and entire families. Even teachers would come out to the highway and give classes there."[38]

Analyzing piquetero actions in Córdoba, Argentina, Pablo Pozzi describes their courage and ability to get the government to the negotiating table: "One of the main elements that forced the state to negotiate with the rioters and blockaders was their collective willingness to confront the security forces" (2000, 67–68). The piqueteros have been successful in bringing state attention to job creation and welfare provisioning, though never at levels to address the severity of the problems faced by poor and working-class people throughout the country.

Regrettably, some women have experienced the subordination of their leadership potential to other agendas. Speaking of the piqueteros movement, Norma Galeano described her militancy in one of the organizations. Her hard work and commitment were eventually rewarded when members voted her to be the training coordinator, a leadership position within the organization. Much to her chagrin, male leaders would call meetings and purposely not tell her about them. She feels she was used so they could say they had a certain percentage of women at leadership levels: "They would plan meetings and not even tell me what day they would be. Therefore, I never got to participate, fulfill the role I had earned. I felt like I had been taken advantage of, used. They will never pay attention to you . . . it seems to me that we see a lot of women taking the initiative at the grassroots level, but in the upper echelons, it's the *machos* who take the leadership positions . . . I ask myself why there are so few women in leadership positions when the majority of those working on the issues are women."[39]

This is why Norma has limited her participation with the piqueteros and dedicated herself to the network of community child-care organizations she now runs.

> Today we are part of a network . . . that is four or five years old called the Federation of Community Childcare Centers of La Matanza (Federación de Jardines Maternales Comunitarios de La Matanza). There are about twenty different institutions and together we take care of about three thousand to thirty-five hundred children a day . . . As the women of the Federation, we are an autonomous group and we decide our own destiny. This is a group of women where power relations are horizontal, and it is hard to work with other groups that aren't run this way. . . . In the childcare center where I am, we were able to start two small businesses with unemployed neighbors—making garbage bags and sewing. The childcare center also distributes food.[40]

Despite the fact that women played leadership roles during the beginning of the piqueteros movement, a variety of factors—traditional gender roles, police brutality, and men's need for protagonist roles—have contributed to curbing those leadership opportunities for women in some organizations. Culturally ascribed activities generally expected of women meant that many women assumed care-taking roles in the movement. So, many women would prepare food, take care of children, and perform secretarial functions, carrying out the support actions necessary to launch these large protest actions. When the movement began to stop traffic on major highways, police responded with violence. This response took many women off the front lines of the protests. In addition, the economic crisis led to the loss of more jobs for men than women, which affected men's self-image, and leadership positions within the movement began to be filled by men. The piqueteros movement is comprised of different organizations, most of which have very progressive platforms on women's participation and issues. Some even have quotas for women's participation in leadership positions. Nonetheless, this confluence of issues has diminished women's leadership opportunities in a number of different organizations in the movement (Svampa and Pereyra 2003).

Nelly Borquez was confronted by a similar experience of discrimination in La Matanza. She described the work she put into the local community development association, the Sociedad de Fomento, before deciding to found a separate women's organization: "We created the Sociedad de Fomento and the health center, but clearly we were never the presidents of those organizations."[41] Nelly has found this contradiction particularly unsettling because the men refuse to see the parallel between themselves and women when analyzing the neoliberal model and its impact on communities: "So you criticize neoliberal capitalism but you can't change it. Why? In the patriarchal system, you are very comfortable because you have all the rights. How can you change a system if you're not willing to change yourself?"[42] Men, though they benefit from patriarchal norms, are not able to avoid the impacts of global capitalism and neoliberal policies. As Susy Casaurang reminded me during our interview, men and women live and act in complex systems that, though patriarchal, are subordinate to the capitalist system: "The system holds the power, not them. So, they believed they had the power and they didn't face the contradictions created by this. So, each man has been working in a capitalist society trying to produce more and more. But as the crisis continues, they can't keep it up and this is what gave them their identity."[43] Yet, as the experiences of the women interviewed demonstrate, women create their own organizations when faced with obstacles in male-run organizations. The needs of marginalized and working-class communities have become so urgent that women do not have to remain in organizations that do not facilitate their participation. Rather, they can get together and create their own associations, NGOs, and movements.

Given women's long history with family and community commitments, they have adapted more easily than men to these times of economic crisis and loss of formal employment. In many communities, this is creating identity crises for men. María Rosa Martinez describes how this phenomenon is affecting men: "I believe that in a few years we are going to have to work to strengthen men's leadership abilities because men are more lost every day. At least here in Argentina, we women generate income, take care of our families, covering whatever roles we have to, from providers to organizing our homes and administering resources."[44] Many men, accustomed to being the primary income earners, have not been able to find full-time employment, and this has left them disoriented, experiencing low self-esteem and identity crises. Who is a man if he is no longer the provider, the primary source of income for my family? Women—who have historically carried out the community and family work—have simply added income generation to their list of daily activities, moving into survival mode and looking for alternative economic opportunities. Marta Manterola, active with Christian base communities, reflects on this phenomenon: "When one looks in the barrios, one sees that it is women doing more of the community work than men. Men are self-absorbed, trying to figure out how they lost their provider role. And it's as if they can't stand the fact that women are maintaining the households, running the communal kitchens, getting money for the projects, for their homes, for activities, for the children's centers."[45] When a group of people have occupied the dominant position, they are often not prepared for crisis. Viviana Fridman's reflections corroborated this conclusion: "We've faced crisis after crisis and the self-esteem of men has taken a beating. Men feel like they are failures as heads of households . . . So, women, who didn't have that image of themselves, have had to become the providers and take leadership."[46] Men do not have the same flexibility that women have because cultural messages as well as masculinist ideologies have conspired to bind their roles in family, community, and society to being the provider. When their jobs are taken from them, they also lose their identities. Describing a similar phenomenon in Peru, Norma Fuller concludes, "There is a narrow association between masculinity and work. That they [men] be unemployed . . . severely challenges manhood" (2003, 3). Given women's care-taking roles, they are often able to earn money on the side or participate in community development projects with absolutely no loss of face during economic or political crises.

Many unemployed people turned to the informal sector—income-generating activities outside of the formal economy—and to recycling used materials, in particular, which has led to the emergence of another social movement, also with far-reaching implications for civil society and women in Argentina. The cartoneros recycle cardboard, paper, and other disposable materials found in the garbage of wealthier neighborhoods. In contrast to the piqueteros movement, the cartoneros movement has involved numerous cross-class collaborations between cartoneros and the people of the neighborhoods where they collect their materials (Hirsch 2004). The cartoneros also grew as the economic crisis deepened. More and more people began walking the streets looking for goods to be recycled. As conditions worsened, community associations in the cities began to look for alternative solutions to ameliorate the situation. This led to a number of projects between middle/upper-class neighborhoods and cartoneros that involved establishing soup kitchens, initiating advocacy actions, and prompting political organizing efforts. Women, both from the communities and the cartoneros, play leadership roles in these activities.

Though the economic crisis has in many cases encouraged men and women's participation in civil society movements and organizations, gender discrimination against women in these spaces has to be examined to understand the barriers women face in exercising their leadership abilities. Bringing attention to sexism in progressive social movements needs to be handled delicately; the challenge is the following: if sexist ways of behavior emerge out of socially accepted gender hierarchies, often developed over centuries, all of us—no matter our level of consciousness of sexism or commitment to equality between genders—can fall victim to sexist behavior. This contradiction is not just Argentine; it occurs throughout Latin America. Elisabeth Friedman (forthcoming) recognizes that "historically . . . the political left has an uneven record on women's rights and the fostering of gender-based solidarity." In her sociological study of the Chilean exile community and the role Chilean women played in the solidarity movement in exile, Julie Shayne describes how social movements are informed by gender roles and hierarchies just like any societal institution:

> Social movements and their actors are not immune from assigned norms established by gender. Using gender to study social movements helps one understand the convergence of behavioral expectations and available resources which ultimately sheds light on how social movement actors create and sustain their movement. For example, are women expected to be leaders or followers? How do social movements encourage or discourage women to transgress from those expectations? Are women presumed competent enough to have access to formal political and financial resources? If not, how do women subvert these restrictions? (2009, 134)

Just because a person may choose to support the political goals of a particular group, it remains important to examine its practices in the light of its
actions. This contradiction is not new to Argentina, as evidenced by the
ambivalent and outwardly hostile response early feminists within the
Anarchist movement received from male militants in the late nineteenth
century (Molyneux 1986). Though early anarchists supported women's liberation in theory, they were seldom supportive of women who brought it
up, claiming that class issues had to be addressed before women's issues.
This was not a unique occurrence and has continued to resurface when
women's demands are seen as a distraction to the long-term goals of a
movement.

Conclusions

Argentina presents an intriguing setting for observing women and civil
society leadership; their civil society contributions continue to increase,
and their level of interaction across class boundaries is increasing.
Working-class women and women from marginalized communities have
led the way in community organizing efforts across a gamut of areas,
including microenterprise lending, income-generating projects, health
education, anti–domestic violence campaigns, education for marginalized
youth, consciousness raising, community safety and security, child-care
centers, and fighting environmental degradation. Many women running
nationwide NGOs are reaching out to their community counterparts, treat-
ing them as equal interlocutors; there are examples of community organizers gaining access to elite spaces and national women's meetings
bringing women together from different backgrounds to discuss difference
and find common ground. The interviewees show that women are leading
organizations and communities to challenge social inequalities, and they
are doing it using diverse leadership styles.

In the case of Argentina's past and ongoing economic crises, many
working-class and poor women, who had never been activists previously,
joined neighborhood associations and other social movements to protest
government policies and gain goods and services for their families and
communities. Referring to an earlier Argentine economic crisis, Feijoó
describes the phenomenon of women's transformations in hard times; her

words remain hauntingly relevant for the present: "By sending women to the streets to satisfy basic necessities, which displaces them from the traditional private sphere to the public realm, the crisis has the potential for positive effects and may convert the invisibility of women's work into an unavoidable political and public fact" (Feijoó 1994, 110). Given the widespread activism of women in response to economic hardship, state agencies and international donors cannot ignore their contributions and must take this into account in their programming. This has policy implications for Argentina at the local, provincial, and national levels: governmental agencies will have more effective programs if they treat these women leaders—whose training and field experience is extensive—as important stakeholders in planning and programming. This means involving them in setting priorities, strategic planning, project implementation, and evaluation efforts. Given the extensive amount of funding that CSOs received from the state, state agencies that provide funding for civil society efforts need to make sure that their own gendered understandings of potential grantees do not blind them to seeing the contributions being achieved by women and women-led organizations.

International development agencies and foundations—providing financial support and institutional strengthening to civil society organizations in Argentina—need to make sure they use a gender perspective as they search for leaders and organizations to support; otherwise, they run the risk of missing the real protagonists pursuing social change. If the ideal leader for a foundation is a man who demonstrates masculine leadership qualities, the foundation will obviously identify male leaders more readily than female. This kind of stereotype must be transformed, and donors can make a big difference by proactively promoting women's leadership and addressing the barriers they face. For international agencies, this translates into not only making sure they are not giving male leaders preferential treatment, but also raising the importance of intentionally supporting the transformation of the obstacles to women's leadership development. Argentina's civil society is in good hands, but women civil society leaders still need support in their struggle to lead their communities and organizations toward more equitable forms of development.

4

Chile

I am president of the community . . . I have almost as much power as the *lonko* [the cacique or chief]. He knows a lot about the rituals, but I know more about the history of the community and how to relate to institutions outside of the community. He and I have a good relationship, as we always support each other.

—Petronila Catrileo, community president, Pocuno

Civil society in Chile—particularly the women's movement—was in great part responsible for achieving an electoral transition from the dictatorship to democracy in 1990; since then, though, the women's movement appears to have dissipated, divided by social class differences, accusations of cooptation, and competition over limited funding sources. However, new forms of civil society leadership are emerging on the edges of Chilean society. This chapter is about a renewal within Chilean civil society and the Mapuche women leading the transformation. Living on the very margins of Chilean society, these leaders teach the women of their communities the weaving and knitting techniques of their mothers and grandmothers; they organize their communities to reclaim lands taken from them; they reach out to other marginalized groups to build coalitions and advocate for improved services from state agencies; and they invite strangers into their homes to talk about Mapuche culture. These women are providing a model of leadership that could bring people together, transforming a culture of individualism into a culture of democracy and intercultural celebration.

Initial interviews with women civil society leaders in Santiago and Concepción called attention to a need for new leadership models from civil society to build networks and have more impact on "socio-political projects . . . [and the] institutionality of the state" (de la Maza 2003, 2), and they frequently mentioned the innovative work of the Mapuche women. Rita Moya, codirector of CET-Sur, an NGO working with marginalized populations in south-central and southern Chile, described the kind of leaders Chile needs: "The idea is to look for and work with people who have a different sensitivity—who don't just work with women but with all kinds of people. And this is where women leaders can be found, for example, what we call women healers, or women who work with natural plants and herbs, or women who raise and share seed stock."[1] When I asked where I might find examples of this kind of leadership, Rita mentioned the self-sustaining efforts of Mapuche women to empower other Mapuche and rural women near Cañete. She also proposed I visit communities outside Cañete where Mapuche women are leading efforts to reclaim ancestral lands. In Santiago, Nicole Etchart, cofounder and CEO of the Nonprofit Enterprise and Self-Sustainability Team (NESsT), recommended I visit a group of Mapuche women outside of Temuco successfully marketing their weaving in national and international venues. Pati Jara of Pewman Ruka Hostal encouraged me to visit the alternative tourism circuits outside of Temuco and near Puerto Saavedra, which include culturally sensitive tourism activities, many of which are run by Mapuche women. These recommendations and others led me to southern Chile, where I interviewed Mapuche women about their lives, work, and leadership experiences.

Ten percent of the population of Chile is made up of Mapuche indigenous people.[2] And though the Mapuche often think of themselves as a rural people who draw their power and inspiration from the native forests of southern Chile, 79 percent of the population has left the countryside seeking better economic opportunities in the major cities and 43 percent live in the capital city of Santiago de Chile. Paradoxically, the presence of the Mapuche in the major cities and in the countryside has not decreased the discrimination they experience for being Indians. "In Chile, the Mapuche are invisible," explained Pati Jara, who works on a nationwide campaign to promote increased consciousness about Chile as a multicultural country. This blindness to the non-European peoples of Chile continues, even after the founding of the state agency for indigenous affairs, the National Corporation for Indigenous Development (Corporación Nacional de Desarrollo Indígena—CONADI), in 1993. Often the issues that the Mapuche request CONADI resolve—such as land rights, water rights, cultural survival issues, and demands for increased citizen participation—are ignored, or even repressed, if they adversely affect state priorities and macro-economic plans as substantiated by state subsidies to the forestry companies, the mining and water rights granted to mining concessions, and the electrification projects involving damming rivers, often on Mapuche land (see Reuque Paillalef 2002, 309; Richards 2004, 134–135). Instead of an acceptance for the different cultural backgrounds of the country's citizens, "there is the widespread belief among Chileans that theirs is a racially homogenous society of European origin" (Richards 2004, 44). The only repeated reference to the contribution of the indigenous peoples is a superficial nod to the savage Indian who refused to be subjugated by the Spanish. As Pati Jara explained to me, Chile is a country that has never celebrated its indigenous peoples, preferring to stereotype indigenous men as boorish, illiterate thieves and drunkards or political subversives, and indigenous women as docile maids and child-care providers.[3]

Though a number of mixed-gender organizations—such as the Mapuche Cultural Centers (Centros Culturales Mapuches), founded in 1978, and the Ad Mapu[4]—were founded by the Mapuche to organize, lobby, and advocate for the respect of their human, cultural, and land rights, and to protest against the dictatorship, many women leaders have left to form women's organizations, preferring to work with other women rather than face gender discrimination within the male Mapuche-run organizations. In talking about Mapuche men and why women are creating their own organizations, Isolde Reuque Paillalef, a Mapuche leader herself, said:

> [The men] don't give you the floor when it's time to speak. It's the men who deliver the speeches, who discuss what's happening, not the women. And who are the secretaries, who does the cleaning, who does the work, who does the thinking, who designs the projects? Generally, almost always, it's the women. In Ad-Mapu, Nehuen-Mapu, Choinfolilche, Kallfulikan, Roble Huacho, Rehue: it's women who do it all. They're the secretaries, the treasurers, the program directors; they make the proposals and the projections; they write and they transcribe. And men show off, presenting the projects and reading the proposals. (2002, 233)

Many Mapuche women—in the capital, other cities, and the south—are simply refusing to be overlooked, be it by men in their own communities or by the broader society. Through the effectiveness of their actions, they are getting elected to community positions, and when men try to hinder their work, they create women-only organizations. They are challenging men in their own communities, state organizations, and *winka*-led nongovernmental organizations as they seek a more equitable and culturally and environmentally sustainable form of development.[5]

This chapter focuses on the lives and experiences of six Mapuche women leaders active in communities outside of the cities of Cañete and Temuco, in south central and southern Chile respectively. Before describing their efforts and leadership experiences, background information on Chilean civil society, the women's movement, and Mapuche organizing is necessary to contextualize the stories of Mapuche women leaders. This chapter begins with a brief depiction of Chilean civil society in general and an assessment of the contribution of civil society to achieving a democratic end to the dictatorship of General Pinochet. The women's movement was particularly active during this period, bringing together women across differences of class, ethnicity, and political ideology; however, the pluralistic nature of the movement has declined today, due in part to the loss of a unifying vision, competition over funding sources, and the fact that the state agency, the National Service for Women (Servicio Nacional de la Mujer-SERNAM), has absorbed many former activists into its ranks. Following these sections, I describe Mapuche women's organizing efforts and then present the leadership experiences of Silvia Nain, Petronila Catrileo, Amalia Quilapi, Irene Huelche, Jaqueline Caniguan, and Julia Matamala.

Civil Society in Chile

The Johns Hopkins University is the only institution to have conducted a major quantitative study based on 106,880 organizations about the composition, nature, and challenges faced by Chilean civil society (Irarrázaval et al. 2006, 23). For this study, a civil society organization is an organization outside of direct state control and does not generate income. A major weakness of the study is the fact that it does not include indigenous associations because of their productive nature or income-generating activities such as arts and crafts workshops and agricultural projects. Many of these organizations/businesses are cooperatives or projects that generate income, but many civil society organizations—such as women's and indigenous organizations and community development corporations—generate income to support their activities without being profit-driven; rather, they are dedicated to improving the populations they serve. Published in English and Spanish in 2006, the Johns Hopkins study describes a vibrant sector of Chilean society with some surprising characteristics. Compared to other Latin American countries, Chilean civil society provides paid employment for thousands of Chileans, much higher than many of its neighbors. "Paid employment alone represents 2.6% of the economically active population" (Irarrázaval et al. 2006, 5). Furthermore, Chile has one of the highest levels of volunteerism in Latin America; the study calls Chile "a country of volunteers," where "an average of 7% of the adult Chilean population contributed part of their time to volunteer work . . . 47% of total civil society employment is made up of volunteer workers, making Chile the country with the highest volunteer participation in Latin America, even outranking developed countries" (5). The claim that Chile is "a country of volunteers" is further substantiated by the fact that 42 percent of all people interviewed for the study claimed to have performed volunteer work at some time or another during their lives (29).

The study describes the following breakdown for sources of civil society funding: 18 percent from foundations and other philanthropic sources, 36 percent from membership fees, and 46 percent from the Chilean government (35). Most of this funding, especially state funds, is destined for educational institutions, which often translates into less state funding for organizations in other sectors of civil society. On one hand, the state provides funding unavailable from other sources, but on the other hand, this tendency can create dependency on state funds and priorities, thus influencing the actions and agendas of the organizations and jeopardizing the sector's independence and ability to act as a watchdog monitoring state practices. De la Maza summarizes the risks inherent in state funding for CSOs: "many of these organizations change their roles, missions, to implement these [state-supported] projects" (2003, 10). Chilean civil society organizations receive less international foundation and multilateral aid

dollars because of the perceived level of democratic development and economic prosperity in the country, thereby making civil society groups
dependent on state funds often provided via state-sponsored, competitive
request-for-projects. This reality has severe repercussions for organizations whose staff or volunteers do not have grant-writing skills or experience deciphering the complexities of grant application processes; this
restriction is particularly relevant to indigenous, rural, and low-income
groups. Even though SERNAM, the state agency for women, and CONADI,
the state organization for indigenous people, were created to improve the
status of women in Chile and contribute to the development of indigenous
communities respectively, funding opportunities from these agencies are
often awarded to intermediary service organizations administered by
urban professionals. Francisca Rodríguez, national leader of ANAMURI
(National Association of Rural and Indigenous Women), a countrywide
network, succinctly summarizes the problems that this dependence on
state funds generates: "We are not going to run behind the merry-go-
round of being summoned for projects, because that is the characteristic
of the subsidiary state, which is every day summoning [organizations] for
different projects, and the whole world chases after these projects because
of a lack of resources and ends up applying the policies of the State and
abandoning the political proposals and plans for their own organizations"
(Franceschet 2003, 25). This dynamic also leads to resentment between
grassroots organizations and nongovernmental organizations, endorsing
the model of the service organization run by urban professionals to the
detriment of resource-poor organizations working at the informal, local, or
grassroots level.

The Chilean Women's Movement

The women's movement became a major civil society protagonist during
the dictatorship and began to organize around women's rights, human
rights, and the economic rights of marginalized communities. Bringing
together human rights groups, feminist groups, self-help groups, and economic survival organizations from the marginalized neighborhoods
around Santiago, the women's movement was "one of the most important
new political actors to emerge" (Chuchryk 1994, 66), culminating in mass
organizations of women such as Women for Life (1983) and Coalition of

Women for Democracy (1988) (Friedman, forthcoming). Under its unifying theme of respect for women's rights and a return to democracy, women's organizations flourished, and they received extensive international support and funding for their activities. During this time, there was a lot of international money for activities from international foundations and communities of exiled Chileans. Over one million Chileans were forced to abandon Chile and seek asylum in over 140 countries during the dictatorship (Shayne 2010, xv). These communities of Chileans were active in raising awareness about the situation in their country and raising funds for the organizations that continued to function there.

The encounter between this growing movement of working-class women activists and feminists from the city coalesced into a formidable, diverse, yet unified force of women struggling for social change. "What bound all of these groups and enabled them to work together was the struggle for the return to democracy" (Chuchryk 1994, 79). Many scholars agree that this panoply of women's groups—bridging differences of class and ideology—was central to creating a movement capable of pressuring the government to call free elections (Baldez 2002; Chuchryk 1994; Franceschet 2003; and Richards 2004). Baldez summarizes this achievement: "Women's organizations leveraged their ability to mobilize supporters into demands for policy change on the agenda of the opposition. They achieved a level of political clout unprecedented for Chilean women" (2002, 168). However, the same scholars that argue that the Chilean women's movement was one of the primary forces that brought an end to the dictatorship also describe a present-day women's movement that has not been able to sustain what it had achieved by 1990. Today's women's movement in Chile is described as "disappearing" (Chuchryk 1994, 91), having "lost its momentum . . . cohesion and articulation as well as its visibility" (de la Maza 2003, 19), and as being "weakened or in a state of latency" (Franceschet 2003, 26). Richards goes as far as to question whether or not a women's movement exists in Chile anymore: "All of this fragmentation leads to the question of whether a women's movement exists in Chile today" (2004, 60). Given this kind of consensus among scholars, one must assume that the women's movement has lost a certain amount of its power as a movement capable of bringing together different parts of society for a common purpose. Nonetheless, attention must be brought to the structural and individual factors that influence this retreat, as well as the potential that remains crystallized in women's organizations and networks today.

This phenomenon of demobilization is not unique to Chile; massive mobilization against state repression tends to dissipate once democracy has returned and often has a gendered component—detrimental for women and beneficial for men—that manifests as a return to "'business as usual,' where the political scene is dominated by men" (Richards 2004, 56). Once a return to democracy has occurred, official political parties can resume their activities, and in Chile many women focused their energies in this direction. "As democratization processes unfold, however, traditional actors such as political parties re-assume their central role, and a formal political arena is re-constructed and (once again) sharply delineated from the social sphere" (Franceschet 2003, 10). Some Chilean women demobilized because the goal had been achieved and they wanted to dedicate themselves to other activities. For instance, some women left movement-oriented, informal groups and went to work for nongovernmental organizations, becoming paid employees or *femocrats*, to use Richards's terminology. Many pobladora activists left the women's movement because they felt it no longer reflected their needs and aspirations, preferring other forms of organizing. They were critical of feminists for their perceived focus on solely eliminating gender discrimination; they resented how much easier it was for college-educated feminists to get paid employment in newly formed feminist nongovernmental organizations. Divisions along class and ideological lines appeared, creating fissures along preexisting differences between women (Baldez 2002, 168).

Though scholarship on the topic indicates that the Chilean women's movement is less visible and influential than it used to be, there are a number of factors that provide insights into the complexities of post-transition societies and challenge the conclusion that the women's movement has dissolved. As terrible as periods of repression and dictatorship can be, it is problematic to use these times as a baseline with which to compare other time periods. Especially in the case of Chile, which had a strong democratic tradition through most of the early twentieth century, it does not make sense to compare civil society organizing using the dictatorship era as the norm. Moreover, with a return to democracy, there is greater diversity of needs and goals, and it becomes harder to establish a common cause that unifies across differences. Groups that worked together during the dictatorship chose to ignore certain differences among themselves in order to reach a common goal, but once democracy had been achieved differences surfaced. Civil society groups, too, had to adapt to the new context, either transforming into nongovernmental organizations—a process called NGO-ization, in which informal groups chose to professionalize, becoming formal NGOs staffed by employees instead of volunteers or activists—or continuing as informal groups with decreased funding, or changing priorities to find funding. Additionally, many women active at the community level remained active in their communities but lost regular contact with the broader movement.

Despite these issues, however, numerous networks of women's organizations have emerged that connect dispersed groups. ANAMURI is a national network of rural and indigenous women's groups working throughout the country to transform the discrimination faced by the women it serves. REMOS and the Women's Initiative Group unite women's organizations across the class spectrum to identify goals and create a common action agenda. And SERNAM is a state agency that has brought increased attention to gender discrimination, generated funding for women's initiatives, and provided employment for many former activists. Its impacts have been both positive and negative.

SERNAM

Many women who left the movement took positions within SERNAM so they could participate in determining the direction of the new national government and its institutions. Founded in 1991 to promote women's equality and help integrate a gender perspective into other ministries and state agencies, SERNAM is an important government initiative and an indicator of the women's movement's ability to pressure the state (Chuchryk 1994, 87; Franceschet 2003, 22; Richards 2004, 46). In recent years, SERNAM's annual budget has increased; "[President] Bachelet increased its budget by 13 percent in 2007," and the organization has lobbied and gained legal reforms promoting women's equality in Chilean society (Friedman, forthcoming; Richards 2004, 53). But because SERNAM is not a ministry in its own right—being housed within the Ministry of Planning—it is prohibited by law from implementing its own programs. This mandate limits the scope of SERNAM's impact because its staff can only implement their own projects in the pilot stage; otherwise, they serve as advisors or depend on other state agencies or NGOs to implement their ideas.

SERNAM's lack of implementation is not its only detracting feature: the institution has been accused of usurping much of the organizing voice and actions of the women's movement, because it has "replaced the women's movement as the key interlocutor in the public discourse on women's issues" (Chuchryk 1994, 88). This lobbying and advocacy role has contributed to alienating many of the working-class, indigenous, and rural women activists who would like to see more resources for grassroots empowerment and initiatives. They see SERNAM as preferring to support feminist, professional NGOs, which stems from the amity, camaraderie, and shared history among SERNAM employees and women in the NGOs. "The well-developed relations between feminists in SERNAM and the NGO community mean that professional women in NGOs enjoy greater access to gender policy networks than do non-professional activists in grassroots women's organizations" (Franceschet 2003, 35). Nonetheless, there has been extensive discussion within a number of women's and feminist organizations in Chile about the risks of working in state agencies or mixed-gender organizations and the significance of remaining autonomous from state organizations. Sadly enough, these kinds of tensions create fissures that destroy alliances and multisector movements. Friedman (forthcoming) summarizes the tension and fallout: "The division between the self-proclaimed *autonómas*, who continued to work in movement arenas, including those of the political left, and those they identified as *institucionalizadas*, who sought change through more formal institutions, marked another painful rending of feminist energies." Instead of institutionalizing gender equality and bringing together Chilean women, SERNAM has become a contested institution supported by many urban professional feminists and harshly critiqued by other women's groups, especially those comprising indigenous, rural, and working-class women.

Mapuche Women's Civil Society Activism and Leadership

The ethnic blindness of many Chileans—ignorance whether genuine or feigned about the multicultural nature of Chile—can also be perceived in the actions of the state—its policies and institutions—as well as in the work of Chilean women's movement scholars. "Indigenous women are seldom mentioned in scholarly work about women's interests and the women's movement in Chile. This omission reflects the deeper-seated denial of eth- nic and cultural diversity" (Richards 2004, 44). For scholars interested in studying Mapuche women, a number of methodological and ethical issues have to be confronted. How must the researcher adjust her methodology when doing research with a colonized people? How does the researcher confront her own racism, having been raised in a racist paradigm? How does the researcher negotiate what black feminist scholar Patricia Hill Collins (1991, 15) calls "the politically contested" nature of intellectual work? There are no easy answers, especially for a researcher like myself. I am white and privileged to have had the opportunities and education I have received. I am also from the United States, not necessarily a country known for its cultural sensitivity, either domestically or in the arena of for- eign affairs. Furthermore, the United States has a long history of genocide and blindness vis-à-vis the native peoples that inhabit its own borders. And while I do speak fluent Spanish, my ability to speak Mapudungun is very basic. However, I never ask a question I am not willing to answer myself. I never make a commitment to the women I am interviewing I am not able to fulfill. In addition to individual interviews and follow-up to return transcribed interviews and seek feedback on initial conclusions, I seek group opportunities to gather feedback about my conclusions, be it using a formal focus group methodology or taking advantage of celebra- tions, meetings, and community projects where women have gathered. This process of using field notes and interview transcripts with research participants opens the opportunity for Mapuche women to comment, co- construct, and deconstruct with the scholar. As Bacigalupo recommends, "We need to attend to theories that start from the 'Margin' and see how they analyze and position themselves with regards to the 'Center'—and in turn look at how the presence of the Other creates the 'Center'" (Bacigalupo 2003, 11). I also seek to establish ties with Mapuche women's organizations, and I put my contacts and knowledge at the disposal of the individuals and organizations I get to know. Following the example of such scholars as Florencia Mallon and Patricia Richards, I work collaboratively with Mapuche and local scholars whenever I can.

Ethnic blindness does not just exist in scholars or state institutions; it can also be identified in the women's movement and NGOs. Many of these efforts were led by professional women whose worldview has been influenced by the culture and political climate in which they are immersed; often people interiorize and replicate racist behaviors without even being aware of it. Though well meaning, their actions are often influenced by stereotypes, prejudices, and the predominant cultural paradigm. "I have observed women NGO directors and professional women deal with women they perceive as 'different' in a prejudiced way," said Nicole Etchart of NESsT. "I see this all the time in Chile. Many progressive women have maids. Even though they have lived in solidarity at times, or given a lot, they can still segregate their domestic responsibilities from their commitment to working with women." In most cases the maids are Mapuche. Pati Jara describes the migration pattern: "Many Mapuche women work as child-care providers or *nanas* in the cities. They come to live in the working-class communities of Cerro Nabia and La Pintana on the outskirts of Santiago." The female director of an international foundation active in Chile describes this phenomenon: "None of our women partners who has young children can live without someone who helps them in the house; it's unthinkable not to do it." And if professional women can only be active in social movements or NGOs if they have a Mapuche woman doing their housework, what do the Mapuche women do who want to be activists or work in a civil society organization?

Mapuche women activists are aware of these contradictions. In addition to the invisibility of the Mapuche women who care for many civil society activists' homes and children, many Mapuche women have chosen not to consider themselves part of the women's movement but as activists with multiple causes. For Mapuche women—similar to pobladora and other marginalized groups—they disagree with feminists who only see the struggle in terms of gender. As Richards cogently assesses: "Unfortunately the assertion of difference between men and women has not always translated into recognition of differences and inequalities among women themselves" (2004, 2). Mapuche women critique the women's movement, especially the feminist NGOs who choose to focus solely on gender discrimination. "Indigenous women, of course, were never really integrated into the Chilean women's movement. Like pobladoras, rural and indigenous women from organizations like ANAMURI (National Association of Rural and Indigenous Women) and other organizations are increasingly vocal about the ways they are excluded and how their own interests and priorities differ from those of middle-class, urban, non-indigenous women" (60). However, in the case of Mapuche women's organizing, it has unfolded in the context of the Mapuche movement, not like the pobladoras who joined the women's movement. For many Mapuche women, their struggle is multifaceted; they are struggling as Mapuche for social, cultural, economic, and political rights, land-tenure rights, *and* women's rights. They are struggling for economic survival, cultural preservation, *and* respect as women in their families and communities.

For many activists, motivation stems from their commitment to safeguard Mapuche identity from Chileanization and global consumer culture. Originally a rural, nomadic culture in south-central and southern Chile, the Mapuche have experienced radical cultural change since the arrival of the Spanish and their internment in *reducciones*, or reservations, at the end of the nineteenth century by the Chilean government. Yet, through all the different forces they have had to confront, they have been able to preserve some essence of their culture, such as their relationship with the land and the importance of family and lineages. This cultural adaptability draws part of its inspiration from their pre-Spanish history of moving their communities in accordance with the seasons and availability of game and food. "For indigenous peoples, this pattern of spatial mobility is nothing new. Since time immemorial the Mapuche in Chile, for example, have moved within their territories and within adjacent national and international spaces" (Bello 2007, 5). From present-day Santiago to the island of Chiloe in southern Chile, from the Pacific Ocean to the pampas on the other side of the Andes, the Mapuche have moved frequently, developing an ability to adapt to new environments from before the arrival of the Spaniards. From this time onward, the Mapuche have demonstrated a remarkable capacity to incorporate change in order to survive. They became expert warriors and cowboys upon observing Spanish warfare and horse and cattle raising.

When experiencing population depletion due to the spread of European diseases and famine brought on by the wars to preserve their independence from Chile, they adjusted their marriage practices so one man, capable of supporting larger groups, could have numerous wives and protect the children. The introduction of polygamous marriage practices, however, has not been without its complications, as the testimonies of Mapuche women show in the next section. Though the Mapuche have fought for their rights to native forests since the 1500s, they have had to transform the literal bond between community and native forest to one of a need and celebration of green spaces for connection with *newenes* (friendly nature spirits) because so much of the population lives in urban settings. This cultural fluidity facilitates maintaining a Mapuche identity even in today's interconnected, globalized, consumer society. "The notion of 'being Mapuche' is extremely fluid and context specific. Belongingness often depends less on a person's knowledge of traditional lore and more on their ability to recreate their identity and that of others; to adapt themselves to situations; to manipulate competing systems of knowledge and reality; and to negotiate between realities" (Bacigalupo 2003, 6–7). For example, many Mapuche women have assumed leadership roles in their communities and regions because they speak Spanish and are agile in negotiating the bureaucracy of governmental agencies. They take advantage of opportunities from Chilean or winka culture if it behooves them and their communities. As we will see in the case of Petronila Catrileo, who as president of her community works hand in hand with the *lonko*, the male chief of the community.

Mapuche women were active in Mapuche organizations that formed during the dictatorship. Organizations such as the Mapuche Cultural Centers and Ad Mapu were formed under cultural auspices so as to not raise concerns with regime authorities. They often carried out cultural activities, such as *ngillatun* and the polo-like sport *palin*, but they also took advantage of the gatherings to organize on behalf of a return to democracy. And since the return to democracy, Mapuche organizations have continued to grow: "The contemporary Mapuche movement has proliferated since the creation of CONADI and the Indigenous Law . . . over 60 associations in Santiago, and about 175 associations in the rest of the country" (Richards 2004, 129). Richards goes on to cite a 1997 SERNAM paper in which Mapuche women participate more in civil society groups than other Chilean women and that they are more likely to attain leadership roles in these organizations than other Chilean women (164). In addition to participation in a range of mixed-gender organizations, a growing number of Mapuche women are creating women-led and women-serving organizations such as ANAMURI, based in Santiago; Rayen Voygue in Cañete; the House of Mapuche Women in Temuco; and Keyukleayn pu Zomo also in Temuco . This is a delicate issue. Organizing their own groups shows that there may be certain gender-related issues that require separate organizational spaces for their treatment; however, the fact that they are forming their own organizations also raises the issue of sexist discrimination against women within male-led organizations and Mapuche culture in general. The fact that some Mapuche women activists speak of discrimination is often perceived as a rejection of Mapuche culture by Mapuche purists. So women who choose to work only with women often face antagonism in the broader Mapuche society. Mapuche scholar A. Millaray Painemal tackles this issue:

> The appearance of organizations of Mapuche women in recent years is due to the lack of space in mixed gender organizations where men make the decisions. And on the other hand, it comes from the need to address specific issues such as discrimination and abuse that women suffer in their communities as well as the violence against women when they experience unlawful entry by state forces due to conflict with the forestry sector. We feel that from this participation in women's-only organizations, women can develop leadership skills, strengthen ethnic identity and Mapuche women's rights, thereby contributing to the construction of the idea of a Mapuche nation. (2005, 2)

Similar to black or Chicana feminists in the United States, many Mapuche women see that their struggles are multi-sited and interrelated. They will fight for the preservation of their culture, they will fight against sexism within the Mapuche culture, and they will fight to regain tenure of land taken from their ancestors. "The gaze of Mapuche women encompasses the worlds they live in and their own culture. Mapuche women are defenders of their culture but they do not ignore the need to improve their

situation in their own culture, combating discrimination and violence"
(Painemal 2005, 2). Given the precarious situation that Mapuche culture
finds itself in—hemmed in simultaneously by a Chilean vision of a
European country and global consumer culture; concerned by the declining numbers of fluent Mapudungun speakers; confronted with a culturally
insensitive educational system; and aware that they are no longer a rural
culture due to heavy migration to the cities—Mapuche women activists
often frame their work in cultural terms. "They are insistent that even
when they make specific claims as women, their central objective is to
achieve recognition of the rights of the people as a whole" (Richards 2004,
193). Even so, this act of placing particular struggles against the background of Mapuche cultural preservation is seldom easy; for some
activists, their work draws its inspiration from a deep commitment to
transforming sexist practices that have limited their own lives, as well as
other women's. Evident in my interviews with Mapuche women, and corroborated by Richards, Mapuche women activists face many challenges:
"the tension between seeking recognition as a people and dealing with the
specificities as women is present in the discourse of almost all women
I interviewed" (188).

Participation in mixed-gender and women-only organizations is
increasing the leadership skills of Mapuche women, creating a cadre of
articulate, empowered, networked women committed to meeting their
goals. "In present times, these organizations are growing stronger in
tandem with a new generation of leaders—functional and traditional"
(Painemal 2005, 1). The concept of functional leaders refers to the presidents of communities, the directors of women's organizations, board
members of women's organizations, and the leaders of training programs;
but Mapuche culture also has traditional leadership positions reserved for
women. Though women play a number of important roles in religious ceremonies such as the *ngillatun* and *machitun*, the most respected leadership
position for women in traditional Mapuche culture is the *machi*, who
bridges the human and spirit worlds to heal members of her community.
Machi, almost always women, are "people who heal with herbal remedies
and the help of spirits ... Machi are also mediators and negotiators
between different cultural realities" (Bacigalupo 2003, 1). In addition to
the mediator and healing role, the machi holds an immense knowledge of

medicinal plants and herbs; this respected role in her community, along with her practical healing knowledge, means that machi are consulted by Mapuche and non-Mapuche alike (Bengoa 1992, 116). The machi—feared and revered by communities fortunate enough to have one—have control over the spirit world and this gives them power in their communities, helping to balance some of the gender inequalities with local men, who are often afraid of the spirit world. The traditional role of the machi is one of the leadership options that Mapuche women exercise; other functional roles—often in civil society organizations—are also occupied by Mapuche women.

The phenomenon of Mapuche leadership in civil society organizations is well exemplified by the testimony and life story of Rosa Isolde Reuque Paillalef, based on interviews with historian Florencia Mallon. A respected elder in her community near Temuco, Chile, Reuque Paillalef said, "Leaders, I think, should be like mirrors in which the people can see their own reflections" (2002, 239). Raised with little knowledge of her own Mapuche heritage, she has dedicated her adult life to learning and disseminating Mapuche culture. During the dictatorship, she was active in Mapuche organizations that challenged the regime. After the democratic transition, she was a leader of the Christian Democrats and then founded a Mapuche women's organization to address the discrimination Mapuche women face. Criticized by some of her people as having moved too far to the right, and by others of moving too far to the left, she was accused of abandoning her people in exchange for feminism. "I've had to develop a thick skin," she said. "Many times I've thought that, as a leader, I have a double, no, even a triple, personality. First I'm my parents' daughter; then I'm my husband's wife; and finally I'm the leader who must answer to her people. But maybe there's yet a fourth identity, that of the Mapuche woman who has to live in a non-Mapuche society that demands many things of you that aren't part of your culture, things for which you're not prepared and don't have the resources" (141).

The Reflections of Mapuche Women Leaders

The Mapuche story-telling style is such that I have chosen to use entire excerpts from individual interviews so the reader can appreciate the way

Mapuche women tell their stories, often building a story around a particular moral or lesson learned. As Florencia Mallon points out in the introduction to Reuque Paillalef's testimony, "Isolde arranges her story around particular incidents or watersheds . . . moments that then become nodes of meaning" (Reuque Paillalef 2002, 11).

Silvia Nain Catrilelbún (Fifty-five Years Old)

I first interviewed Silvia in the small city of Cañete at the arts and crafts gallery run by Rayen Voygue, a local organization serving indigenous and farming women. Our conversation at the gallery was punctuated by sales of handmade baskets and weavings to local shoppers. Like many of the women I interviewed in south-central and southern Chile, Silvia grew up in extreme poverty until her father was able to form a cooperative under the agrarian reform and obtain land for the first time. Though her parents believed in the importance of getting an education, all twelve of their children had to contribute to the family's income by helping their father in the fields and their mother with the chickens or with weaving. As the oldest, Silvia had to help her mother raise the younger children; she saw how her mother lived her life always pregnant. She remembers,

> As a little girl, I suffered because I was mother to my other brothers and sisters. And in the house, I was the only help they had. And when my mother was expecting a baby, she never went to the hospital. She had them at home. My father would be the midwife and I would be his assistant. My father would say, "Heat the water." And I would say to myself, "Why do I have to heat the water?" I had to heat the water because everything had to be clean and sterilized, including the scissors to cut the umbilical cord. . . . I did all these things. And my father would tie my mother up so she could push the baby out. . . . I would suffer so much watching this, because as women, it can be terrible, and for this reason, I never wanted to get married. . . . My mother always told me, "If you get married, don't get married so young." "No," I would say, "I am not going to get married because I want to be a professional and go to work."[6]

Even though it was not common for girls to go to school when she was little, Silvia knew that it was her only path out of poverty. When she first went to school, she only spoke Mapudungun and had to learn Spanish. Given the rejection and abuse that young Mapuche of Silvia's generation received when they arrived at Chilean or Catholic schools, many decided not to speak Mapudungun with their own children so they would not have to feel ashamed at school like they did. This has created a generation of Mapuche who have had to learn their native language as adults. In addition to pursuing her studies for her own advancement, Silvia also wanted to succeed at school and then seek employment so she could help her younger brothers and sisters get an education. Yet it was not until she was doing an internship to become an agrarian technician that she discovered her commitment to working for the empowerment of rural and indigenous women. She was sent to the countryside near the city of Chillán to work with women: "I taught them to work in the garden, to work in the kitchen, and all the crafts of weaving, embroidery, and dying the thread. From this time, I decided to work with indigenous women. I saw that the women were dedicated and hard working, they could learn new things, and I said, 'Why don't we do something given we know so much?' I wanted to recover the lost crafts. I worked for two years with the women in Chillán. One of the obstacles was generating income; another was getting permission from the husbands."[7]

Realizing that empowering women meant working with men on their conceptions of gender roles, she began facilitating discussions among the husbands of the women she was serving so they could see the benefits of having their wives learn new skills. It was not until two decades later that masculinity and gender-related issues for men would become international development priorities and early proponents of gender and development policies made the same connections as Silvia. Gender does not equal women; gender sensitivity is about understanding how gender hierarchies and gender roles of women *and* men inform development.

Upon returning to Cañete with her degree, Silvia cofounded Rayen Voygue in the 1980s. She was president when they took over an abandoned building in Cañete for their offices. She led the campaign asking CONADI to intercede and assist the women in buying the office, and part of that effort involved organizing a *ngillatun* outside of Cañete in support of the cause. Silvia recounts the meaningful event: "We invited a machi, and in the part where she went into a trance, she had a dream which she shared with us. She dreamed that we would be able to keep the building. So we found the strength and everything worked out well in the end."

Silvia played a leadership role during this foundational period of Rayen Voygue in which they eventually gained ownership of their offices and became a legally inscribed organization in 1994. Now she manages the guest house and the crafts store. The organization generates enough income to cover their expenses and provides services to rural farming women, who face many of the same challenges as Mapuche women. The guest house produces income for the activities of Rayen Voygue, especially important in times of decreasing state and international donations. And the crafts store generates income for local women. The store takes 20 percent of the final sale price and the craftswomen keep the rest.[8] This strategy of self-sufficiency means that the organization has the autonomy to make its own decisions about which priorities to pursue.

Silvia also works in a nearby community, teaching knitting and weaving techniques; her commitment is to being a multiplier of cultural wisdom. Yet she does it critically. She has chosen to focus on the aspects of her culture that create much-needed income and empowerment for women and their families.

Petronila Catrileo (Fifty-nine Years Old)

In a rural hamlet near Cañete, Petronila lives with her winka husband, René. They work the land Petronila inherited from her family. She takes care of the garden and the animals, and René farms and takes care of the pigs and cows. Like Silvia, Petronila grew up very poor. Watching her mother's hard life motivated her to keep studying even without the support of her father:

> I was born in 1950. I started school against the wishes of my father. For him, women are meant to get married, have kids, and work the land. I was seventeen when I decided to leave home. I wanted to have a job; I wanted to buy my own things. I wanted to help my little brother study.
>
> I was the oldest child. I always had a lot of chores. I fixed breakfast. I went to the river to wash the diapers. And then I had to go with my father to work the land. We did not have any money to buy

anything. For example, my father did not have oxen. Someone had to loan us oxen so we could harvest the wheat. Once we had completed the harvest, there were twenty bags, ten to the rich man who owned the land, five sacks to the owner of the oxen, and that left us with only five sacks. This was not enough.

My dad would hit my mother and always left her pregnant. Now he lives far away, practically alone and in complete poverty. He had to pay for how he lived his life. So I decided that I would get out of there no matter the price. I had luck. I got two scholarships.[9]

After graduating as an agricultural technician, Petronila went to work near the city of Temuco in the small town of Chol Chol; she worked for the Fundación Chol Chol training men, women, and children in how to farm the land, put up the crops, and take care of the animals. The hardships she faced as a child, along with the abuse she witnessed between her parents, influenced her decision to seek a winka as a partner. She returned to the Cañete area with René to farm the land. Once she and René returned to have their family, she began to participate in a mixed-gender Mapuche organization, where she met Silvia. Soon thereafter the women began to grow more radical as they reflected on the situation of the country and their own marginalization as Mapuche women; differences started to appear between the women and the men who were more conservative and afraid of Pinochet's regime. The men stopped attending, and the Mapuche women's organization Rayen Voygue was born; Petronila provides an account of this process: "In the 1980s, I participated in the Rayen Voygue organization. The priests helped us; they let us use rooms in the church. I was interested in participating in an organization because I was not in agreement that Pinochet govern the country. The organization started out as a mixed organization, but in the end, we were just women because we kept arguing with the men. Few of them were honest; sometimes they were even in agreement with things that Pinochet did. Often men do not suffer as much as women. Who had it the worst off were women."[10]

Because of her technical training, Spanish skills, and participation in the founding of Rayen Voygue, the community kept asking her to take on more responsibility. As the introductory quotation to this chapter describes, Petronila is the president of her community and she works closely with the lonko. Instead of functional and traditional leadership roles entering into conflict, as happens in some communities, Petronila and the lonko work together, complementing each other.

Petronila is leading her community to take over one thousand acres that were taken from the community a hundred years ago. When the Chilean state finally subjugated the Mapuche in the late nineteenth century, their lands became state property. In 1904 land-grant titles were handed out to some lonkos, but in many cases the land was given to European settlers. It was during this time that the community of Petronila's grandparents lost the land in exchange for a sack of wheat. After speaking with the elders in the community, Petronila pieced together the following story:

> It is said that a spinster sister of Juan Segundo Marileo, whose name was Señora María Inés, leased the land to a family called the Prietos. They were the first non-Mapuche to take over the land. And María Inés leased the land to them for a sack of grain. And from then on, the land was passed on or sold to other winka families. This continued on for 150 years. And eventually they became the owners. And because the Mapuche had no papers, there was nothing they could do about it.
>
> For many years I have said to the community leaders, "Don't let those lands be planted, don't let the landowners plant again. These lands belong to our community; we have to fight for them." But they didn't pay me any mind because they were cowards; they don't stand up for their rights.[11]

Petronila finally convinced the community to take action. And on October 12, 2006, el Día de la Raza—a day celebrated throughout Latin America as the day that Christopher Columbus "discovered" the Americas—Petronila and her community marched up to the mountain that had been taken from María Inés. They called a press conference on the mountain, performed sacred rites, prepared a meal, and issued their intention to regain the land legally.

The community remains hopeful that CONADI will help them negotiate the return of the land. The current owner of the land has forested the mountain, half with pines and half with eucalyptus trees. Because of the worth of the trees, Petronila is negotiating that the owner harvest the trees and sell them, then return the land without the trees to the community. Not only will this make the land cheaper to buy back, but it will not include trees that bring death. For the Mapuche, the native forest—with its diversity—promotes life, contains the good spirits, and takes care of the water, while mono-cropping pine and eucalyptus species does not. "This form of forestry dries up all the water. There is not as much water as there used to be when there wasn't just pines. Like I said before, in the summer the river was so much higher. But not now. You have seen where the water is now and we're not even at the height of summer yet. And the pines go right up to the river's edge."[12] Reforesting with single crops not only affects the water levels but also kills the spirits: "The *newenes*—the good spirits— are getting lost when there is deforestation or the planting of exotic trees. The spirits don't like this. It is not good what is happening to the Mother Earth. That is where our strength is. There would not be any Mapuche left if everything were just pine and eucalyptus. What will the Mapuche live on if there is only eucalyptus and pine?"[13]

Petronila raises an issue that is at the center of the present-day conflict between the Mapuche and the forestry industry. There are a few forestry companies that follow international standards for protecting ecological diversity and respecting the land claims of the Mapuche; but there are other companies that do not. They simply seek to maximize their profits regardless of the ecological or cultural cost.

Amalia Quilapi (Seventy-three Years Old)

Amalia, her husband, Luis, their daughter, Dominica, and I stepped out of the summer sun into the shade and coolness of the family's *ruka* to have our interview. Amalia built the ruka—a traditional Mapuche house—on her property and furnished it just like the one she and Luis lived in when they first moved in together over fifty years ago. One must duck down to enter at one end, and the long building, covered by thatch, is arched. Just inside sits a fire pit and a suspended drying rack, and surrounding the pit are stools made from tree stumps covered with sheepskin. Wooden bed frames lean against the far wall.

A community leader, farmer, and weaver, Amalia frequently invites community members and tourists to the ruka to learn about Mapuche culture. Luis, her husband, is the community lonko. He works the land and helps Amalia with her weaving. Dominica, one of their eight children (six daughters and two sons), has built a house next door. She is the president of Rayen Voygue and has just assumed a leadership role in ANAMURI.

When Amalia was twenty, she met Luis at a ngillatun, a ceremony carried out to ask the gods to reinstate well-being and balance to the community (Catrileo 2005, 204). In those days, courtship was different. A girl did not speak to a boy because it would have been considered too forward for a girl. But once the boy had spoken to the girl, it was up to the girl to decide whether or not the conversation continued. Amalia remembers admiring the way Luis danced; she reminisces:

> We met at a ngillatun ceremony. That's how I met him. He was dancing. He danced well, the *purun* mapuche, in the ceremony. It was a delicate thing, how a girl got to know a boy. We didn't have friends back then like young people today. It was all very private. It was said that it was bad to spend time with boys. So there were absolutely no friends who were boys. They would have the celebrations, the ngillatun, and then it was the boy who had to speak first, back then it was the men who spoke first. Today, I think, it's the women who talk first to the men.
>
> I was twenty-years old, young. That's why I have so many children. We waited to get legally married. We already had four children when we got married. This happened often. We were together a couple of years. You didn't get together and get married right away. Nor did you register your children right away.[14]

Gender roles were fairly rigid when Amalia and Luis were young. She remembers that her parents never had her baptized, nor did her father want to put his name on her birth certificate, because he was upset that he had too many girls.

> My parents never baptized me when I was a baby. It wasn't until I got married, that I got baptized and I had four children by then. It was my dad, over everyone else, who did not want me baptized. It was that way before. He was angry because he only had mostly girls: three girls and one boy. He wanted more boys than girls. So he

got angry and refused to register my birth or baptize me. I didn't really go to school. I probably attended school, all told, for about two weeks. I had to help my mom out at home. Girls were expected to help their mothers. Work consisted of helping cook, make the bread, go out and harvest the wheat, weave at night. In addition to this, we had to work in the fields. Go to the machine, put on the sacks, and drag the sacks home. And always help our mom back home. I learned very young how to cook.[15]

From the moment they began living together and having children, Amalia and Luis were poor. Dominica recounts, "When my mother and father were young, it was very hard for them to rise up and overcome their circumstances. My father always told us about how poor they were. They had one iron pot that was old and broken." As Amalia and Luis raised their children, they were finally able to get land through agrarian reform, but they had only their hard work to make the most of the land. Together they describe the conditions of the early years of their relationship together. "Because we worked so hard, when we arrived we didn't even have a hoe," said Amalia. "Nothing, no oxen, nothing. Just all our girls." Luis continues,

I remember the day we arrived. Some Chileans made fun of us. "Look at the Mapuches and their carts." They laughed, but look, they are no longer here today, they have all passed away. It does not serve to laugh at other people. My god listened and today, thanks to the prayers and hard work, we are in good health even though we are very old. It's not worth it to do those things, talk that way and make fun of people who are poor. Because we were poor, we were born poor. And now our lives are different because we worked. This was our big commitment. We worked and worked. If we hadn't, it would have just been us and a whole bunch of kids. We were smart. First we are going to do this, and we did it. Then we are going to do that, and we did it. That's how we progressed. We met our goals. And at the end of the day, we don't stop. At night, Amalia keeps working, she weaves. One day I thought, "Look, I am going to help you. I will turn the thread." So at night, I help her by turning her thread for her.[16]

As Amalia and Luis remember their history, they tell it with a moral. Hard work gets you ahead. They are critical of Mapuches who have not taken advantage of opportunities; they are critical of how winkas discriminate against the Mapuche. Yet they both know that the Mapuche have always had to fight to keep the little they have been able to achieve. And many Mapuche have not been able to get access to sufficient land or have had to leave the land to find work in the cities. Luis and Amalia were able to gain land, and land is the key to Mapuche survival. Today their house, weaving studio, and ruka are frequently full of their children, grandchildren, and visitors interested in learning more about Mapuche culture.

Jaqueline Caniguan (Thirty-three Years Old)

Jaqueline is one of only a few Mapudungun linguists; she got her master's degree in linguistics in Mexico. Jaqueline is not only a Mapuche intellectual but also a member of Identidad Lafkenche, a group that brings together Mapuche from the coastal region. She and her husband and son have moved back to Puerto Saavedra, her hometown on the Pacific Ocean. Many Mapuche leave their homes to seek education and work and seldom return. Jaqueline is the exception; she has returned to Puerto Saavedra and lives in the house where she grew up. She reflects on how complicated it is to live in a Chileanized or Western world:

> There's another issue that Chilean society does not see which is that the war—for the Mapuche—only ended a hundred years ago. And a hundred years in the history of a people is nothing. My mother would talk to me about her grandmother who survived the war. So for me, history arrives fresh. For example, in the town I am from—Puerto Saavedra—the war ended in 1896. The war had begun in 1881 under the leadership of General Cornelio Saavedra. This may sound like a joke, but I always forget the name of my town because it is named Puerto Saavedra in honor of Cornelio Saavedra who was a murderer, an evil man, who never kept his word, a man who said that for him the war was more about wine and alcohol than about gun powder. So you see our history is recent. And when it is a history of defeat, I think that it is easy for the losers to not want to be seen. The pattern of discrimination—how the small towns,

especially those where the few people with money are not
Mapuche—emerges . . . "Indians are like this and that," and eventually people don't want to be Indians anymore.[17]

Jaqueline comes from a long line of strong women. Not only was her
mother a machi, but her grandmother and great-grandmother were leaders and challenged the gender stereotypes of their times:

> It is a family line where women have played a strong role because
> the grandmother of my mother [Jaqueline's great-grandmother]
> was the only child of the lonko of the community. . . . They had the
> land that today is the town of Puerto Saavedra. I always joke with
> people that someday I am going to get angry and throw them out
> because it is my land. So we are talking about the year 1850, a little
> before. So this man had a wife and one daughter. His wife died, so
> he sought another wife with whom he had two boys. So his only
> daughter [the child of his first wife] had the same name as my
> mother, Margarita.
>
> As was tradition, negotiations occurred between her father
> and another lonko from El Budi in the area of Piedra Alta. And so
> he gave her to this other lonko in marriage. But my great-
> grandmother, Margarita, had been raised as an only child. And
> when she arrived to her husband's ruka, she was the third or fourth
> wife. In front of the husband, the older wives treated her well,
> but when he wasn't home, the treatment was awful. I question the
> idea that four wives are going to get along and live in harmony. But
> if I said this to a Mapuche, he would say that I am criticizing my cul-
> ture, and I don't know what else. Back to the story, so my great-
> grandmother was not being treated very nicely by the other women,
> and so she escaped. She fled via the beach and made it home to her
> father. And she told him she was never going back there. This is a
> big step for a woman of her time. She left her husband and returned
> to her father [and she was not forced to return].
>
> So she assumed the leadership of the community when her
> father died. She had a few common-law husbands over the years and
> had children with a number of them. But she never married again,
> and all her children were daughters. When she came home after

leaving the lonko, she was pregnant with my grandmother. And since the first child tends to spend a lot of time with the grandparents, when my mother was born, she spent a lot of time with her grandmother for whom she was named, Margarita. So this is where she learned to stand up for herself.[18]

Jaqueline's mother was a machi, a respected healer whose services were sought by people throughout the region; she would travel far to see patients, and these patients would also journey great distances to come and visit her. To this day, people remember her mother, though she passed away a number of years ago. When Jaqueline was growing up, she would accompany her mother as she visited patients and performed healing ceremonies. Jaqueline preserves many memories of the conversations she was witness to as the daughter of the healer; she shares some of those stories she heard women tell her mother:

Because of my mother's work as a machi, I listened to the stories women would tell; I visited the sick, and listened as my mother treated people. Together we traveled all over, visiting many communities. My mother treated people from Tirua to Teodoro Schmidt, people came from as far away as Neuquén [in Argentina], they came from all over. I heard thousands of stories, and got to know many cases.

I am critical of a more [purist or] culturalist approach [to Mapuche culture], because I believe that all cultures of the world have their good parts and not-so-good parts, their bad parts. It is necessary to reflect critically about how women are treated and not attempt to justify violence or abuse because it is "cultural." For me, repeating a history of violence cannot be justified by saying it is "cultural." There is no justification for violence. And I speak from experience; I lived it up close and personal when I was a child.

I clearly remember being about seven or eight years old and listening to the case of an old woman who cried a lot when she spoke of how she got married. The marriage had been arranged between two families, like it used to be for the Mapuche. She was taken from her family when she was still a fourteen-year-old girl. She remembered that she was taking care of the sheep when her older brothers came to her and said that the next day some men were going to take her away, that she should get ready and pack her things. She spent that whole night awake, scared. The next day, the men arrived and there was a big party, and they took her. And in the night, she did not know what was going to happen. When she arrived, the whole family was waiting for her in the ruka. As the night progressed, she saw that the guests were starting to depart, leaving them alone. And something inside of her knew what was going to happen. She was wrapped up in a long dress and she put it in between her legs so that he could not touch her. And even as an old woman she cried because during that first night of her marriage, her first sexual experience had been a rape. And it had been violent. We are not talking about someone who was aware that she was an innocent girl. And afterwards so she wouldn't escape, they cut the bottom of her feet so she couldn't walk. So for six months she had to crawl around the house.

I am not able to justify this behavior. . . . Violence is violence no matter where it occurs, but it is for these reasons that I rebel against certain aspects of my culture. And this is when I'm accused of having become Westernized, become a feminist.

Many of the women I interviewed described feeling ostracized by Mapuche who romanticize or encapsulate their culture, wanting things to go back to an idealized, pre-conquest moment that no longer exists. When Mapuche women leaders use a gender lens to examine certain traditions or behaviors, such as marriage between an old man and a girl, they are often made to feel like they are betraying their culture. However, Jaqueline maintains that being critical of certain aspects of one's culture or history does not mean one denies one's culture, rather the opposite: one is engaged in and wants to continue being a part of that culture. Jaqueline is not pessimistic regarding gender relations between Mapuche men and women. She sees many positive signs of change:

But you know, I am optimistic in this sense. A few years ago I carried out an interesting evaluation of a women's organization in Puerto Domínguez that had received funding to implement a vocational workshop for women. Together we reconstructed the history of the workshop which had been going for ten years, but there had been a change in the men, in the husbands of the women who participated in the workshop. When I interviewed the husbands, they recognized that ten years ago they did not want their wives to go to the workshop. They thought that they would just waste time and gossip. But they began to see that their wives were learning new things. And later, the men began to get involved, helping the women, coming to agreements on schedules, time commitments, etc. The fact that the men got to the point of coming to agreements is a big step, because we are talking about men in their sixties . . .

   I see that there is a lot of feminine presence in [civil society] organizations, and I feel that the organizations—be they independent or aligned with political parties—would have nothing if it weren't for the women. The support is provided by the women. A woman puts things in order. She is committed and a hard worker. There is still a ways to go in terms of women being respected for themselves, but I think the next big step is going to be when we women are recognized for how important our participation is. This is lacking: that women be recognized for all that they do.[19]

When I visited Jaqueline to return her transcribed interview and share some of the conclusions from my analysis of all of the interviews, she described her work with women, neighbors, and townspeople to recognize that women have rights, that they see they are entitled to respect in their relationships. According to Jaqueline, more equitable relationships between men and women depend on both sexes changing their behavior. These sentiments echo the conclusions of Mapuche scholars like America Millaray Painemal and point to how vital women's contributions are to CSOs. They also serve to illuminate why some Mapuche women are choosing to leave mixed-gender organizations to found women's-only organizations.

Irene Huelche (Fifty-five Years Old)

Irene is from a rural community outside of Temuco, Chile. Though she worked for a number of years in Santiago as a domestic worker, she returned to her community after the coup in 1973 and has been a community organizer ever since. Irene articulately conveys the challenges she faced as an idealistic, young woman who began to comprehend how severe and extensive the discrimination was against the Mapuche:

> Similar to the women you mention in Cañete, I am motivated to make a difference because of all the poverty I have seen. We have had to walk the path of poverty, of humiliation, marginalization, in schools, in offices, at work. So we don't want our children to have to face the same thing. Our parents did not know about their rights, sometimes even letting people marginalize them because they did not know better. And even teachers marginalized us, punishing us for speaking Mapudungun or for playing. Many times I would work hard but still get bad grades, but the teachers were Westerners and the best students of the class were Westerners. And they always got the best grades. We were always the ones that did poorly. So I believe that at some point I began to want to do something about this situation. The injustice was too big.
>
> I saw that a man would work from sunup to sundown in the rural estates, and they didn't pay him with money, just with wheat or flour. He hardly had time to eat lunch. I saw this with my uncles and my parents. And the owner would sit there on his horse holding a whip while the workers ate as quickly as they could. And if they didn't eat fast enough, they would feel the lash of the whip or get fired.[20]

Yet Irene's witness to discrimination and injustice extended beyond seeing how Chileans treated the Mapuche in general to seeing how Mapuche men treated women, especially witnessing the relationship between her parents. She began to see that oppressive gender roles were inhibiting the lives and aspirations of women in her family:

> And women were like the slaves of their husbands. "You can't go out," "You have to stay here because I have something to do." So the women were nothing more than slaves. The first person that I rebelled against was my father. I saw that my mother was a slave and she worked so hard and so much, like an ant. She worked and worked with her arts and crafts, her weaving, and then she would go

into the city to sell what she had made. She would bring her earnings back to the house. She bought all the clothes for us. She made cheese, blankets, rugs; she gathered eggs and sold them, she raised chickens and sold them. She did whatever she had to do to make money. My father did not treat her well. I saw all of this and my sense of rebellion began to emerge. So I reached a point in my studies, when my mother could no longer pay for me to keep going to school. I had made it to third grade and I needed a notebook and a pencil, but my mother did not have enough to help me. I knew my father would not help me. He was very *machista*. For him, a woman was supposed to stay at home and not go to school or get a job. So, I rebelled against him and left the house to go to Santiago and work as a domestic servant. And I saw a different world, but still a world of discrimination.

Irene's experience of the world was greatly broadened by going to Santiago to find work. She had never lived outside of her Mapuche community and did not know a lot about Western culture. Though she had to work long hours, she saw a dynamic within the family she took care of that was different from her own family:

I was new to the Western world, but I saw that they didn't trust us Mapuche, but I also didn't trust them; I saw how I was marginalized and exploited by them. Because I had to get up at six in the morning and work until two in the morning, sleep a little bit, and then start all over. Because on the weekends they would invite fifteen people over to dinner and there was no one to help me, just "do this and do that."

I did see that there were things about their world that I hadn't known. I saw that the Western man treated his wife and kids very well. And this is when I thought, "Oh, I am not going to marry a Mapuche. The Mapuche treats his woman poorly. And I am not going to get married. I want to have children but as a single mother. I don't want anyone telling me what to do. I don't want anyone to hit me. I don't want anyone to scold me. I will have children, but I won't get married."

As described above in the introduction to this chapter, many progressive Chilean families—often activists, leaders, and participants in civil society organizations—employ Mapuche women as domestic workers to take care of their children and clean the house. In the case of Irene, the family she worked for obviously demonstrated blindness to the amount of work they were giving her, but they did show some sensitivity to her ethnicity and the importance of the Mapuche struggle.

> My employer would give me advice, asking me why I was scared to admit that I was Mapuche. It was Christmas, and he sat down with his family and with me and he said the following to me: "Irene, don't you ever feel shame for being who you are. It should be the opposite. You should feel proud." He said this to me after I told him I did not speak Mapuche when I did. So he said to me, "I know that you know how to speak Mapuche. But for some reason you don't want to tell me. But I am going to give you some advice. That language is very rich and not everyone can speak it. Whether you are in front of the Minister or the President of the Republic, whoever it may be, you need to speak to them in your language."
>
> In 1973 the family had to separate because he had to go into exile. He had worked in a municipal, public office [under Allende]. His wife was a special education teacher. They worked for a cause on behalf of poor people, so he had to go into exile and was soon followed by the family. I had to return home because I could not leave my children.[21]

When Irene returned home to her community, her vision of her people, of political causes, and of the rights of women had evolved; not only had her worldview been broadened, but she felt different, almost a stranger to her community. Her initial rebellion against her father had been transformed by her experience of living with a progressive Western family in Santiago and her anger over the death of Allende and the coup by Pinochet. She returned to her community wanting to share her new insights and help her people. From the beginning she was called a communist, and though she has participated in numerous women's organizations over the years, she still had not found an organizational space from which to contribute to

her community. It was not until she realized that her gift lay with introduc-
ing Chileans and foreigners to the Mapuche culture that she finally began
to find her contribution. She came to alternative tourism by accident.
Initially her community had been approached to host a small delegation
from Sweden in 1995, but after a series of misunderstandings, the group of
Swedes all arrived to stay at her house. Her house was very rustic: "No electricity, no potable water, not a lot of room to sleep, but we had just enough
to receive nine people plus the translator and the guide." She enjoyed the
visit but did not think anymore of it until she received another request to
host a delegation; and then one delegation followed another. Each time the
logistics got easier, and she learned to create a budget so she knew how
much it was going to cost to host a group. With the next group, she said to
her family, "Look, we've got another group coming to visit on such-and-
such a date, but this time more people are coming. We are going to have to
build another house." Finally she began to think that this kind of exchange
might be a way to earn a living and disseminate important Mapuche cultural wisdom to other people: "And it was then that I began to turn over
this idea, a way of sharing my culture with others, a way of getting to know
other people. A way of showing a different vision of the Mapuche; transforming that idea that we are 'drunk Indians' or 'lazy Indians.' We said, 'We
can't visit the world, but the world can come to us.'"[22]

Today Irene has two houses and a ruka for guests, as well as latrines
and chairs. She reflects, "I was a pioneer in this. When I inaugurated the
ruka, the media arrived, even mayors from nearby towns, they came to the
opening." Irene's history of sensitivity to social issues has found an outlet
that uses her leadership skills, promotes increased understanding of the
contributions of the Mapuche people, and attracts significant economic
resources to the community.

Julia Matamala (Thirty-three Years Old)
Julia built a ruka near Puerto Saavedra, along a tourist circuit through
the lush landscape to the ocean. Tourists stop for horseback riding, sailing
on the lake, shopping for arts and crafts, and camping or renting cabins.
Julia, her mother, and her grandmother live down the hill from the ruka,
but during the summer she spends her days there, knitting and weaving
and selling her arts and crafts to people who drive by. On Sundays the

community theater group she started with the help of the Karukinka Human Development Center, an NGO based in Temuco, holds its meetings there. She describes the group:

> Right now we are a group of twelve people from the community, Mapuche and non-Mapuche, children, adults, a little of everything. This is the first organized group I participate in. I don't like to work in groups that get together to ask for handouts or donations. . . . So, I have always been reluctant to be in groups for this reason. But now I form part of a different kind of group because we don't get together so someone will give us something, rather we get together because we have fun, and because through the theater, we recover our histories and share them with the community.
>
> The first big play we did was more than a history of the community; we wrote and performed a play about the past four hundred years; we went back in time before the winkas—or non-Mapuche had arrived. . . . Now we are working on a play about the history of the Mapuche wedding. So we began to investigate about what this meant, how were the weddings before, what kind of clothes did they wear. And just if people speak Mapudungun in real life, then they speak it in the play. So we discovered that there are different kinds of Mapuche weddings. . . . One form of Mapuche marriage is when the young man comes and steals the woman in the night. This form of marriage is generally of mutual agreement.
>
> The kind of marriage we chose to focus on for this play is the following: a well-off man with good prospects, from a different community, will arrive to the ruka and the family will invite him to come in. When he sees a baby, he asks is this a girl or boy child? And they tell him it is a girl. And he says, "Well, I am going to reserve her (*dejarla pedida*). When she is eleven or twelve, I will come to get her and make her my wife." And the parents can't say no. If he has chosen her, then she will be his wife. So when the girl is twelve-years old, the man comes back for her. Sometimes they are linked by some form of kinship and sometimes not.
>
> This is how my great-grandmother got married to an older man. He was from Cañete and his last name was Nain. He requested her

hand from her parents when she was just a child. And when she was eleven years old, he came to find her and took her away against her will. What eleven-year-old child would want to get married so young? This is the bad part that few Mapuche ever talk about. Often people from afar romanticize the Mapuche culture as something unearthly and all good. But just like any other culture, it is sometimes contradictory. Because this great-grandfather came and took my great-grandmother away. He raped her. And my great-grandmother did not want to stay there so she escaped, and they went out to find her. And so she would not escape, they cut her heels so she would stay put. She never forgave him, always referring to him as "that man who hurt me."[23]

By using the dramatization of Mapuche history and cultural assumptions, Julia is leading a process in which her community—either as actors or as audience—has the opportunity to reflect on their culture, its evolution, and discuss what it means to be Mapuche together. With the play about one of the historical forms of marriage, Julia facilitates a reflection for her community about what it means to be a Mapuche woman, a Mapuche man, how men treat women, and how women want to be treated. Julia, like Jaqueline, believes that you can be Mapuche and critical of your culture at the same time. If some action or habit entails oppressing a certain subgroup of the culture—women in this case—then Julia has taken a major step forward by encouraging her community to reflect critically about former marriage practices.

Julia and her mother frequently talk together about the inequalities between men and women. They wonder where the machismo comes from. According to Julia, it is not that men are bad or that they are all to blame. She points out that it is women who raise girls and boys into women and men, thereby making women complicit in reproducing a macho society:

Mapuche culture is machista. But machista in quotation marks because at the end of the day it is women who raise the children. She is completely in charge of the house and what goes on there. It is the man's job to work. So women have some responsibility in how men treat women if they are raising the men. I can speak from my own family history. My grandfather only had daughters. And he would get angry whenever a new daughter was born. The only thing he wanted was a boy child. And my grandmother said the same thing too. So they had the idea that only a man can get things done, but that is just not the case. Because we were raised in a house with all women, we were always more women than men. . . . But everything from raising animals to building something, we women can do it.[24]

As Julia's reflections demonstrate, Mapuche women are as capable as men; they can perform productive and reproductive activities. Julia and the women in her family are transforming oppressive gender roles by celebrating their independence and questioning traditional expectations of women. On one hand, they do not hesitate to question women's and men's collusion in the maintenance of webs of certain roles that inhibit women's contributions, but they also move beyond questioning, organizing their family and the community to reflect critically and consider new alternatives.

New Models for a New Chile

The life stories and leadership experiences of these six Mapuche women leaders speak to a vibrant yet often unrecognized leadership emerging in Chile. All six women work with their local communities, promoting an appreciation of Mapuche culture, from a ruka museum, to alternative tourism, to a local theater group. There are radical elements to each of these women's stories that challenge conservative, rural Chilean values. Silvia chose to have children but never marry or have a partner. Julia has remained single. Petronila and Irene decided to marry winka men to avoid suffering like their mothers. And in the case of Amalia and Luis, Luis has taken up what is traditionally considered women's work, turning Amalia's thread as she weaves in the late evenings. Jaqueline has gotten an advanced graduate degree and returned to her home town, raising her son within a family setting in which she and her husband reflect frequently on gender roles and what kind of role models they want to be for their son. All the women interviewed agree that it is crucial for women to have the space to develop leadership and organizing skills. Silvia and Jaqueline believe that a critical aspect of women's freedom lies in generating their own income and gaining economic independence from their husbands. Many of the women interviewed spoke critically of certain Mapuche male-led organizations that exclude women, and they feel that sexist behavior does not need to form a part of their culture. They remain committed to transforming unequal power relations between men and women. All of the interviewees spoke to the need to transform certain aspects of their culture that contribute to the subordination of women, arguing that there is nothing cultural that justifies violence against women. Though these women challenge certain aspects of Mapuche culture—which may have been adopted from Western culture—they are working to assure a future in which Mapuche culture can thrive, even in times of globalization, and Mapuche men *and* women can place more value on women's contributions.

Amalia, Petronila, Silvia, Irene, Jaqueline, and Julia, their families, the women and community members with whom they work, and the women leaders they network with in other parts of the country show that indigenous culture in Chile is capable of surviving and flourishing—and not to the detriment of one gender over another, of one segment of the population over another. They are creating spaces for women to empower themselves as individuals and as members of communities. They are challenging economic interests that do not take a sustainable approach to cultivating the land. They are reclaiming lands taken from them. They are encouraging their children to take something from their native culture even when they have to leave the community for the city to find employment or continue their schooling. They are building new models of leadership that confront the Chilean status quo and may just generate the renewal that civil society in general and the women's movement in particular needs. Rita Moya describes this vital contribution: "These women leaders, with different characteristics than male leaders, allow us to see truly that one can build something in a new way."[25]

5

El Salvador

I struggle for two goals: to reduce the gender gap so women have equality and equity and to reduce the gap between the rich and the poor. . . . Instead of choosing between them, I have taken them both on. I am convinced that El Salvador would be different if we could reduce these gaps even if just a little bit.

–Blanca Mirna Benavides, activist, San Salvador

El Salvador is a small country of big contradictions: violence and poverty alongside commitment and hope. These same contradictions inform many of the efforts of Salvadoran civil society organizing in general and the women's movement in particular. In El Salvador the women's movement—comprised of a diversity of groups, organizations, and networks—remains determinedly committed to transforming the violence and poverty that confront so many Salvadoran women, men, and children. Both in civil society organizations and the women's movement, women's participation and leadership has been extensive before, during, and after the civil war. The scale of suffering during the civil war and the ongoing violence and poverty that threatens the country continues to test the very stability of the democracy established by the peace accords in 1992. Even though the peace accords heralded the end of the conflict, today homicide rates remain as elevated as during the war, having grown 25 percent in the past five years (U.S. Department of State 2008). The peace accords led to a democratic opening for the former guerrillas, the Farabundo Martí National Liberation Front (FMLN, now a legally inscribed political party), but most wealth remains in the hands of a few, and the economic model remains unchanged since the Nationalist Republican Alliance (ARENA), the far-right political party, first came to power in 1989. El Salvador stays an extremely poor country: 20 percent of the most poor only enjoy 2.4 percent of the national income, and only 53 percent of the country has access to potable water (Hopkins Damon 2008, 68). Forced to find income for their families, over 2.6 million Salvadorans have emigrated in order to send their families over $1 billion every year in remittances (Silber 2004, 562). Even with so much emigration, El Salvador remains one of the most densely populated countries in Latin America due to its population of six million and small, geographic size.

Many of the women interviewed for this chapter honed their leadership skills during the war, making great sacrifices for the causes they believed in. Interestingly enough, today these women face a constant negotiation between past identities as revolutionaries and present-day identities as feminists or women's activists, confronting the often ambivalent acknowledgment that peace came at a very high price and that there is still much to be accomplished before El Salvador can be considered a democratic country for all of its citizens.

The Role of Women in Salvadoran Society

Women have been primarily responsible for the survival of the Salvadoran family during times of economic and political crisis (Cosgrove 2001). "All women in El Salvador were affected by the war, whether or not they were part of an organized constituency. As those responsible for generating income (during the war, up to 51% of households were female-headed), providing child care, and securing medical assistance, food, and shelter for the family, women were profoundly affected by living in an unstable social, political, and economic environment" (Ready, Stephen, and Cosgrove 2001, 184–185). Today, as during the war, women are often responsible for taking care of their families, generating income, and participating in community projects. Virginia Magaña directs the Agency of Local Economic Development (Agencia de Desarrollo Económico Local—ADEL), a community development organization active in the western department of Sonsonate, and is also the president of the National Association of Women Municipal Council Members and Mayors (Asociación Nacional de Regidoras, Síndicas, y Alcaldesas Salvadoreñas—ANDRYSAS). She believes that women are the primary motors of the family and society: "I am convinced that women are the principal protagonists in the family, whether it is has a male provider or not. But it is also women who exercise leadership through income generation, community development, and social networks. . . I am even more committed than ever to working with women because of the conditions I have seen in Sonsonate."[1] Blanquita Orellana, mayor of the small town of Caluco in the department of Sonsonate, considers that women are more astute than men and better at multitasking. She says, "Look, I can be here working with you, but I can also be thinking about what I left on the stove in the kitchen. Men, on the other hand, just work and arrive home, expecting to be served."[2] Blanca Mirna Benavides, longtime activist and program officer at FUNDE, a respected Salvadoran think-tank, describes the role of women in Salvadoran society in the following way: "Women are the protagonists, the motor that promotes activities to resolve the problems that the communities face, whether this is lack of water, access to credit, you name it. They are active, go to meetings, negotiate, administer. Women are the protagonists in all community activities, but not when it comes to making the decisions. Because when it comes to electing community boards, things change. The president is a man, the vice president too."[3] Blanca Mirna is referring to how common it is for formal leadership positions to go to men even though women design, implement, and organize much of local development work. This form of discrimination is frequently reinforced by the government, state agencies, and their programs. Blanca Mirna provides an example of how government programs only see women for their traditional roles: "Here the Solidarity Network program is a government project that provides women with US$40 every other month so they can better educate their children, improve the family diet. But the money supports women in their domestic role as mothers, not as women. Why? Because what does society value? It values the mother, the wife, but not the woman for herself."[4]

The fact that certain leadership positions are reserved for men is paradoxical when one considers how much Salvadoran women leaders, and the groups working with them, have achieved. In addition to supporting families when men are gone (emigration, prison, death), raising children with little male support, and leading and participating in community development projects, Salvadoran women have been active politically and militarily. Throughout the century women have been active in NGOs, teachers' unions and associations, and political parties, but their presence in the FMLN—the largest female presence in a guerrilla force—reached 30 percent by the end of the war (Silber 2004, 571). They were combatants, comandantes responsible for logistics and reconnaissance, nurses, doctors, and cooks. Many of today's Salvadoran women leaders gained valuable leadership experience during the war, be it through their participation in the FMLN, community associations, micro-credit communal banks, NGOs, or the broad-based social movement for peace.

The Role of Civil Society

From women's organizing to peasant organizing, from labor organizing to environmental advocacy, from local community associations to nation-wide NGOs, and from clandestine political movements to open social movements, civil society organizations have fostered civic spirit; they have catalyzed protest efforts from the twentieth into the twenty-first century. Today civil society organizations address a range of issues, such as community development, sports and recreation, women's issues and gender-related matters, religion and spirituality, research, education, and human rights; they cover the ideological spectrum: some organizations are openly allied with the right, others with the left, some with political parties, and others with autonomy. Though many scholars researched Salvadoran civil society and argued that it is a potent force in the country, few quantitative studies—similar to the Johns Hopkins studies for Chile and Argentina and the CENOC data for Argentina—exist for El Salvador that provide numbers of organizations, categories of organizations, numbers of volunteers, and a breakdown of funding sources (see Cosgrove 2002; Foley 1996; McIlwaine 1998b; Stephen 1995).

Describing civil society efforts in the postwar reconstruction period, Michael Foley claims that the role of civil society was at the very core of the civil war: "The armed conflict that racked El Salvador from 1980 until the signing of the Peace Accords in January 1992 began and ended in a still unresolved struggle over civil society: over what expression civil society would be allowed to take, over its influence in public debate, over who would control it, and how" (1996, 67). I have developed a slightly different interpretation than Foley's; according to my analysis, the unresolved issue was not civil society, per se, but access to the state and to determining how wealth and land were to be distributed more equitably. During the conflict, civil society organizations *were* at the heart of the conflict, but this occurred because they brought attention to the marginalization and suffering of the majority of the people of the country. Unions called for better working conditions; students called for an increased budget at the National University; farmers called for access to land and credit. It is true that many activists incorporated into the FMLN because the repression of the Salvadoran security forces against civil society groups was so extreme in the 1970s. Although many of the organizations had concrete demands, the long-term goal revolved around becoming political stakeholders and influencing the economic priorities of the country. It is true that with the support of the Salvadoran Catholic Church hierarchy on the side of the popular movement, the security forces turned against the Church as well, but again the key issue was democracy for Salvadoran citizens, respect for human rights, and the obligation of the state to attend to the social needs of its people. During the war, many civil society organizations were aligned with different tendencies on the left and right. For this reason a lot of the research on Salvadoran civil society has concentrated on questions about the political autonomy of civil society organizations from the armed left or political parties. The other major issue that scholars focus on is the development and service role that civil society organizations have assumed during and after wars.

Political Autonomy of Civil Society Organizations

The political autonomy of civil society organizations has been a charged issue for activists, researchers, analysts, and development practitioners alike. Foley comments that "who works with what NGO or civil group in El Salvador conveys a distinct political connotation, even when the organization in question is most successful in avoiding political entanglements" (1996, 84). During the 1970s and 1980s, the military and government accused organizations on the left of being no more than fronts for the guerrilla forces. They used this accusation to justify repression against the organizations and their adherents. In some cases, links did exist between organizations and the guerrilla forces that extended beyond mere political sympathies to include passing information and money to the guerrilla forces. The present-day version of this trait is the misdirection of funds destined for a specific purpose to the priorities of a particular political party. This is also the case for the right and many civil society organizations with ties to the government whose funding sources depend upon following a far-right agenda. Foley describes the phenomenon: "The government continues to direct its resources, almost overwhelmingly, to inefficient and, at times, corrupt government agencies, ARENA party mayors, and the 'private sector' NGOs" (1996, 89).

After the war many civil society organizations, leaders, and activists began to question the historical political affiliations of their organizations. Some organizations declared their autonomy, seeing that a wartime necessity was no longer appropriate in peacetime. In the case of individual activists or leaders who found themselves in organizations still preserving historical affiliations, some chose to move to other organizations, as illustrated by the following testimony from a woman civil society leader who left an FMLN-affiliated NGO to seek employment elsewhere: "One of the reasons I decided to quit was because I did not agree that we should divert funds received for a communal project to personal or political interests. The organization became more interested in its own political agenda and survival than building democracy in the country."[5] A growing commitment to distinguishing between political sympathies and the diversion of funds has occurred in many Salvadoran NGOs over the past fifteen years due to aspirations on behalf of the organizations for the autonomy to serve their target populations as they see fit without party interference, combined with international donor pressure for transparency and accountability. A number of women's organizations were founded at the end of the war by women militants from the FMLN, and most of them have declared their independence from the FMLN. Autonomy became a crucial issue for the development of the struggles and organizational strategies of many women's organizations (Herrera et al. 2008, 51). Rosibel Flores, former executive director of the women's organization the Mélidas (Association of the Movement of Women Mélida Anaya Montes) recounts how the autonomy process unfolded there:

> In 1992 we emerged as an organization and we became a part of the party, even included in the party's statutes . . . But after a while, we

decided to leave the party. Of course, there was a lot of internal
debate on the issue and the party called us traitors, and told us we
were ungrateful, that they had helped us get funding, that they had
helped us form, but we said, "Well, that may be, but now you don't
have to support us and we can get by with what we have achieved."
And it has been this way since then . . . The Mélidas is fourteen
years old, and we have now been autonomous for thirteen years.[6]

Many of the leaders I interviewed recounted similar experiences to
Rosibel's. Morena Herrera, who cofounded the Dignas (Women for Dignity
and Life), an organization that declared its autonomy from the FMLN soon
after its founding in 1990, describes the wariness that exists to this day
between some women's organizations and the left: "There is still a certain
amount of mistrust. [When autonomy was proposed, the men said,]
'Autonomy, hahaha, that won't be allowed. This will divide the struggle.
You all are traitors.' To this day, the left hasn't told us we were right."[7]
    In addition to political autonomy, civil society organizations have also
had to navigate the complexities of an exceedingly polarized, national context. Though the peace accords ended the war, much bitterness and mutual
recriminations haunted attempts to build consensus and bring together
antagonistic sectors of the society. In 1996 Foley grimly declared that "politi-
cization has rendered minimal the effects of cooperation which does exist"
(89). Today the panorama appears more optimistic as there are some pluralistic efforts that have led to cross-party and intersectoral collaboration,
such as the civil society/public sector collaboration on the National
Women's Policy that led to the founding of the state agency, the Salvadoran
Institute for the Development of Women (Instituto de Desarrollo de la
Mujer—ISDEMU). ISDEMU has offices throughout the country and is one of
the few state agencies providing services for battered women; they also carry
out research on women's issues that they disseminate nationally. Another
example of pluralistic collaboration can be found in the National Association of Women Municipal Council Members and Mayors (ANDRYSAS).

Civil Society Organizations and the "Shrinking State"

The remainder of the scholarship on Salvadoran civil society tends to focus
on the extent to which civil society organizations have assumed increased

responsibility in society as the state has made cuts in its spending to reduce expenditures and fulfill its neoliberal economic agenda. Silber describes the ramifications associated with this tendency: "international assistance coupled with parameters set by neoliberal structural adjustment contributed to a shrinking state apparatus and thus an elision of state accountability in rebuilding, ultimately undermining 'development'" (2007, 169). Due to this, some CSOs have moved into service provisioning— distributing food, running day centers, staffing health centers—activities that the state formerly would have performed because the organizations can get much-needed funding for these activities. Other civil society organizations have undertaken serving low-income communities because the effects of the economic model—increased prices of basic food stuffs, loss of jobs, increase of costs of education and health—fall so adversely on the poor. Because of state inattention to social issues and the history of state-sponsored violence, a number of organizations have become social watch organizations: "Numerous recent activist and NGO efforts have worked to render visible patterns of neglect and irresponsibility on the part of the state and on the part of corporations" (Moodie 2006, 74). Therefore, civil society is expected to absorb the former responsibilities of the shrinking state and simultaneously act as a watchdog demanding state compliance with environmental laws, labor laws, and international treaties. Many of the women's organizations and all of the feminist organizations have been active in lobbying and maintaining pressure on the state and political parties to address discrimination against women.

The Salvadoran Women's Movement

There is more research on the composition and impact of the Salvadoran women's movement and the organizations it comprises than there is on civil society organizations in general. According to a recent FUNDE study, there are a total of 526 women's organizations in El Salvador.[8] These organizations include community organizations—self-help groups, consciousness-raising groups, productive projects for women—that connect women together at the local level (51 percent), formal NGOs serving women (26 percent), national networks (4 percent), women's committees within political parties (4 percent), sports teams (3 percent), regional offices of feminist NGOs (1 percent), and ad hoc groups (1 percent) (Bena-vides, Hopkins Damon, and Herrera 2008, 126). The FUNDE study can-vassed women's organizing efforts across the country, demonstrating that women's organizing is not limited to the cities. Many of these organiza-tions—especially local ones—subsist with little external funding, while the large NGOs acquire their funding through income-generating activi-ties, consultancies, and international sources such as foundations, multi-lateral aid agencies, and international NGOs. The study argues that the women's movement has achieved national scale and scope for its activi-ties: "We start from the fact that the women's movement of El Salvador has become one of the strongest social and political actors in the country; it is capable of challenging authoritarianism with its demands and pro-posals in political, economic, social, and cultural spheres" (Herrera et al. 2008, 29).

Authors substantiate their claims by describing the contributions of the women's movement. In politics they point to the numerous bills and legislation on behalf of women's rights that feminist lawyers and women's organizations have drafted and presented to the National Assembly; gender-sensitive demands presented to political parties; the founding of ANDRYSAS; the extensive involvement of women from women's organiza-tions in municipal and legislative elections; and lobbying for changes to public policy. Women's organizations participated in the preparation of the National Policy for Women and served as key stakeholders in the founding of ISDEMU, a state agency for women. Across the country, women's organizations have designed and implemented numerous income-generating initiatives, business startups, agricultural cooperatives, and microenterprise lending programs; plus they have provided technical assistance to women's productive projects. Targeting Salvadoran society with nationwide media campaigns, the women's movement has brought attention to the rights of women, including women's health and reproduc-tive rights, as well as promoting responsible fatherhood; they have raised consciousness about the predominance and adverse effects of domestic violence, and through their organizing efforts and press coverage they have made progress in reaffirming an image of Salvadoran women as work-ers, professionals, protagonists, and citizens, in addition to their tradition roles as mothers and wives.

Some feminist women's organizations—such as the Dignas and the Mélidas—have concentrated on expanding women's leadership skills and experiences. The Mélidas has a leadership program that complements its microlending program in poor neighborhoods in the capital and in a number of sites in the countryside. The Dignas, and its spin off, the Feminist Collective for Local Development (Colectiva Feminista para el Desarrollo Local), have worked to encourage women to participate in election politics. Morena Herrera, cofounder of the Dignas, sat on the city council for San Salvador for a term before founding ANDRYSAS to provide more assistance to women in local government. In a study on the women's movement in El Salvador, she writes how vital leadership training and experiences has been to the movement: "The process of building the leadership abilities of women involves analyzing functional and relational dimensions . . . This means applying democratic styles to achieving and sharing leadership opportunities. It also means handing over leadership positions. It means building relationships that support women leaders, help women achieve leadership positions, and it means moving on once you've held your position for a while" (2008, 57–59). Herrera also contends that generating leadership opportunities for women in civil society organizations and recognizing the multiplicity of contributions of women's leadership are vitally important to the process of democratic consolidation in which the country presently finds itself (57).

The Limitations of the Peace Accords

Soon after the signing of the accords, fissures began to appear in the surface of the "successful international model for how to 'negotiate a revolution'" (Silber 2004, 569). Sadly enough, political concessions alone were not sufficient to address the structural inequalities in the country; crucial elements were missing from the very inception of the peace accords, such as participation of civil society in the negotiations, not to mention revisiting the economic model being pursued by the government. Many of the women leaders I interviewed made reference to the contradictions of the peace accords and the negative impacts of the economic model. Blanca Flor Bonilla, former NGO director and FMLN legislator in the National Assembly, describes the risks associated with pursuing an inequitable economic model: "while there are great disparities, marginalization, exclusion, and violence in a society, it is impossible to have development."[9] Celina Monterrosa, a former National Assembly deputy who now works for the municipality of Nejapa on local income-generating projects for the town and its citizens, articulates the frustration many feel:

> It is still hard for me to understand that we live in a time when one can go to the moon, but there are still people who cannot read, or don't have access to potable water, or not even enough food to eat. And this goes on around the world . . . but here in El Salvador, we sacrificed so much so that you don't get killed for saying things, for doing political organizing, which is a significant achievement, but as regards the economy, there has been little progress. Economically the situation continues the same as it was before the war. This is what has to be dealt with now.[10]

If, as McIlwaine argues, "it is broadly accepted that the roots of the civil war in El Salvador . . . lay in deep-seated inequalities between those representing the small land-owning elite and the popular classes" (1998b, 658), then how long will peace last if the inequalities between the wealthy and the poor appear only to be increasing?

The peace accords transpired as a negotiated settlement between the respective cupolas of the FMLN and the ARENA-led government; there was not significant participation by the civil society organizations most active during the conflict. "The organizations of civil society played no role in the negotiations, and almost no role in the deliberations of the rival parties, except to remind all sides that peace was a necessity. If this was a 'negotiated revolution,' it was a very limited revolution indeed" (Foley 1996, 77). It could be argued that negotiations like this require limiting the number of participants at the negotiating table due to the polemical nature of the issues under discussion; even if this were the case, there should have been greater attention to implementing a nationwide process of forgiveness and reconciliation in order to transform polarization and hatred and directly address the trauma and grief of affected sectors of the population. Lessons learned from other countries—such as Chile and Argentina—indicate that an intersectoral and broad-based initiative of reconciliation and forgiveness has to be implemented in order to foster the process of healing the loss, trauma, and prejudice that can linger after this kind of conflict as well as dispensing government moneys in compensation to the victims and families of torture and disappearance, but civil society activists in these two countries also argue that fear and distrust remain on the surface—*a flor de piel*—from the dictatorships.

Though the 1993 United Nations Truth Commission report was made publicly available in El Salvador, few cases were brought to justice; in fact, not even in the most high-profile cases were the intellectual authors of the crimes punished. "For the most part no one has been held accountable for violations to human rights" (Silber 2004, 563). Many Salvadoran, human rights activists contend that impunity, rather than justice, has been the official response to the human rights abuses carried out during the war. Though there was a trial for the 1989 assassinations of the Jesuits, their housekeeper, and her daughter by members of the Atlacatl Battalion, the intellectual authors were exonerated, and only a colonel and lieutenant were imprisoned for their role in the deaths. Evidence of systemic impunity can be found in the fact that the United Nations Truth Commission had proof that the Minister of Defense, along with the consent of most of the Army High Command, had ordered the Jesuit killings, yet nothing occurred to see them tried for this crime (Popkin 2004, 112). A general amnesty law was passed in 1993 pardoning those who had committed human rights abuses, under the pretext that the Truth Commission had addressed the collective suffering, but the lack of reform only reconfirmed the commonly held perception of the impunity of the armed forces and the other security forces.

As mentioned, another fundamental difficulty with the peace accords was that the economic model and distribution of wealth and land was not effectively addressed, or if it was treated behind the closed doors of the negotiations, it was forfeited, which is precisely what many scholars argue: "Elites conceded political democracy and the FMLN, gaining full participation, conceded a liberalized market economy" (Silber 2004, 569). Foley takes the analysis even deeper: "But the core institutions of the Salvadoran government remained untouched, and the core interests of the FUSADES wing of the ARENA party were guaranteed, at least until the next elections" (1996, 77).[11] Though elites have been able to increase profits from investments and business ventures—like the construction of malls and large gated communities, expansion of the banking sector, and infrastructure development—this income has not trickled down to the marginalized sectors of the country. Since women are primarily responsible for the well-being of their families, they often have it harder than men, especially if they are poor. Silber describes how "[neoliberal structural policies] disproportionately affect women's lives" (2004, 562), and she provides an evocative, ethnographic description of just how hard women have to struggle to get by, especially single mothers in the former war zones:

> Martina and Sandra were each raising four young children alone, and rumour had it that both were pregnant again. While they each received direct benefits from the negotiated peace, such as small, distant and poor quality land through the land transfer program, their households were desperately poor. . . . As Martina and Sandra sat on hammocks, speaking softly into my tape recorder . . . they launched into stories about the post-war gender-based violence they were living through as single mothers and the obstacles they had to redress. They blame the community councils that organize the repopulated communities, and describe the injustice of post-war stratification as a result of corruption; the unequal distribution of development projects for example. . . .
>
> In an effort to find redress, Chalatecas [women from the department of Chalatenango] have turned to popular community structures and new post-war institutions established to implement legal reforms . . . such as child support. Martina and Sandra both recount how they have been accused of evil actions, of leaving poisoned foods . . . for their former partners, after they fought back for legal redress. . . .
>
> And Sandra's poverty is extreme, on the borderline of survival: "I feel a great deal of suffering. Weeks pass without even tasting beans . . . So, I start really worrying. And I say, if I start making a list of all the things I need, I'd probably go crazy." (Silber 2004, 572–576)

For poor women living in former war zones, the types of violence—poverty, domestic violence, lack of support from fathers of children due to death or negligence, exclusion from development projects and housing and health-related initiatives due to personal vendettas or political agendas—inform their daily struggles for the survival of themselves and their families. These challenges are often not recognized due to the myth that "things should be better under democracy and peacetime." Silber suggests that "a daily and gendered violence is rendered invisible. This constitutes a suffering that many women cannot communicate in the context of memories of war" (2004, 564). So these women will say "estamos peor que antes" (we are worse off now than before [during the war]) (Silber 2004, 564), because the sacrifices and traumas suffered during the war were supposedly for a noble cause, but the violence has become pervasive, embedded in gender stereotypes, and entrenched in the economic model of the country. The economic hardships—combined with the postwar challenges of governance and grassroots democracy—present gendered ramifications. Due in great part to ethnographic work, like that of Irina Carlota Silber and Ellen Moodie, that describes the everyday hardships of what it means to be Salvadoran, the devastating effects of structural adjustment policies and many of the unfulfilled promises of democratization have begun to be treated as human rights issues in which human security becomes a human right.

High Levels of Violence in Salvadoran Society

Alarmed by the poverty and violence prevalent in El Salvador, many of the women leaders I interviewed see links between the violence and the structural inequalities; they are alarmed by how this affects vulnerable sectors of society. Blanca Flor Bonilla is especially concerned about the high levels of violence in the country. She explains that "the violence has not been overturned [since the end of the war]. Yes, it is true that there is no longer a military dictatorship; there is no longer a civil war, but the violence has tripled since the armed conflict. Because now the violence is right on the surface, a flor de piel."[12] Moodie confirms Blanca Flor's analysis: "After peace accords were signed in 1992, the mass of violent death in El Salvador expanded. Murder rates matched or surpassed war counts of casualties" (2006, 63). El Salvador has one of the highest rates of homicides per year of the world . . . rivaled only by Venezuela, Colombia, and Iraq. Even the U.S. State Department warns travelers to be careful in El Salvador: "The U.S. Embassy considers El Salvador a critical crime-threat country. The homicide rate in the country increased 25 percent from 2004 to 2007, and El Salvador has one of the highest homicide rates in the world" (U.S. Department of State 2008). Writing six years after the signing of the peace accords, McIlwaine describes the violence and how it inhibits civil society organizing: "Despite the obvious historical antecedents, violence remains a debilitating force in the associational life of contemporary El Salvador. . . . This culture of fear, which has been displaced from the ex-conflict zones to the major urban centres, is now one of the major barriers to the functioning of associational life and social capital, which in turn feeds into the operation of informal civil society organizations in particular" (McIlwaine 1998b, 663). Writing over a decade after the signing of the peace accords, Silber also calls El Salvador one of the most violent countries in the world in which "violent crimes are estimated to range between 100 and 150 per 100,000 people" (2004, 563). The violence involves more than gang violence and common crime; Blanca Flor Bonilla says, "And there are more arms and guns. And today, even in the most remote community, there are drugs. El Salvador is not just a pass through place for the drug trade, but a consumer and distributor of drugs. So this means that the youth is affected more. It ends up looking like this is the option the right wants to give kids."[13]

Wartime violence evokes a different response than common violence in the mind-sets of the people directly affected by the violence as well as the international community. Salvadorans and the international community assign certain values to the sacrifices made during the war; but in peacetime the violence of gangs and poverty simply does not have as much suggestive power to create solidarity as it did during the civil war. Since the end of the war, gang membership has flourished in El Salvador due to the deportation of Salvadoran gang members from the United States. Wartime violence in El Salvador followed a chain of command; there were structures in place that informed how the violence would be deployed. In some cases, civilians were able to avoid the violence by circumventing contact with the armed group in question or code switching and using language, body language, and appearance to avoid suspicions. However, in the widespread warfare of gang violence, drugs, and arms trafficking, there are more opportunities for people to get caught in the crossfire. With the demobilization of the former guerilla forces and the depuration of the

army, a large group of former soldiers were expected to quietly slip back
into civilian life, in an economy with few opportunities for them. As a
result, many got involved in related spirals of violence—gang warfare, the
drug trade, arms trafficking.

Alba América Guirola, director of the feminist organization CEMUJER
(Instituto de Estudios de la Mujer "Norma Virginia Guirola de Herrera"),
expresses how violence appears as a common thread in the services they
provide to battered women, and she points to women's vulnerability to a
violence that is culturally embedded:

> Whether it is working with the women who come to our offices for
> assistance or the men and women we meet in the schools and in the
> police stations, the common element is the violence, the daily vio-
> lence in the family. Violence that they didn't even know was vio-
> lence. To the simple act of wanting to sit down and having to go and
> attend to someone else because that is your role . . . What has hap-
> pened is that we have been sold the idea that this is our destiny,
> obligation, and role. So if we don't fulfill these obligations, we are
> failing as women.[14]

Violence against women is also prevalent in Salvadoran society. Morena
Herrera, cofounder of the Dignas, told me that there are no official, nationwide statistics that accurately describe how pervasive domestic violence
really is. ISDEMU keeps a record of the cases reported to them and the news-
papers cover some of the more sensational ones, but many feminists feel
these number fall short of the reality. In the 1990s the National Coordina-
tion of Salvadoran Women (CONAMUS) estimated that domestic violence—
referring to physical and psychological abuse within the household—affected
60 percent of Salvadoran households. Attempting to find a rough figure for
El Salvador, Morena Herrera referred to a Mexican study in which 76 percent
of Mexican women have experienced domestic violence at least once in
their lives.

Both in interviews and subsequent conversations, the leaders I interviewed describe the violence and its detrimental effects on women and the
poor, but they also point to how certain sectors of society are benefiting
from the violence. Blanca Flor Bonilla discusses the connection between
the state and the security industry: "For example, the director of the

national civil police, Rodrigo Avila, is the owner of many of the stores that sell arms. He and others are also involved in the private security business. More insecurity, means more people buying their services."[15] Morena Herrera describes how the inequality and exclusion is spawning this lucrative sector of the economy dedicated to arms sales and security systems: "Yes, the country is more insecure, more exclusionary, and there is greater insecurity. But the insecurity is fomented for financial ends. Selling arms, security systems, and body guards. There are economic sectors that benefit from the insecurity. Insecurity generates wealth for them. Just recently a law was passed that makes it illegal to sell arms and hold high public posts in the government."[16]

The women interviewed did not disagree that El Salvador is a violent country, but they also recognize that the ongoing levels of violence have created a security industry in which many of the owners and investors in these activities hold leadership positions within the government and security forces. Possibly the legislation that makes this kind of conflict of interest illegal will deter public employees or people with government posts from directly benefiting from the very insecurity they are supposed to be fighting. Salvadoran and foreign feminists and scholars have brought attention to how the postwar violence and economic policies of the government have had a negative impact on women and poor sectors of the country, exposing them to violence and the effects of structural inequalities. However, the peace accords did provide an opening in Salvadoran politics for the left, and maybe this participation will generate possible solutions to the problems of poverty and unequal distribution of wealth and land. Women from civil society organizations have been particularly active in politics, participating as candidates and gaining access to the government.

Gender and Salvadoran Politics

Most of the civil society leaders I interviewed have participated in politics in one way or another: Celina Monterrosa was a legislator in the National Assembly for two periods for a total of six years. In 2000 Morena Herrera joined the city council for San Salvador, El Salvador's capital. Blanca Mirna Benavides was on the city council of Soyapango for one electoral period.

Virginia Magaña is presently on the city council of Santa Tecla. Blanca Flor Bonilla was a legislator in the National Assembly for the past nine years, and in 2009 she successfully ran for mayor of Ayutuxtepeque, moving from national politics to the executive position at the local level. CEMUJER, the organization that Alba América Guirola leads, has dedicated many of their resources to lobbying and writing bills on behalf of women's rights. Angela Rosales, a microentrepreneur and advocate for market women, sat on the city council of Nejapa for one period, and she has worked closely with René Canjura, the mayor of Nejapa, and the city council over the years to help build a local economy that revolves around the town marketplace and women's microenterprises. The propensity of the women civil society leaders to participate in politics is reflective of the trend for other civil society women leaders and activists: their commitment to ameliorating the marginalization and poverty—in which the majority of Salvadoran women and men find themselves—has compelled them to get involved in politics, with the expectation that they can address some of the structural problems from within the state. Of the civil society leaders I interviewed, however, only one has chosen to make politics her career, though the rest remain active in their local communities and continue their advocacy work from civil society. This eventual disillusionment with participation in the Salvadoran National Assembly and local municipal governments resonates with a similar phenomenon described in other Latin American contexts by Elisabeth Friedman (forthcoming): "Though women gained political access, women were seen as the 'housekeepers' of the public sphere, responsible for the daily life of the party organization rather than the promotion of their own interests."

Since the peace accords were signed, women's formal participation in electoral politics has increased. Hopkins Damon explains that, "yes, there has been progress for women in the creation of formal mechanisms, but there are worrisome retreats as regards substantive democracy and equal opportunities" (2008, 65). For this reason, scholars and analysts are not only focusing on elections and competitive party politics as indicators of a strong democracy, but also on other factors, such as the distribution of power, structural inequalities, and cultural stereotypes that exclude certain sectors of the population from participating. This "wider distribution of power in society" needs to be addressed, especially as disregarding this can lead to ignoring the importance of pursuing gender equality (Luciak 1998, 40). In his meticulous examination of the gender commitment for the parties on the left of Guatemala, Nicaragua, and El Salvador, Luciak argues that "gender equality is a central indicator in assessing whether the revolutionary left is fulfilling its promises toward its female constituents" (39).

From its inception as a political party, the FMLN appears to have responded positively to the pressure applied by its members and the women's movement who demand equal opportunities for women. Approximately 30–35 percent of party members are women, and the party has adopted the policy that 35 percent of electoral candidates need to be women (Luciak 1998). However, many women are not satisfied with the quotas due to the proportional representation electoral system of El Salvador in which parties create lists of candidates, and depending on the number of candidates elected only the candidates at the top of the list actually get elected.

Luciak contends—and many of the women I interviewed agree—that "the improvement in the female candidates' chances of election was not an accident but evidence of the female militants' hard work to persuade their male counterparts to accept gender equality within the party" (1998, 52). Women party members and the women's movement have been effective in keeping pressure on the political parties to include women at the top of candidate rosters; as a result, women have increased their participation in elected positions with municipal and national politics compared to before the war. In 1994 the FMLN won twenty-one (five of which went to women) of the eighty-four seats in the National Assembly; ARENA won thirty-nine seats (three of which went to women). In 1997 the FMLN won twenty-seven seats (nine of which went to women); ARENA won twenty-eight seats, of which only four went to women. Therefore, as of 1997 one-third of the FMLN seats were held by women compared to only one-seventh of the ARENA seats. At the municipal level for the mayoral elections the percentages decrease: in 1994, 13.3 percent of FMLN mayors and 14.5 percent of ARENA mayors were women, but in 1997 FMLN women mayors decreased to 12.5 percent and ARENA women mayors to 9.9 percent.[17] San Salvador, both a municipality and a department because of its size, has achieved the highest number of women deputies in the National

Assembly, whereas the participation of women decreases in rural departments and municipalities. Voting patterns indicate that departments with
greater rural populations tend to vote more conservatively as regards
electing women, though this might also be affected by fewer women being
included in the candidacy rosters for these areas.

In the January 2009 municipal and legislative elections, women now
hold eleven of the thirty-five FMLN seats and four of the thirty-two ARENA
seats in the National Assembly; in total, 19 percent of the seats are held by
women. At the municipal level, 11 percent of mayors are women (Departamento de Sociología y Ciencias Políticas 2009, 2). Since the 2000 elections,
women's participation at the national level is barely increasing. Though
women mayors have doubled since 2006, the overall percentage is still
low. According to analysts at the Jesuit University, la Universidad Cen-
troamerica "Jose Simeon Cañas," "Albeit the increase of towns governed
by women is encouraging; nonetheless, this does not show in any way that
the gaps between women's and men's political participation are lessening.
It is the political parties that should generate real opportunities so women
can choose to run for public office, but party actions show that gender
equity as regards this issue is just rhetoric" (2). Virginia Magaña also has
doubts about the authenticity of the left's commitment to gender equality.
She says, "It's all about the lists and nothing about promoting the leadership of women on the left. I have lived this, and I know that there are quotas, but often not even this is respected, especially at the municipal
level."[18] Celina Monterrosa, having been purged from the FMLN, is wary of
the commitment of the FMLN and affiliated organizations; she says, "There
are a lot of speeches, but in reality, nothing. The whole world tells you that
they are sensitive to the issue of gender, but when it might affect their own
interests, they don't respond. Always the revolution is above all other concerns. With the left, you think you are in good company, but in actuality,
the gender agenda is at a standstill."[19]

The most successful example of how a multipartisan coalition of
organizations from the women's movement influenced the political platforms of parties and promoted the inclusion of a gender perspective in
politics was the 1994 lobbying effort called the National Platform of
Salvadoran Women, an initiative that included seventy-two demands for
the political parties participating in the elections. The platform included

the following demands: that the state create and implement policies to address domestic violence, incest, rape, and sexual violence against women; that women have the same rights as men in access to land, credit, and technical assistance; that measures be implemented to assure that women occupy half of government posts; that women be able to choose if they want to be mothers; and that improvements be made to the health care system, housing, education (including sex education), and child support enforcement (Hopkins Damon 2008, 65). With this platform of demands, the women's movement obtained the commitment from ARENA and the FMLN, the two main political parties, to addressing the demands after the elections. Clearly, it is one thing to gain a commitment from politicians during the campaign period and another that the elected government, or the party with the majority of legislative seats, for that matter, actually implement the commitments. But in the case of ARENA—which won the presidency and the majority of seats in the National Assembly—the National Policy for Women was enacted in 1997 following the creation of ISDEMU in 1996 (ISDEMU 2005, 9).

Luciak argues that the women's movement has not been as successful since the mid-1990s in having an impact on Salvadoran politics; he blames infighting within the women's movement for this decrease in effective lobbying. Though the issues he cites—*doble militancia* (belonging to a feminist organization and a male-led political party) or the question of political impartiality (supporting women across the political spectrum or just women on the left)—have been genuine polemical issues for the women's movement, I would argue that these discussions have helped the movement distinguish between what holds a movement together and what should be considered individual beliefs (Luciak 1998, 44, 45). The issue of doble militancia was already being addressed by women's organizations formed by the FMLN in the mid-1990s, when autonomy from the FMLN was established, but members of the organizations could choose to be militants or vote as they pleased. The question of political impartiality did occupy the women of the Dignas, but rather than immobilizing action, it facilitated reflection and led them to found ANDRYSAS. Instead of putting the blame on the women's movement—a civil society movement that has made much more progress than other parts of Salvadoran civil society to open politics to women and generate solutions to the polarization of the country—I would look at why Salvadoran women have had to maintain the struggle to keep political parties and governments sensitive to their participation. One would think that it would be in the best interests of political parties and governments to want 51 percent of the population to participate actively in their ranks, electoral lists, and government posts. There is a lot of fluidity and movement of Salvadoran women between Salvadoran civil society and the public sector; even with the shortcomings and contradictions generated by the peace accords, the women interviewed for this book feel that political space has been opened and needs to be taken advantage of; they have participated in local and national politics. The two main issues that emerged in the interviews and in later conversations are the pluralistic achievements of ANDRYSAS and the challenges women civil society leaders face when they leave politics and return to civilian life.

The best description of ANDRYSAS comes from my interview with Virginia Magaña. Now the executive director of ADEL Sonsonate, Virginia is also a city council woman for the city of Santa Tecla, a prosperous city to the north of San Salvador, and the president and legal representative of ANDRYSAS. She describes ANDRYSAS in the following way:

> ANDRYSAS was founded in 1999 as an initiative of a group of women who occupied public posts at the local level, which is to say women politicians at the municipal level. Women are active as mayors and city council members throughout the country. So, this organizational space was formed out of a concern for how to generate more opportunities for women in municipal governments. Our association sustains itself with membership dues from members, from member municipalities, and projects we get funded.
>
> Presently, our membership is 512 women mayors and city council members. The majority of our members are from the FMLN, the left. The second group, about 30 percent, comes from the right, ARENA. Why do these two parties make up most of the membership of ANDRYSAS? Because these two parties hold the majority of the municipalities between them.
>
> ANDRYSAS's mission is to build plurality, help women to see what we have in common outside of political differences, political

currents, or ideology. As women politicians at the local level, we all share a problem and that is to struggle for more opportunities for women in politics. In this country, as in the other Central American countries, there is not a lot of support for women who want to participate in local politics . . . The challenge that ANDRYSAS faces is to provide training and formation for the women so they have the qualitative and technical skills necessary for their posts.

ANDRYSAS has shown that it is possible to build pluralism, identify issues in common outside of political differences, and work together as women . . . And the inequalities, the closing of opportunities, and how we overcome these obstacles are what all Salvadoran women—be they from the left or right—have in common. And I, as a woman on the left, have learned to respect difference. So, when I attend a meeting with ARENA, for instance, I don't wear any color or article of clothing that denotes my party [red and black for the FMLN]. . . . So when we are together we don't wear party colors or talk about "my party this, my party that," and I believe that this is a mechanism that helps us build democracy.[20]

In addition to Virginia, I interviewed three women politicians from across the political spectrum about why their participation in ANDRYSAS has been so meaningful for them. Blanquita Orellana, the mayor from the small, impoverished municipality of Caluco represents the National Conservative Party (PCN). She says,

I have been the mayor here for thirteen months. Through the municipality's work with ADEL, I met Virginia and learned about ANDRYSAS. This has been very important for me. . . . Many people say there is no pluralism in El Salvador, but I believe that if you apply yourself, you can make it happen. For example, in the last assembly of ANDRYSAS . . . I met a woman from ARENA, and I couldn't believe it, because we got along so well and had so much in common. Or I would realize that a woman I shared a lot with was from the FMLN . . . and there is an important connection within ANDRYSAS because irrespective of the political party, we have so much in common.[21]

Women like Morena Herrera, cofounder of ANDRYSAS, and Angela Rosales, who is active in the town of Nejapa, have achieved a lot during their experiences in municipal governments. Morena, elected to the city council of San Salvador in 2000, reflects on what she achieved while in office:

> I believe I achieved three things during that period in San Salvador. First, I helped facilitate the flow of information between local organizations and the city council . . . [second], I helped concretize the gender policy for the city. So, we created three centers, the women's municipal office, budget lines for this, and made sure that the policy document was complete . . . these efforts are still functioning to this day. I was not alone, there were other women with me . . . and the third contribution was promoting more citizen participation; and we passed new bylaws to promote this.[22]

Angela was on the town council of Nejapa for one period, but before and since then, she has remained active in town politics. She runs a small restaurant stall in the marketplace and has led microcredit initiatives, the committee to rebuild the marketplace, efforts to reforest the hill behind the town, and she accompanies the Nejapa soccer team on all its games, home and away. She talks about how the mayor asked for her help in designing the new marketplace: "I was one of the first who began to complain because we didn't have water or light. I went right into the town hall. The mayor asked me, 'Do you think you can get the people together in a meeting?' So my daughters helped me photocopy the invitations and I put them up. Yes, all the people [from the market] came. So, they asked us how we wanted the market building."[23]

With Angela's leadership and the input from the women, the mayor had an architect draw up designs and the women reviewed them, making suggestions. "Sure, I was the one leading the women from the market, I spoke for them." Angela came up with an interim plan to house the market in a nearby building on the main street while the building was under construction, and then she helped the municipality assign market stalls in the new building in an equitable fashion.

In the cases of both Morena and Angela, they remained active politically even after their terms on their respective city councils ended.

Morena returned to the Dignas and helped found the Feminist Collective for Local Development. Angela continues organizing on behalf of women marketers from her market stall restaurant. Other women, who have been active in politics, have sadly enough experienced more difficulty integrating back into civilian life; in some cases, being a politician effectively blacklists women who return to civil society. Blanca Flor Bonilla and her family have founded a foundation, so when she is done with politics she has a place to work. Celina Monterrosa—who spent two periods as a legislator in the National Assembly—lost her political prospects when she was purged from the FMLN accused of "entertaining politically conservative ideas."[24] Afterward, she spent six months looking for a job. No one on the right wanted to offer her a job because she was associated with the FMLN, and few on the left wanted to risk the possible political consequences of hiring someone who had been purged. She comments sadly, "And then you are left alone, finished, blacklisted. And no one, not the left or the right, wants to work with you." Morena Herrera analyzes the challenges that women politicians face when they leave politics—often they have been abandoned by the organizations they came from: "The organizations encourage them to run for office, and then break the ties. It gets worse when these former politicians return to civil society and find themselves without employment" (Herrera 2008, 58). In a focus group session to review my initial conclusions, Rosibel Flores mentioned a number of women in politics—Celina included—who have had to face the situation Morena described. "Yes, women can have a political career, make it their way of life, but they always have to watch the party line, and going back into civilian life can be very hard. You stick to the party line; you keep your seat and your salary, political survival at any cost." If the Salvadoran women's movement is committed to helping more women get into politics, maybe more attention and support needs to be offered to these women when they transition out of politics.

Gender and Leadership

Many Salvadoran women leading civil society efforts got their first leadership experiences during the war, some as FMLN combatants and others as students or activists in civil society movements; they feel their leadership

styles are primarily informed by the context and circumstances in which
they find themselves—for example, the current juncture of events, or
coyuntura. This is to say that the times tend to determine the leadership
style one pursues. According to Blanca Mirna Benavides, whether women
pursue a "more collective or more authoritarian style depends on the
times."[25] Others alluded to having had to be more masculine than men in
order to prove themselves as leaders, especially in groups of men during
the war. Describing her early years as a guerrilla leader, Rosibel Flores
reflects:

> At the time, I did not think of myself as exercising a position of
> power. But I did figure out how to get around in a world of men.
> I only worked with men. And when I was put in charge of groups of
> men, I established good working relationships with most of them.
> And they accepted that a woman would be telling them what to do.
> Generally the leadership was in the hands of men, but nevertheless,
> I figured it out, even until the end [of the conflict], because thank
> God, I am still alive today. . . . There was no softening, no crying, no
> expressing yourself emotionally.[26]

Exercising their leadership skills during the war, the women explained to
me that they used a more linear, masculine leadership style. Morena
Herrera recounts how this was the case in El Salvador: "The context and
circumstances informed leadership styles. For instance, before the civil
war, I was a pacifist, antimilitary, but when the repression got so fierce, the
only option was to form a people's army. So, I militarized myself, not just in
deed but in thought. And a more top-down leadership style was required
because peoples' lives were in danger." Celina Monterrosa agreed with
Morena, concluding that "different historical moments require different
styles. During the war, results mattered, this required a more vertical
approach."

When speaking of their leadership styles in the current political
climate, the women provided examples of how they lead and the challenges they face in their organizations; today they tend to pursue participatory styles. Morena Herrera discussed the importance of democratizing
leadership and management roles within civil society organizations.
"You have to differentiate between leadership and the position. It is also

important to think about how we can make our organizational spaces more democratic." Today the leadership styles of many of the women I interviewed revolve around the importance of consensus-oriented, collective approaches within organizations and movements. Silvia Larios, the coordinator of a potable water network composed mostly of men, speaks about how she has figured out how to lead men effectively:

> Most members of the network are men; they are engineers because the issue that brings us together is water and sewage. I used to wonder how much they would let me make proposals because I am an economist and not an engineer. But we built a flexible working environment, and I have had the full support of all the members of the water network from the beginning. I try to avoid saying things I know they might find offensive, like privatizing the water. It is important to understand what is important for the people with whom you are working. [When there is a potential disagreement] I go up to the person and say, "Yes, that is true, but you know, you can also look at it another way." . . . So, basically, I don't take a confrontational approach or a direct "no," rather I find something to agree with and then introduce other ideas.[27]

A director of an international NGO in El Salvador describes her leadership style, which includes many empowering elements: "More important than constantly checking up on someone or telling them what to do is to provide training so people understand the cause. . . . I need my teams to grow stronger, and I need to help them develop their capacities. . . . This is the role of a leader, how to help people grow and move down their paths. My biggest satisfaction is when I start with someone, and they achieve an outstanding performance."[28] Women can use authoritarian forms of leadership, but in the case of the women interviewed in El Salvador, their sensitivity to the necessities of the Salvadoran context and their own experiences of discrimination have made them want to be the kind of leaders they would like to see more of in El Salvador.

When one of the women interviewed left the women's movement to work in a progressive, mixed-gender think tank, she felt criticized by some of her former feminist colleagues: "They asked me, 'Where are you going?' and I have felt a certain amount of rejection since then." After cofounding and participating in the leadership of the Dignas for ten years, Morena Herrera felt it was time to let other women lead by encouraging younger women to take on new responsibilities, so she prepared an exit strategy for herself. She returned to school to earn a master's degree in local development and was considering participating in local politics. In two and a half years she moved from being part of the executive committee of the Dignas to managing the program for political participation and local development. However, after her time on the city council of San Salvador, she finally phased herself out of the Dignas so she could dedicate herself to research and local organizing efforts in Suchitoto, the small city where she lives. It is not an easy balance:

> I get asked "Why are you still here? Why are you participating if you left? You can't leave; we need you." How do you leave but still keep contributing to a project you spent so much time building? But you have to be creative and find alternative ways to keep contributing because we need renovation. For instance, at ANDRYSAS, I only served as the president for one period and since then, there is a new president every period. Over the past ten years, there have been three different presidents. If I stay, I create a culture of staying. Now I don't have a position anywhere and nothing depends on me for its existence.[29]

This concept of ceding leadership positions is a fascinating characteristic in a leader as it speaks to the long-term commitment of the leader to a particular cause or organization; Morena sees that she has to cultivate new generations of leaders to continue the work. She thereby focuses on expanding leadership opportunities for women as well as working for their greater inclusion in local politics.

Though a few of the women I interviewed were raised in middle-class homes, the majority come from rural or working-class backgrounds. Speaking to why the efforts of many Salvadoran feminists do not generate some of the class contradictions found in other countries, Blanca Mirna explains how in a small country like El Salvador "many of us who live in the city today come from rural, poor settings. And we frequently go to our home communities to visit friends and family. There is a constant coming and going." Yet, I also perceived an immense sensitivity concerning people

excluded from society, whatever the cause; their commitment to transforming sexism coexists with their commitment to transforming poverty
and its causes. Morena Herrera said, "On the one hand, I am a feminist,
and I intend to live my life more and more as a feminist, but at the same
time I am part of the women's movement in El Salvador that is also concerned with economic relations and class. I have both identities" (Stephen
1997, 86). Morena's analysis helps illuminate what is unique about
Salvadoran feminism. Many Salvadoran feminists understand the links
between class-based struggles and women's rights given their past participation in grassroots organizing, Christian-base communities, labor movements, and/or the armed left. The following quotation from Blanca Flor
Bonilla's interview encapsulates this point: "Here in El Salvador there are
different barriers, according to the situation and position of the person.
A woman can face barriers because she is a woman, because she is from
a poor community, which is to say because she occupies a particular
social position. It could be because she is indigenous or because of her
age."[30]

Angela Rosales has had to face a lot of barriers, but she goes to great
lengths to put her knowledge and that of others at the service of market
women. She has a lot of advice for how to handle Salvadoran men: "I always
say that a woman has to be smart. She shouldn't fight with her husband, or
tell him what to do, rather show him that each person in the couple has
duties and involve him in household chores by getting him to feel as if it's
his responsibility too. But if a man just wants to run around with you in
secret behind closed doors, it is because he's just going to leave you with a
growing belly."[31]

For this reason, birth control is a very important issue to Angela. As
I sat with Angela at her market stall in 1996 and 1997 attempting to learn
more about her business, she would repeatedly engage me in public discussions about safe sex and birth control, encouraging nearby market
women to participate in the conversations. One day Angela invited a
young woman selling toilet paper from a basket nearby to talk with us.
Obviously committed to convincing the woman of the importance of waiting to have children, Angela asked the woman if she used birth control
with her new partner. At first terribly embarrassed, the woman said little
but listened avidly as Angela asked me very direct and personal questions

about my sexual relationship with my husband and our birth control practices. Soon the three of us were discussing different strategies for how to convince Salvadoran men to use condoms. Ten years later, I recently had the opportunity to ask Angela why it is so important for women to hear about birth control, and she said, "They always know that if the man does not want to put it on, they can put it on him. That they take care of themselves. I always tell women that they have to work so they don't have to depend on a man. If they have husbands, then those husbands should fulfill their obligations."[32] Though many Salvadoran women activists and feminists come from underprivileged or working-class backgrounds, another factor in the class integration of the women's movement is the fact that communities across the country have organizers like Angela as well as their own women's organizations and that national NGOs headquartered in the capital have regional and city branches throughout the country. Furthermore, an active set of networks of women's organizations keep them interconnected throughout the country.

Conclusions

In 1992 Robyn Braverman and I interviewed Morena Herrera soon after the signing of the peace accords. It is uncanny how germane her words remain for the El Salvador of today. She said, "In this transition from war to peace, we understand that peace is not just the silence of arms, but rather the end of all impunity and the elimination of all forms of violence, from political violence to domestic and sexual violence, of which we women have been the principal victims. The struggle has only just begun."[33] This enduring commitment remains palpable in the actions of the women I interviewed for this book and in the research and scholarship of feminist social scientists in El Salvador and abroad; women's civil society activism and leadership in El Salvador remains a vibrant force addressing the contradictions of the peace accords' unfulfilled promises and El Salvador's incipient democracy.

6

Policy Implications of Women's Civil Society Leadership in Latin America

> This is why we have made such an effort to work with types of leadership other than classical styles. Sometimes they are more subtle or delicate, hidden in the social base. But they are there, producing and building a distinct way of life.
>
> –Rita Moya, CETSUR, Penco, Chile

Obviously one's judgments, opinions, and priorities evolve over time, and so have mine during the eight years it took to write this book. My dedication to Latin American women whose efforts are making a difference in their communities and spheres of action—even though they face discrimination due to class, ethnicity, gender, or other forms of difference—continues to deepen. As a researcher, I feel an urgency to broadcast the results these women are achieving—this way I can contribute to undoing the invisibility generated by gender subordination and other forms of discrimination. I have been aware of women's contributions to development and democracy in Latin America since the mid-1980s, when I lived in Nicaragua and El Salvador. I saw women ensuring the survival of their families and communities during periods of conflict and economic crisis while men were fighting with one side or the other: with the Sandinistas or Contras (counterrevolutionaries) in Nicaragua, or with the government armed forces or the FMLN in El Salvador. During my graduate studies in the 1990s gender studies played an influential role in my coursework and informed my master's and doctoral research as I tracked the impact of microcredit loans on women marketers, their communities, and the organizations serving them. Through my years in Central America and ensuing research trips to the region during graduate school, I came to recognize the catalytic role that leadership can play in community development, especially women's leadership. After graduation I chose to join the staff of AVINA because of their focus on leadership and sustainable development throughout Latin America. I had found an organization that contributed much-needed resources and capacity building to Latin American civil society leaders.

In 2000 I was working as a project analyst for AVINA when Stephan Schmidheiny, AVINA's founder, stopped by my desk and asked, "Serena, what is the gender breakdown of AVINA leaders?" This one question has led me to discover a series of lessons, the first of which was the significance of disaggregating project and partner data by gender; if an organization's files do not include the gender of the individual, then the only way to know how many men and women the organization serves is to go through files one by one. So, with the help of an intern I began to comb through the files, and we came up with a very disquieting result: only 23 percent of AVINA leaders were women. Since that initial shock, a number of institutional responses have transpired at AVINA. First, the institution implemented a series of changes in data management that allowed files to be disaggregated by gender, education, and age. Today 39 percent of AVINA leaders are women, and every year the foundation raises its goal in an attempt to reach parity. This one simple question about women and men leaders raised a deeper set of unanswered questions for me about women's civil society leadership. Are women leading as much as men? What are women's civil society leadership contributions in Latin America? What challenges do women face that men do not? Does gender affect how people lead? Since that day in 2000, I have dedicated my research time to tracing the extent of—and attempting to measure the impact of—women's leadership in CSOs in Latin America, which has coalesced into this book's focus on Argentina, Chile, and El Salvador.

Common Trends between Argentina, Chile, and El Salvador

Although some progress has been attained for women in health, education, and income generation, women still lag behind men in terms of political representation, financial remuneration for work, and access to

formal leadership opportunities. Many women perceive political representation as vital for democratization, and when a culturally marginalized
group such as women occupy political positions, commonly held stereotypes can be transformed. Furthermore, the more that marginalized
sectors can gain access to the state, the more that they can contribute
to determining state priorities, thereby making these institutions more
responsive to citizen concerns. This does not mean that all civil society
leaders should cease their activities and become politicians. Civil society's
independent, social watch role remains imperative for strengthening weak
democracies. Yet, as many of the experiences of the women interviewed
from El Salvador indicate, Salvadoran women activists have interspersed
periods of participation in elected positions followed by a return to civil
society. Morena Herrera and a number of the other women interviewed in
El Salvador spoke to how civil society organizations support their activists
running for office, but then distance themselves from the candidates once
they are elected. This ambivalence about holding elected posts or working
for state agencies is not a new one for feminists, as the Chilean state
agency SERNAM demonstrates; this concern is best articulated in Audre
Lorde's influential and oft-quoted poem about how "the Masters' tools will
never dismantle the Master's house." The argument being that if a political system is sexist, what genuine possibilities exist to achieve long-
lasting, effective change from within? For women civil society leaders
who do choose political careers, many do not consider their decisions as
betrayals of the different causes they have championed in the past, rather
they see themselves as having taken the struggle inside the state. For this
reason, support from other women in politics can be very important to
women politicians, as evidenced by the comments about the importance
women members assign to the work of ANDRYSAS.

In Latin America, both women and men are vulnerable to the effects
of macro-level policy changes such as structural adjustment policies, but
women are the first to lose formal sector employment and the ones that
make up most of the informal sector—selling from stalls in marketplaces,
preparing food for sale, or running microenterprises. In the formal sector,
women's presence tends to cluster in the textile/assembly plant and service sectors, where they are often forced to work long hours at low pay.
Income generation within the informal sector exposes women to overwork

and underpayment for their efforts, as they frequently have to make many sales to show a profit. Especially in times of social upheaval or economic crisis, women are likely to become the primary income generators within their families and have to cope with additional responsibilities—such as guaranteeing the well-being of children, washing clothes, completing domestic chores, preparing food, and participating in community projects—and they find themselves working brutally long hours, often into the night. In Argentina, women like Nelly Borquez and Norma Galeano are building organizations to address violence against women and creating employment opportunities for women in the working-class city of La Matanza.

In El Salvador, women are responsible for implementing many of the community development projects in the country, but when it comes to formal leadership positions—for civil society groups or community development efforts—men are often chosen over women. Leadership in this culture is often associated with public speaking and giving orders, which are both considered masculine activities. Nevertheless, in El Salvador and Chile—where conservative values often inhibit formal civil society leadership opportunities—women are taking advantage of different opportunities, be it in local women's groups, women's organizations, or their protagonism at the community level, which includes citizen participation in municipal politics as well as contributing to building and implementing integrated local development plans. Regardless of whether they hold formal positions, they are leading and making change happen. Petronila Catrileo in southern Chile called upon the male leadership of her community to stop acting like sheep and do something about the lack of land for community members, especially the younger generation. As this book has shown, women in Argentina, Chile, and El Salvador are leading marches, giving orders, and talking into the microphone, but they are also networking, mentoring, and using empowering or participative strategies.

Beyond Argentina, Chile, and El Salvador

This book revolves around women's leadership experiences in Argentina, Chile, and El Salvador, but there are numerous examples of women's civil society leadership throughout Latin America. Lynn Stephen's *Women in*

Social Movements in Latin America: Power from Below explores women's contributions in El Salvador, Chile, and Brazil. In her article on Rigoberta Menchu and Mayan women in Guatemala, Victoria Sanford (2001) describes how Guatemalan indigenous women's activism and participation has informed recent historical developments in the country. And Sonia Alvarez (1990) has described the contributions of the women's movement to transition politics in Brazil. There have also been a number of multiauthor volumes that address the impact that women's civil society leadership and organizing has accomplished in countries across Latin America and the Caribbean (see Jaquette 1994; Jelin 1990; Nash and Safa 1985).

A number of international movements across different issues unite women throughout the region creating extensive networks, concerted actions, and knowledge sharing from the Southern Cone up through Mexico. Many of these movements comprise different kinds of women, not just from different countries but from different class backgrounds, ethnicities, sexual orientations, cities, and rural areas. The Latin American Federation of Associations for Relatives of the Detained-Disappeared (FEDEFAM) brings together civil society organizations composed of relatives of the disappeared—whose leaders and activists tend to be women—throughout Latin America, including Argentina, Bolivia, Brazil, Colombia, Chile, Ecuador, El Salvador, Guatemala, Honduras, Mexico, Nicaragua, Paraguay, Peru, and Uruguay. The federation and its member organizations continue to demand respect for human rights, and many of the organizations have begun to address women's rights, specifically targeting domestic violence.

In Latin America, the highest levels of poverty and lack of access to potable water can be found in the countryside, yet it is rural women around the world who produce 50–80 percent of the food grown. The Network of Rural Women in Latin America and the Caribbean (Red LAC) was initiated by Maria Vanete Almeida in 1985 in the northeast corner of Brazil. Inspired to confront the deplorable living and working conditions rural Brazilian women like herself were facing, Vanete began organizing rural women laborers in northeast Brazil (Red LAC 2007, 16). Today, thousands of rural women participating in local organizations across twenty-five countries throughout Latin America and the Caribbean are working together, both nationally and across national boundaries, to transform the discrimination that rural women face. As Vanete and her colleagues have demonstrated, rural women are organizing themselves, working together, and reaching out to their sisters in other countries to demand increased state services, income-generating opportunities, and the right to be full participants in the development of their regions. Support to form the network of rural women was generated at one of the Latin American and Caribbean Feminist Meetings held every couple of years throughout the region; the first meeting, in 1981, and the eleventh meeting, in March 2009, occurred in Mexico City. According to Sonia Alvarez et al. (2003, 539), these meetings (*encuentros*) "have enabled activists to exchange differences in perspectives and construct alternative political and cultural meanings. . . . They have been crucial in challenging masculinist, nationalist cultural norms and in creating a common (if always contested) feminist political grammar." Furthermore, they have led to the formation of other regional networks composed of local and national women's organizations. Examples of thriving networks include the Latin American and Caribbean Committee for the Defense of Women's Rights (CLADEM); the Campaign for the Decriminalization of Abortion in Latin America and the Caribbean; the Network of Afro-Latin American, Afro-Caribbean, and Diaspora Women; and the Latin American and Caribbean Feminist Network Against Domestic and Sexual Violence.

Policy Implications for Organizations Committed to Gender Equity

There are many examples of women's groups and organizations attaining goals that other mixed-gender or male-led groups have not been able to achieve. In Argentina the Madres de Plaza de Mayo were one of the few organizations that openly challenged the dictatorship. They played a significant role in discrediting the dictatorship and have continued to be a voice for the marginalized, advocating for people with little recourse in the face of economic and political crisis. In Chile the Mapuche and rural women of Rayen Voygue created a sustainable organizational model dedicated to cultural preservation and economic survival, and they keep widening the circle of women who benefit from their efforts. El Salvador is so polarized by political difference that militants from each side still refer

to the other side as the enemy. Yet ANDRYSAS is building a strong, mutually supportive network among women politicians, irrespective of their
political parties. The members gather together because what unites
them—overcoming the challenges that face women politicians—also holds
the possibility for long-term democracy in El Salvador, which is to say,
working together across difference. These are just three examples, but
many more exist throughout Latin America.

The point is not that men do not stand up for the voiceless, nor is it
that men do not try to empower others by recovering long-lost crafts; and
it is not that men cannot work across difference. The point is that to
increase women's visibility their achievements as leaders and generators
of innovative solutions must be illuminated. If these women had more
support for their endeavors or help to address the obstacles they face, their
efforts could accomplish more. There is much that organizations—be they
local, national, governmental, international, or even bilateral and multilateral—can do to encourage women's civil society efforts in the countries
where they operate.

Nonetheless, before looking out into the societies where they are
active, organizations need to examine their own organizational cultures,
hiring practices, promotion procedures, and management systems before
attempting to change the world. Setting goals for equity at all levels of the
organization is a good place to start and sends an important message to
the organization about the importance of this issue. By committing to equity
and making transparent the policies that guide performance review and
promotion, these institutions can show their staff that male employees are
not receiving preferential treatment over women. Thus, they can embody
the change they envision for the communities and populations they serve.
Having goals does not mean that parity will necessarily be reached in the
immediate future, but it does help the institution plan and organize for
change so that the workplace is managed in a more equitable manner. The
very organizations that want to promote women's leadership, or to address
the obstacles women face, also have to scrutinize their own internal practices and systems, assuring that they are promoting the advancement of
their employees, regardless of gender or other forms of difference.

For organizations who want to promote leadership for men and
women, they must examine how their conceptions of what it means to be

a leader might be informed by a cultural lens that preferences a leadership model informed by characteristics associated with the masculine. There is a growing body of research that discusses the importance of such skills as networking, mentoring, and collective processes, many of which are culturally ascribed feminine traits (see Brodkin Sacks 1988a, 1988b; Erkut 2001; Freeman, Bourque, and Shelton 2001).

Setting diversity goals for the identification of partners or beneficiaries is an important step for donors, but goals need to be accompanied by strategies to reach them. Training can be helpful for donor staff to increase their understanding about why these strategies are important plus learn how to implement the strategies. There are many international consultants—including Caroline Moser, Aruna Rao, Rieky Stuart, and David Kelleher—who have extensive expertise in helping organizations incorporate a gender perspective. Consultants or experts can provide advice and offer strategies for consideration, but the change has to be led by the organization itself. A change management process has to be implemented, and the active buy-in of key stakeholders—for example, the leadership or management—in the organization is key to long-term success.

Within an organization, certain members of the staff may manifest resistance to change; participative workshops where staff can become aware of how gender—or race or class—stereotypes affect peoples' lives may help open minds to considering new ways of interpreting social constructs like gender. For some it is effective to hear emotional explanations for why this is the inclusive direction that should be pursued; others need rational proof. This is where the extensive literature about women's roles as motors of development is useful. Many of the United Nations agencies have carried out this research and demonstrate why it makes sense to include women—even to focus exclusively on women—given their community contributions, dedication to family welfare, and productive and income-generating activities. Disseminating these findings can contribute to changing perceptions within a donor agency about the importance of including gender in the mission or approach of the organization.

For organizations committed to strengthening civil society or leadership in Latin America, they can choose to do more than just try to increase the number of women partners or partner organizations that work on women-related issues for there are multiple structural and cultural barriers that keep women, indigenous, and others from participating fully in society or that limit their abilities to provide for their families. For a state agency, ameliorating these conditions can translate into enforcing and implementing fair labor practices or enforcing sexual harassment laws; for international organizations, it can mean using international standards for gender sensitivity or training; it can mean facilitating conversations about difficult topics. International organizations' staffs can discuss taboo issues such as domestic violence, violence against women, and birth control.

Ultimately gender is about how men and women negotiate their roles and responsibilities. Many Latin American men suffer from heavy societal expectations about being the provider, especially in times of economic crisis, when formal jobs become a rare commodity. Men often turn to alcohol or other forms of self-medication when their livelihoods or self-esteem are endangered because societal beliefs and values have created expectations for their behavior that cannot be sustained during political or economic crisis. Men are often chastised or sanctioned for acting feminine, whereas women face consequences for challenging societal expectations. Men and women can suffer from oppressive gender stereotypes, and change depends on both genders. As Julia Matamala in Chile pointed out, there may be extensive machismo in Latin America, but who has had the primary responsibility for raising men? Women themselves are part of the system that reproduces exclusionary beliefs, values, and actions. Thinking about how gender or ethnicity or class affects our lives raises difficult questions that should not be shied away from. Out of this difficult conversation, new, more inclusive ways of being can emerge that allow women to get a respite at home, where men do not feel they have to always be the provider, where people are held accountable when they commit violent acts. A good first step for changing behavior is becoming conscious of the issue. Donors and state agencies sensitive to the importance of women's empowerment can do a lot to foster this awareness.

Topics for Further Study

Obviously, entire books could be written on the women leaders in each of the three countries examined here. While working on this book, I came upon many gaps in the research about the breadth of Latin American civil society in general and women's civil society organizing and leadership in particular. However, this is not due solely to a lack of coverage or attention to these noteworthy topics; rather, it stems from the inaccessibility of some of the research—stored in databases to which only universities and academics have access—or the research has not been made public due to lack of resources or contacts of the researcher. Often research is carried out on a country-by-country level, but seldom does it receive attention or dissemination outside local networks of like-minded people. In some cases, I was only able to find valuable research by searching the libraries of women's organizations, online feminist journals, and the archives of think tanks in each of the countries under study. But this required extensive phone calls and visits to local organizations, publishing houses, and scholars; it also entailed developing local knowledge of civil society organizations and their activities in each country. The Internet has helped disseminate research, allowing researchers to publish in blogs and online journals, but successful searches are often the result of hours of attempting one string of key words after another.

Research remains uneven regarding the extent, role, and impact of civil society organizing in Latin America as a whole. There are a number of topics that could use additional qualitative and quantitative research. Though many theorists, development practitioners, and researchers reference the important role that civil society plays—especially vis-à-vis the public and private sectors—few comparable, country-by-country studies exist that document the different types of civil society organizations or the scope of their activities, sources of funding, or challenges that the sector faces. Civil society organizations have to negotiate a complicated terrain when it comes to assuring their financial sustainability or institutional capacity necessary for achieving their goals. How to avoid depending on major donors? How to keep mission-critical issues in the forefront as funding sources become available in other areas? Some organizations turn to generating their own income; this has worked for the Mapuche women of Rayen Voygue, but what about small NGOs that have their staff take on consultancies or income-generating activities that take them away from programmatic foci?

Additional resources need to be dedicated to making research about the impact of women's leadership in feminist and women's movements more broadly available and to consolidating, comparing, and analyzing existing research to identify common themes at the continental level. Women's movements are such important sites of learning, skill development, and leadership experiences for women that leaders, organizers, and activists are applying their knowledge within the movement and in other civil society groups. This use of knowledge and leadership skills learned from participating in organizational spaces just for women is a topic that necessitates further research.

A few committed historians are researching the histories of disenfranchised groups, but much of this research remains local, disconnected from broader processes at the regional or continental level. There needs to be more research on the macro-level impacts of the organizing and contributions of marginalized groups like women, indigenous peoples, workers, and groups from the past.

In a time where authoritarian regimes in Latin America have given way to more democratic and leftist governments, the conceptualization of human rights needs to be updated, or at least expanded, to include human security issues such as the right to not suffer from domestic violence, insufficient infrastructure, or the effects of the shrinking state. During authoritarian regimes, the focus of many democracy movements has been to reestablish political citizenship, but today the relevance of social citizenship—the right to find viable and meaningful employment, the right to live in a family or community not racked by violence, the right to healthcare and education—is attracting more and more attention. Dense ethnographic description—such as Irina Silber's (2004) research about how former revolutionaries negotiate broken dreams in the mountainous, former war zones of El Salvador or Ellen Moodie's (2006) description of how a fatal bus accident represents the failure of both the state and the business sector to protect Salvadoran citizens—challenges readers to reconsider assumptions about peace, democracy, and revolution. Ethnographic portraits help us expand our understanding of preconceived concepts that need to be updated because ethnography—the descriptive form of research and writing favored by anthropologists and other social scientists—can provide insight into what it means to work in an assembly plant in a free-trade zone in a country with no welfare safety net or little investment in infrastructure. It can tell the story of what it is like to be a Mapuche woman and watch your children leave the countryside for the city because there is no land for them to farm. It can evoke what it means to live in an urban, marginalized area and avoid getting caught up in the culture of violence. We live in an interconnected, globalized world in which our lives and the challenges we face are often linked or related to those of people from other places: the shirt I wear was sewn by a woman from El Salvador; the computer I use was assembled on the U.S.-Mexican border; the pollution I create affects an atmosphere that surrounds the world. Research about these other realities articulates the tensions, inequalities, and possible solutions, calling us to expand our notions of what kind of a world we want.

Final Thoughts

The goal of this book is to bring visibility to the efforts of women civil society leaders in Latin America. I have written about the inspiring work that women in Argentina, Chile, and El Salvador are accomplishing as they transform their communities, countries, or spheres of action. I have chosen this focus because women's invisibility inhibits recognition of their contributions, impedes generating additional support for the work they are doing, and hampers efforts to transform gender subordination. In many places, gender indicators are slowly improving due to the commitment of women and men throughout the hemisphere, and this achievement needs to be acknowledged. Many women, however, continue to face discrimination for their gender, race, ethnicity, and/or economic situation, which makes them particularly vulnerable in times of social, political, or economic turmoil. Transforming the obstacles that exclude women from fully participating in society has become a priority for UN agencies and should be for all state agencies, private foundations, bilateral aid and multilateral agencies. In many communities, women are the motors of development; they are also the negotiators and mediators of the necessities of everyday life for themselves and their families. Given the set of responsibilities many women bear—as well as the organizing and leadership roles they play in their communities—it is time that organizations provide greater assistance to women leaders, especially rural, indigenous, working-class, and/or impoverished women. As more and more women take on leadership roles, they are transforming the very societal molds that have created the exclusion they and their sisters face. It is my hope that this positive cycle continues to unfold: strong women transforming their communities and simultaneously contributing to changing oppressive gender roles.

APPENDIX:
ORGANIZATIONS OF INTERVIEWEES

Argentine Printers' Union (Sindicato Gráfico Argentino), Women's Community (Comunidad de Mujeres) serves female union members and the female family members of all union members. Tel. 54-11-4343-6585

Caminos Abiertos provides social services for families in the San Cristobal neighborhood of Buenos Aires, as well as workshops and classes for adults. http://www.idealist.org/if/languages/es/av/Org/198957-258/c

El Agora is an NGO promoting citizen participation, conflict mediation, networking, and increased community security in Argentina. http://www.elagora.org.ar/

Community Organizing Foundation (Fundación de Organización Comunitaria, or FOC) implements social programs throughout Argentina focused on children, youth, and the community. It also has a strong women's health program. http://www.fundacionfoc.org.ar/

Foundation SES works for the educational, economic, and political inclusion of underprivileged teenagers and youth in Argentina. http://www.fundses.org.ar/

Malaver-Villate Cooperative for Housing, Credit and Consumption supports Malaver-Villate community members in their struggle for decent housing and other necessary services. http://www.malavervillate.blogspot.com/

Mothers of the Plaza de Mayo—Founding Line (Madres de Plaza de Mayo–Línea Fundadora) promotes human rights in Argentina and community development in marginalized communities. http://www.madresfundadoras.org.ar/

Network of Child-Care Centers of La Matanza (Red de Jardines Maternales de La Matanza) serves families in the municipality of La Matanza. federacionjardines@yahoo.com.ar and puchetagal@sion.com

New Land Pastoral Center (Centro Nueva Tierra) provides services for Christian base communities in Argentina. http://www.nuevatierra.org.ar/

Rosa Chazarreta Women's Center (Casa de la Mujer Rosa Chazarreta) provides women's empowerment opportunities and attention to men with histories of domestic violence. Bedoya 6315 (CP 1765), Isidro Casanova, Provincia de Buenos Aires; casarosachaz@yahoo.com.ar

Save the Children Argentina is part of the Save the Children global network; info@savethechildre.org.ar, http://www.savethechildren.org.ar/

CHILE

Center for Education and Technology in the South (Centro de Educación y Tecnologías para el Desarrollo del Sur, or CETSUR) is an NGO with offices in Temuco and Penco that works for the empowerment of the marginalized sectors of southern Chile. http://www.cetsur.org

Fundación Chol Chol is an NGO promoting sustainable economic development for rural Mapuche weavers and artisans from the Araucania region. http://www.cholchol.org

Karukinka Human Development Center (Centro de Desarrollo Humano Karukinka) is an NGO based in Temuco that helps rural and indigenous communities use art and culture for community development. http://www.karukinka.org/

Mapuche Women's Center (Casa de la Mujer Mapuche) promotes the development of cultural identity while improving the quality of life for Mapuche women and their families. Tel. 56-45-223-3886; Arturo Prat 289, Temuco, Chile; http://www.allsouthernchile.com/southamerica/southern-arts-and-culture-by-all-southern-chile/house-of-the-mapuche-women.html

National Association of Rural and Indigenous Women (Asociación Nacional de Mujeres Rurales e Indígenas, or ANAMURI) brings together women's organizations throughout Chile who work with rural and indigenous women. comunicaciones@anamuri.cl, http://www.anamuri.cl/

Nonprofit Enterprise and Self-sustainability Team (NESsT) addresses critical social problems in emerging market countries by developing and supporting social enterprises that strengthen civil society organizations' financial sustainability and maximize their social impact. http://www.nesst.org/

Pewman Ruka Hostal is a small hotel in Temuco, Chile that also provides information about eco-friendly, alternative tourism in southern Chile. www.pewmanruka.cl

Rayen Voygue Association of Women Farmers and Craftswomen (Asociación Gremial de Pequeñas Agricultoras y Artesanas Rayen Voygue) was formed to create a space of autonomy and training for craftswomen and women farmers in the Cañete

area. Tel. 56-41-261-1821; Sèptimo de Lìnea 794 – Cañete, VIII Región, Chile; http://www
.biblioredes.cl/BiblioRed/Nosotros+en+Internet/Rayen+Voygue+Canete/Rayen+
Voygue+Ca%c3%b1ete.htm

EL SALVADOR

ADEL Local Economic Development Agency Sonsonate (Agencia de Desarrollo Económico Local Sonsonate, or ADEL Sonsonate) provides services for local economic development to small farmers, craftspeople, cooperatives, and women's groups. Tel. 503-2450-1664; adelsonsonate@yahoo.com

CARE El Salvador serves individuals and families in the poorest communities of El Salvador. Part of the CARE International network, CARE El Salvador draws on strength from its diversity, resources, and experience to promote innovative solutions for community development. http://www.care.org.sv/

The Feminist Collective for Local Development (La Colectiva Feminista para el Desarrollo Local) focuses on strengthening the Salvadoran women's movement and assuring that local development efforts include the participation of women. http://www.colectivafeminista.com/

Las Dignas Association of Women for Dignity and Life (Asociación de Mujeres por la Dignidad y la Vida, or Las Dignas) is a feminist organization that works for an end to the subordination of Salvadoran women. http://www.lasdignas.org/

Las Mélidas Mélida Anaya Montes Women's Movement (Movimiento de Mujeres Mélida Anaya Montes, or Las Mélidas) is a feminist organization committed to the struggle of Salvadoran women for equality; Las Mélidas provides low-income women with training, technical assistance, and microcredit. http://www.lasmelidas.org/

National Association of Municipal Councilwomen and Women Mayors of El Salvador (Asociación Nacional de Regidoras, Sindicas, y Alcaldesas Salvadoreñas, or ANDRYSAS) brings women mayors and municipal council members together across the spectrum of political parties by providing them with technical training and gender empowerment workshops, in addition to promoting the development and implementation of gender policies at the municipal level throughout the country. Tel. 2226-2521; andrysas@integra.com.sv

National Foundation for Development (Fundación Nacional para el Desarrollo, or FUNDE) is an independent think tank committed to the inclusion and development of Salvadoran communities. http://www.funde.org/

Women's Studies Institute (Instituto de Estudios de la Mujer Norma Virginia Guirola de Herrera, or CEMUJER) is an autonomous women's organization in El

Salvador dedicated to improving respect for women's rights through lobbying, legislation, and raising awareness. Tel. 503-2275-7563; http://cemujer.org.sv/institucion/

LATIN AMERICA

AVINA is a Latin American NGO with offices throughout the region, contributing to sustainable development in Latin America by encouraging productive alliances among social and business leaders and by brokering consensus around shared agendas for action, with the support of people and institutions from around the world. http://avina.net

NOTES

CHAPTER 1   WOMEN AND CIVIL SOCIETY
LEADERSHIP IN LATIN AMERICA

1. In Mapudungun, the Mapuche language, *rayen voygue* refers to the flower of the *foye*, a tree that is considered sacred to Mapuche culture.

2. The concept of the empowerment of women is complex. Similar to other concepts—civil society, citizenship, human rights—definitions often vary according to the political or economic agenda and ideology of the user. There are a number of views about what "empowerment" means, resulting in vastly diverse kinds of projects targeting women, from income-generating projects to consciousness-raising groups. These projects use various approaches, from top down to inclusive and participatory. Some researchers claim that increased income empowers women (Blumberg 1995). Although women who earn income tend to invest more of it in their households and children than men, women do not necessarily have control over their income given their subordination to fathers and husbands. Some researchers claim expanding social networks and social capital empowers women, but there is research that raises concerns about how this approach can exclude poor, marginalized women or how this approach ignores how women's networks might be subordinate to men's networks (Mayoux 2001). I have argued that empowerment of women must include gaining the ability to make their own life decisions—about work, child bearing, marriage and family, and community participation—but there must also be a communal aspect to empowerment in which women together come to new insights about their roles in society and demand equal participation at home and in projects, programs, and development plans (Cosgrove 2002).

3. I use Mala Htun's definition of social movements: "sequences of collective action among social actors seeking a variety of goals" (2003, 15).

4. There are no formal statistical records that disaggregate male and female leadership of civil society organizations in the three countries under study. Nonetheless, interviews with civil society leaders and investigators show that parity almost exists in Argentina, followed by Chile, and then El Salvador.

5. See the Rettig Commission Report and Valech Commission Report prepared by multipartisan Chilean government commissions after the return to democracy

for more specific information regarding human rights abuses carried out during the dictatorship (Ministerio del Interior 1991, 2004).

6. In relation to authoritarian regimes in Latin America, the verb "disappear" is used to refer to someone who has been illegally detained and then killed by government armed forces, police, and other state security forces. I quote from *A Lexicon of Terror*, Marguerite Feitlowitz's extensively researched and profoundly disturbing book about the horrors and use of language during the dirty war in Argentina: "Desaparecido/a (n. Something that or someone who disappeared). The concept of individuals made to vanish originated with the Nazis, as part of the doctrine of Night and Fog. 'The prisoners will *disappear* without a trace. It will be impossible to glean any information as to where they are or what will be their fate.' (Marshall Keitel, explaining Hitler's decree to his subordinates.) In Argentina, the model sequence was disappearance, torture, death. 'The first thing they told me was to forget who I was, that as of that moment I would be known only by a number, and that for me the outside world stopped there.' (Javier Alvarez, CONADEP file no. 7332) Most desaparecidos spent day and night hooded, handcuffed, shackled, and blindfolded in a cell so cramped it was called a 'tube.' Some were given jobs. When their shifts were over, they were returned to their tubes where again they were hooded, cuffed, shackled, and blindfolded. Or they were sent to be tortured. Or they were murdered" (Feitlowitz 1998, 51).

7. For an excellent review of how Chilean women supported and protested Allende as well as Pinochet, see Baldez (2002) and Power (2002).

8. Few feminists provide an in-depth analysis of how shared experiences with their informants shape their own constructions of personal experience (for notable exceptions, see Abu-Lughod 2008 and Enslin 1994). Furthermore, few fieldworkers openly discuss their own accountability and responsibility vis-à-vis the people they are studying (for a notable exception, see John 1988).

CHAPTER 2   THE EMERGENCE OF CIVIL SOCIETY IN ARGENTINA, CHILE, AND EL SALVADOR

1. For Chile, see Salazar (1992) and Bengoa (2000); for Argentina, see Molyneux (1986), Guy (1981), Carlson (1988), Lavrin (1995), and Thompson (1994); for El Salvador, see Beverly (1982), Dalton (2007), Gould and Lauria-Santiago (2004), and Ready (1994).

2. For an excellent history of contested truths told from the perspective of the Spanish *and* the local indigenous people, please see Clendinnen (1987).

3. Amalia Fortabat, a businesswoman and philanthropist in her eighties, makes frequent appearances in the society pages of Argentina.

4. See Carlson (1988), Lavrin (1995), and Molyneux (1986) for more analysis of the extent and impact of European immigration on Argentina.

5. There is enormous debate in the political literature on the extent to which social rights are to be guaranteed by governments. Social (and political)

citizenship refers to the many rights and obligations necessary for democratic conditions. Though political rights—the right to vote and the right to assembly—are self-evident, social rights—the right to health-care, education, and minimum wage, among others—are also key components of a democracy (and often overlooked in the rush to declare a country "democratic").

6. Magdalena Jamargo, interview with author, Buenos Aires, May 14, 2003.

7. Sindicato Gráfico Argentino.

8. Cata Jiménez, interview with author, Buenos Aires, May 17, 2003.

9. The Process for National Reorganization was the Argentine army's strategy to justify the coup and systematically commit human rights abuses during the dirty war.

10. Though much has been written about this in Argentina, there is not a lot of information about the actual composition and numbers of guerilla groups due to the lack of historical records and underground nature of the activities.

11. Rosa Nair Amuedo, interview with author, San Telmo, Buenos Aires, May 5, 2007.

12. Ibid.

13. Victoria Matamoro, interview with author, Buenos Aires, July 15, 2003.

14. In the 1800s *mujeres de bajo pueblo* referred to women from marginalized communities. Today they are called *pobladoras* (see Salazar 1992, 64–65).

15. See also http://www.aotc.net/Spencer.htm.

16. Chile is divided into fifteen regions, similar to how Argentina and El Salvador are divided into departments.

17. Asamblea Constituyente de Trabajadores e Intelectuales.

18. *Rotos* here means "broken ones," or "marginalized ones."

19. There is a solid base of research on this topic; I recommend Baldez (2002) and Power (2002).

20. According to Richards, "Neoliberal reform is characterized by an export-based economic strategy, opening of the economy to international investment, elimination of trade barriers, privatization of state industries, devaluation of currency, and elimination of much social spending in favor of more restricted targeting of particularly needy sectors of the population" (2004, 3).

21. For more specific information regarding human rights abuses, see the Rettig Commission Report (1991) and Valech Commission Report (2004) prepared by multipartisan Chilean government commissions after the return to democracy.

22. Laura (pseudonym), interview with author, Chile, September 2006.

23. Santos Zetino, interview with author and Robyn Braverman, El Salvador, 1992.

24. Ibid.

25. Though the war is said to have lasted twelve years, intense civilian opposition, armed combat between the FMLN and government forces, and fierce state repression intensified between 1978 and 1992.

26. Rufina Amaya, interview with author and Robyn Braverman, Segundo Montes and El Mozote, Morazán, El Salvador, 1992.

27. Much has been written discussing the sexism of revolutionary groups. See Morgan (1989) for a more general, global discussion. For Nicaragua, El Salvador, and Chiapas, see Kampwirth (2004). Shayne (2004) provides an excellent treatment of the issue in the countries mentioned. Regarding El Salvador, see Vázquez, Ibáñez, and Murguialday (1996), an account of several women in the guerrillas. See Stephen's (1997) interview with former FMLN comandante Morena Herrera. See also Morgan and Cosgrove (1994) for El Salvador, and Rodríguez (1996) for Central America.

28. Blanca Mirna Benavides, interview with author, El Salvador, July 28, 2007.

29. The first wave of feminism refers to the late 1800s through the mid-twentieth century, when women organized for universal suffrage and social rights. The second wave of feminism occurred during the sixties, seventies, and eighties and focused on an end to discrimination. The third wave of feminist thought was a response both to the limitations of second-wave feminism and the societal backlash generated by feminists. Third-wave feminists challenged the essentialist concept of women, which effectively conflated different kinds of women into one category. This generic concept of woman "obscures the heterogeneity of women and cuts off examination of the significance of such heterogeneity for feminist theory and political activity" (Spelman 1988, ix).

30. Rosibel Flores, interview with author, San Salvador, December 15, 2006.

31. See Ready, Stephen, and Cosgrove (2001) for an in-depth analysis of this process.

CHAPTER 3   ARGENTINA

1. Carlos March, representative of the AVINA Foundation, Buenos Aires, and former executive director of Poder Ciudadano, pers. comm., July 2, 2007.

2. Rosa Nair Amuedo, interview with author, San Telmo, Buenos Aires, May 5, 2007. Raúl Alfonsín was the president of Argentina 1983–1989. Carlos Saúl Menem was the president of Argentina 1989–1998.

3. The total population of the greater metropolitan area of Buenos Aires was 13,827,203, according to official census data taken in 2001, which is 38 percent of the entire population of Argentina (INDEC 2001).

4. Carlos March, pers. comm., July 2, 2007.

5. Carmen Olaechea, interviews with author, San Isidro, Buenos Aires, November 27, 2001, and May 14, 2003.

6. A *villa miseria* is a marginalized community (shantytown) comprising squatters and others who have no other place to live.

7. Gilda Quiles, interview with author, Buenos Aires, May 13, 2003.

8. Victoria Matamoro, interview with author, Buenos Aires, July 15, 2003.

9. Marta Manterota, interview with author, Buenos Aires, May 17, 2003.

10. Matamoro, interview.

11. Ibid.

12. Olaechea, interview.

13. Susy Casaurang, interview with author, Buenos Aires, May 13, 2003.

14. Lina Amat, interview with author, Buenos Aires, May 13, 2003.

15. Amuedo, interview.

16. Matamoro, interview.

17. María Rosa Martínez, interview with author, Buenos Aires, May 12, 2003.

18. Viviana Fridman, interview with author, Buenos Aires, May 19, 2003.

19. Casaurang, interview.

20. Martínez, interview.

21. María Laura Schiffrin, interview with author, Buenos Aires, May 11, 2003.

22. Ibid.

23. Cata Jiménez, interview with author, Buenos Aires, May 17, 2003.

24. Quiles, interview.

25. Ibid.

26. Claudia Laub, interview with author, Córdoba, Argentina, August 6, 2004.

27. Amat, interview.

28. Olaechea, interview.

29. Ibid.

30. Adjective used to describe people from the capital city of Buenos Aires.

31. Olaechea, interview.

32. Ibid.

33. Ibid.

34. Ibid.

35. Nelly Borquez, interview with author, La Matanza, Argentina, May 16, 2003.

36. Matamoro, interview.

37. Another example of women coming together across class differences can be found in the human rights work of organizations of relatives of the disappeared. In all three countries under study in this book, the organizations of relatives of the disappeared comprise women, primarily, from different class backgrounds.

38. Norma Galeano, interview with author, La Matanza, Argentina, May 16, 2003.

39. Ibid.

40. Ibid.

41. Borquez, interview.

42. Ibid.

43. Casaurang, interview.

44. Martínez, interview.

45. Manterola, interview.

46. Fridman, interview.

CHAPTER 4   CHILE

1. Rita Moya, interview with author, Penco, Chile, September II, 2006.

2. Florencia Mallon provides an excellent analysis of Mapuche demographics in the introduction to Isolde Reuque Paillalef's testimony and life history: "In 1992, when the first Chilean census encouraged people to self-identify as members of distinct ethnic groups, many Chileans were surprised to learn that nearly a million people fourteen years or older, or 9.6 percent of the country's total population in that age group, self-identified as Mapuche. Equally surprising, perhaps, was that 79 percent of the Mapuche population lived in urban areas, 44 percent in the Santiago metropolitan area alone" (Reuque Paillalef 2002, 2).

3. Patricia (Pati) Jara, interview with author, Santiago, Chile, December I, 2006.

4. According to Patricia Richards, the Mapudungun phrase "'Ad Mapu' refers to the body of laws and religious traditions inherited from the ancestors" (2004, 22).

5. *Winka* are people of non-Mapuche origin. The words "Chilean" and "Westerner" are also used to refer to non-Mapuche people.

6. Silvia Nain, interview with author, Cañete, Chile, November 29, 2006.

7. Ibid.

8. In the United States, galleries that sell local arts and crafts usually take 50 percent of the retail price.

9. Petronila Catrileo, interview with author, Pocuno, Chile, November 28, 2006.

10. Ibid.

11. Ibid.

12. Ibid.

13. Ibid.

14. Amalia Quilapi, interview with author, near Cañete, Chile, November 29, 2006.

15. Ibid.

16. Ibid.

17. Jaqueline Caniguan, interview with author, Temuco, Chile, August 17, 2007.

18. Ibid.

19. Ibid.

20. Irene Huelche, interview with author, Temuco, Chile, August 17, 2007.

21. Ibid.

22. Ibid.

23. Julia Matamala, interview with author, August 16, 2007.

24. Ibid.

25. Rita Moya, interview with author, Penco, Chile, September 11, 2006.

CHAPTER 5   EL SALVADOR

1. Virginia Magaña, interview with author, Santa Tecla, El Salvador, December 16, 2006.

2. Blanquita Orellana, interview with author, Caluco, El Salvador, July 24, 2007.

3. Blanca Mirna Benavides, interview with author, near San Salvador, July 28, 2007.

4. Ibid.

5. Interviewee name withheld, 2006.

6. Rosibel Flores, interview with author, San Salvador, December 15, 2006.

7. Morena Herrera, interview with author, Suchitoto, El Salvador, December 15, 2006.

8. I enthusiastically recommend *Movimiento de Mujeres en El Salvador 1995–2006: Estrategias y miradas desde el feminismo*, published by FUNDE in 2008 (and available only in Spanish). Each chapter was written by women leaders, three of whom were interviewed for this book (Morena Herrera, Rosibel Flores, and Blanca Mirna Benavides). Although it focuses on 1995–2006, the volume includes the history of women's organizing in El Salvador as well as an in depth analysis of the movement's impact on Salvadoran society. Contact FUNDE directly for additional information (http://www.funde.org/).

9. Blanca Flor Bonilla, interview with author, San Salvador, December 14, 2006.

10. Celina Monterrosa, interview with author, Nejapa, El Salvador, July 25, 2007. I was accompanied by Sylvia Dávila of the Fundación AVINA.

11. FUSADES is a Salvadoran NGO founded during the war with support from the U.S. government; its leaders come from the business sector.

12. Bonilla, interview.

13. Ibid.

14. Alba América Guirola, interview with author, San Salvador, July 27, 2007.

15. Bonilla, interview.

16. Herrera, interview.

17. All statistics are from Luciak (1998) and are corroborated by Hopkins Damon (2008).

18. Magaña, interview.

19. Monterrosa, interview.

20. Virginia Magaña, interview with author, Santa Tecla, El Salvador, December 16, 2006.

21. Orellana, interview.

22. Herrera, interview.

23. Angela Rosales, interview with author, marketplace of Nejapa, July 29, 2007.

24. Monterrosa, interview.

25. Benavides, interview.

26. Flores, interview.

27. Silvia Larios, interview with author, San Salvador, El Salvador, July 27, 2007.

28. Interview with the director of a major international foundation active in El Salvador, July 27, 2007.

29. Herrera, interview.

30. Bonilla, interview.

31. Rosales, interview.

32. Ibid.

33. Morena Herrera, interview with author and Robyn Braverman, San Salvador, 1992.

BIBLIOGRAPHY

Abu-Lughod, Lila. 2008. *Writing Women's Worlds: Bedouin Stories*. Berkeley: University of California Press.

Alexander, Jeffrey C. 2006. *Civil Sphere*. New York: Oxford University Press.

Alonso, Graciela Beatriz. 2000. "Espacios de Mujeres: Acerca de los encuentros nacionales de mujeres en Argentina." Paper presented at the VI Jornadas de Historia de las Mujeres, Facultad de Filosofía y Letras de la Universidad de Buenos Aires.

Alonso, M. Ernestina, Roberto Elizalde, and Enrique C. Vásquez. 1995. *Historia: La Argentina del Siglo XX*. Buenos Aires: Aique.

Alston, Margaret. 2000. *Breaking through the Grass Ceiling: Women, Power, and Leadership in Agricultural Organizations*. Canberra: Harwood Academic Publishers.

Altamirano, Patricia, and Karina Caballero. 2004. "Caracterización del tercer sector en Argentina." *Comunidar (Comunicación y Internet de bien público)*. http://www.comunidar.org.ar/caracterizacion.htm.

Alvarenga, Ligia. 2001. *La situación económico-laboral de la maquila en El Salvador: Un análisis de género*. Santiago: Naciones Unidas.

———. 2002. *A cinco años de la reforma de pensiones en El Salvador y su impacto en la equidad de género*. Santiago: Naciones Unidas.

———. 2004. *Mujeres salvadoreñas en la política de los gobiernos locales: Lecciones aprendidas*. San Salvador: Impresos Quijano / Fundación Dr. Guillermo Manuel Ungo.

Alvarez, Sonia E. 1990. *Engendering Democracy in Brazil: Women's Movements in Transition Politics*. Princeton, NJ: Princeton University Press.

Alvarez, Sonia E., Elisabeth J. Friedman, Ericka Beckman, Maylei Blackwell, Norma Stoltz Chinchilla, Nathalie Lebon, Marysa Navarro, and Marcela Ríos Tobar. 2003. "Encountering Latin American and Caribbean Feminisms." *Signs* 28 (2): 537–579.

Amaya, Rufina, Mark Danner, and Carlos Henríquez Consalvi. 1996. *Luciérnagas en el Mozote*. San Salvador: Ediciones Museo de la Palabra y la Imagen.

Arizpe, Lourdes. 1990. "Foreword: Democracy for a Small Two-Gender Planet." In *Women and Social Change in Latin America*, ed. Elizabeth Jelin, xiv–xx. London: Zed Books.

Auyero, Javier. 2000. "The Logic of Clientelism in Argentina: An Ethnographic Account." *Latin American Research Review* 35 (3): 55–81.

Babb, Florence E. 1993. *Between Field and Cooking Pot: The Political Economy of Marketwomen in Peru*. Austin: University of Texas Press.

Bacigalupo, Ana Mariella. 2003. "Rethinking Identity and Feminism: Contributions of Mapuche Women and Machi from Southern Chile." *Hypathia* 18 (2): 1–17.

Baldez, Lisa. 2002. *Why Women Protest: Women's Movements in Chile*. Cambridge: Cambridge University Press.

Barriteau, Eudine, and Alan Cobley, eds. 2001. *Stronger, Surer, Bolder: Ruth Nita Barrow Social Change and International Development*. Jamaica: University of West Indies Press.

Bello, Alvaro. 2007. "Indigenous Migration in Chile: Trends and Processes." *Indigenous Affairs* (March): 6–17.

Benavides, Blanca M., Christine Hopkins Damon, and Morena S. Herrera. 2008. "Capítulo IV: Las actoras en el movimiento de mujeres: Estructuras, agendas y relaciones." In *Movimiento de Mujeres en El Salvador 1995–2006: Estrategias y miradas desde el feminismo*, 85–175. San Salvador: FUNDE.

Bengoa, J. 1992. "Mujer, tradición y shamanismo: Relato de una machi mapuche." *Revista Proposiciones* 21:95–119.

———. 1996. "Población, familia y migración mapuche: Los impactos de la modernización en la sociedad mapuche 1982–1995." *Revista Pentukun* 6:9–28.

———. 2000. *Historia del Pueblo Mapuche: Siglos XIX y XX*. Santiago: LOM Ediciones.

Beverly, John. 1982. "El Salvador." *Social Text* No. 5 (Spring): 55–72.

Bianqui, Susana. 1986. "Reflexiones sobre nuevas formas de participación de la mujer." In *Movimiento de mujeres en América Latina*. Buenos Aires: Servicio Universitario Mundial.

Binford, Leigh. 1998. "Hegemony in the Interior of the Salvadoran Revolution: The ERP in Northern Morazán." *Journal of Latin American Anthropology* 4 (1): 2–45.

———. 1999. "'After the Revolution': Economic Autarky in Northern Morazán, El Salvador." Paper presented at the School of American Research Advanced Seminar, March 19–24.

Blumberg, Rae Lesser. 1995. "Gender, Microenterprise, Performance and Power: Case Studies from the Dominican Republic, Ecuador, Guatemala, and Swaziland." In *Women in the Latin American Development Process*, ed. Christine E. Bose and Edna Acosta-Belen, 194–226. Philadelphia: Temple University Press.

Blumberg, R. L., C. A. Rakowski, I. Tinker, and M. Monteón, eds. 1995. *Engendering Wealth and Well-Being: Empowerment for Global Change*. Boulder, CO: Westview Press.

Boccara, Guillaume. 1999. "Etnogenesis Mapuche: Resistencia y restructuracion entre los indigenas del Centro-Sur de Chile (siglos XVI–XVIII)." *Hispanic American Historical Review* 79 (3): 425–461.

Booth, John A., and Mitchell A. Seligson. 1984. "The Political Culture of Authoritarianism in Mexico: A Reexamination." *Latin American Research Review* 19(1): 106–124.

Bose, Christine, and Edna Acosta-Belen, eds. 1995. *Women in the Latin American Development Process*. Philadelphia: Temple University Press.

Bowles, Gloria, and Renate Duelli Klein. 1983. *Theories of Women's Studies*. Boston: Routledge and Kegan Paul.

Brasileiro, Ana Maria, ed. 1996. *Women's Leadership in a Changing World*. New York: UNIFEM.

Braverman, Robyn, and Serena Cosgrove. 1993. "Faces of María: Voices of Salvadoran Women in War and Peace." Unpublished MS.

Brodkin Sacks, Karen. 1988a. *Caring by the Hour: Women, Work, and Organizing at Duke Medical Center*. Urbana: University of Illinois.

———. 1988b. "Gender and Grassroots Leadership." In *Women and the Politics of Empowerment*, ed. Sandra Morgen and Ann Bookman, 77–94. Philadelphia: Temple University Press.

Cáceres, Teresa, and Olga Segovia. 2000. "Espacio social y políticas de género." *Boletín del Programa de Pobreza y Políticas Sociales de SUR* 29:1–13.

Capeling-Alakija, Sharon. 1994. Excerpts from the statement made by Sharon Capeling-Alakija, launching the Human Development Report 1994 at the University of Ottawa on June 1, 1994. http://www.ncf.ca/freenet/rootdir/menus/orgs/global/unac-ncrb/newsletters/Aug-94-Bulletin/We-cannot.

Carlson, Marifan. 1988. *¡Feminismo! The Woman's Movement in Argentina from Its Beginnings to Eva Perón*. Chicago: Academy Chicago Publishers.

Carrasco Gutiérrez, Ana María. 2002. "Revisitando Chile: Identidades, mitos e historias." *Comisión Bicentenario*. http://www.bicentenario.gov.

Carrasco Gutiérrez, A., and C. Figueroa Garavagno. 1998. "Mujeres y acción colectiva: Participación social y espacio local (Un estudio comparativo en sociedades minero-fronterizas: Tarapacá, Lota, Coronel, 1900–1920)." *Revista proposiciones* 28:1–23.

Catrileo, María. 2005. *Diccionario lingüístico-etnográfico de la lengua Mapuche: Mapudungún- Español-English*. Santiago: Editorial Andrés Bello.

Censi, Florencia. n.d. "Comparaciones internacionales: El tercer sector debe crecer más en nuestro país." *Cambio cultural-tercer sector*. http://www.cambiocultural.com.ar.

Centro Nacional de Organizaciones de la Comunidad (CENOC). 2006. *Nueva información sobre las organizaciones en Argentina*. Buenos Aires: CENOC.

Cháneton, July. 1992. "Feminismo y movimiento social de mujeres: Historia de un malentendido." *Feminaria* 5:15–19.

Chant, Sylvia, and Nikki Craske. 2003. *Gender in Latin America*. New Brunswick, NJ: Rutgers University Press.

Chejter, Silvia, and Claudia Laudano. n.d. "Género en los movimientos sociales en Argentina." *CECYM*. http://www.cecym.org.ar.

Ching, Erik, and Virginia Tilley. 1998. "Indians, the Military and the Rebellion of 1932 in El Salvador." *Journal of Latin American Studies* 30 (February): 121–156.

Chuchryk, Patricia M. 1994. "From Dictatorship to Democracy: The Women's Movement in Chile." In *The Women's Movement in Latin America*, ed. Jane S. Jaquette, 65–108. Boulder, CO: Westview Press.

Ciria, Alberto. 1983. "Flesh and Fantasy: The Many Faces of Evita (and Juan Peron)." *Latin American Research Review* 18:150–165.

Clendinnen, Inga. 1987. *Ambivalent Conquests: Maya and Spaniard in Yucatan, 1517–1570*. New York: Cambridge University Press.

Cobley, Alan. 2001. "Institutionalized Violence and the Role of Human Sympathy: The Case of the Eminent Persons Group to South Africa." In *Stronger, Surer, Bolder Ruth Nita Barrow: Social Change and International Development*, ed. E. Barriteau and A. Colbey, 127–135. Kingston, Jamaica: University of West Indies Press.

Collins, Patricia Hill. 1991. *Black Feminist Thought: Knowledge, Consciousness, and the Politics of Empowerment*. New York: Routledge.

Comisión de Derechos Humanos de El Salvador (CDHES). 2005a. *Informe 2005 . . . El Salvador 2005: Criminalidad, pobreza y vulnerabilidad*. San Salvador: CDHES.

———. 2005b. "Insumos para un informe alternativo al Comité de Derechos Económicos, Sociales y Culturales: Documento de trabajo." Working paper, CDHES.

Comisión Organizadora XIX Encuentro Nacional de Mujeres. 2004. "XIX Encuentro Nacional de Mujeres 8, 9, 10 de octubre de 2004: Conclusiones." http://www .rimaweb.com.ar/encuentros/conclusionesXIXENMmza.pdf.

Consejo Nacional de la Mujer. 1994. *Las organizaciones no gubernamentales. Informe nacional: Situación de mujer en la última década en la República Argentina*. Buenos Aires: CNM Ediciones.

Cook, Bernard. 2006. *Women and War: A Historical Encyclopedia from Antiquity to the Present*. Vol. 1. ABC-CLIO.

Correa, María José, and Olga Ruiz. 2001. "Memoria de las mujeres . . . Espacios e instancias de participación: Prensa feminista, centros anticlericales Belén De Zárraga y teatro obrero." *Universidad de Chile*. http://www.uchile.cl/facultades/ filosofía/publicaciones/cyber/ cyber19/ correaruiz.html.

Cosgrove, Serena. 1999. "Give Them the Credit They Deserve: Salvadoran Market-women and Micro-Enterprise Lending in Apopa and Nejapa, El Salvador." PhD diss., Northeastern University.

———. 2002. "Levels of Empowerment: Marketers, Micro-Enterprise Lending NGOs, and the Municipalities of Nejapa and Apopa, El Salvador." *Latin American Perspectives* 29 (5): 48–65.

Craske, Nikki. 2003. "Gender, Poverty, and Social Movements." In *Gender in Latin America*, ed. Sylvia Chant with Nikki Craske, 46–70. New Brunswick, NJ: Rutgers University Press.

Dalton, Roque. 2007. *Miguel Mármol: Los sucesos de 1932 en El Salvador*. San Salvador: UCA Editores.

Danner, Mark. 1993. "The Truth of El Mozote." *New Yorker*, December 6. http://www .markdanner.com/articles/show/the_truth_of_el_mozote.

Datta, Kavita, and Cathy McIlwaine. 2000. "Empowered Leaders? Perspectives on Women Heading Households in Latin America and Southern Africa." *Gender and Development* 8 (3): 40–49.

Deere, Carmen Diana, and Magdalena Leon. 2001. *Empowering Women: Land Rights in Latin America*. Pittsburgh, PA: University of Pittsburgh Press.

De la Maza E., Gonzalo. 2003. "Sociedad civil y democracia en Chile." In *Sociedad civil, esfera pública y democracia en América Latina, Andes y Cono Sur*, ed. Aldo Panfichi, 211–240. Mexico City: Fondo de Cultura Económica.

Departamento de Sociologia y Ciencias Políticas, Universidad Centroamericano "José Simeon Cañas." 2009. "Y el resultado de la participación política de las mujeres fue." *El Salvador 2009 . . . en la mira* 22:2.

Díaz, Paula, and Romina Pizzorno. 2000. *XV Encuentro Nacional de Mujeres: 14, 15 y 16 de octubre del 2000, Paraná, Provincia de Entre Ríos, Argentina.* http://www .herramienta.com.ar/varios/14/14–13–2.html.

Di Lisia, María Herminia Beatriz. 1997. "Mujeres, participación y relaciones de género." Paper presented at the II Jornadas de Antropología del MERCOSUR, Fronteras Culturales y Ciudadanía, Facultad de Ciencias Humanas, Universidad Nacional de La Pampa, Argentina.

Dillon, Marta. 2004. "Rebelión en Piquete." *Página/12* (Buenos Aires), July. http://www .pagina12.com.ar/diario/suplementos/las12/13–1297.html.

Dore, Elizabeth, and Maxine Molyneux, eds. 2000. *Hidden Histories of Gender and the State in Latin America.* Durham, NC: Duke University Press.

Drayton, Kathleen. 2001. "A West Indian Feminist Consciousness." In *Stronger, Surer, Bolder Ruth Nita Barrow: Social Change and International Development*, ed. E. Barriteau and A. Colbey, 19–25. Kingston, Jamaica: University of West Indies Press.

Durston, John, and Daniel Duhart. n.d. "Recursos socioculturales de los jóvenes mapuches: ¿Un potencial para el fortalecimiento de los programas de capacitación?" *Red Latinoamercana de Jóvenes Rurales (CIDER).* http://www.iica.org.uy/ redlat/mat/durston_j.htm.

Edwards, Michael. 2004. *Civil Society.* Cambridge, UK: Polity Press.

Enslin, Elizabeth. 1994. "Beyond Writing: Feminist Practice and the Limitations of Ethnography." *Cultural Anthropology* 9:537–568.

Erkut, Sumru, and Winds of Change Foundation. 2001. *Inside Women's Power: Learning from Leaders (CRW Special Report No. 28).* Wellesley, MA: Wellesley Centers for Women/Wellesley College.

Fagen, Patricia Weiss, and Sally W. Yudelman. 2001. "El Salvador and Guatemala: Refugee Camp and Repatriation Experiences." In *Women and Civil War: Impact, Organizations, and Action*, ed. Krishna Kumar, 79–96. Boulder, CO: Lynne Rienner Publishers.

Falú, Ana. 2000. "Noticias." *Boletín CINU (Centro de Información para la Argentina y el Uruguay- Naciones Unidas).* http://www.unic.org.ar.

Faron, Louis C. 1968. *The Mapuche Indians of Chile.* Prospect Heights, IL: Waveland Press.

Feijoó, María del Carmen, and Monica Gogna. 1990. "Women in the Transition to Democracy." In *Women and Social Change in Latin America*, ed. Elizabeth Jelin, 79–114. London: Zed Books.

Feijoó, María del Carmen, with Marcela María Alejandra Nari. 1994. "Women and Democracy in Argentina." In *The Women's Movement in Latin America*, ed. Jane S. Jaquette, 109–130. Boulder, CO: Westview Press.

Feitlowitz, Marguerite. 1998. *A Lexicon of Terror: Argentina and the Legacies of Torture.* New York: Oxford University Press.

Femenía, Nora Amalia. 1987. "Argentina's Mothers of Plaza de Mayo: The Mourning Process from Junta to Democracy." *Feminist Studies* 13 (1): 9–18.

Fine, Michelle. 1994. "Working the Hyphens: Reinventing Self and Other in Qualitative Research." *Handbook of Qualitative Research*. Ed. Norman K. Denzin and Yvonna S. Lincoln. Thousand Oaks, CA: Sage Publications.

Fonow, Mary Margaret, and Judith C. Cook, eds. 1991. *Beyond Methodology: Feminist Scholarship as Lived Research*. Bloomington: Indiana University Press.

Foerster G., Rolf. 2001. "Sociedad mapuche y sociedad chilena: La deuda histórica." *Polis: Revista Académica de la Universidad Bolivariana* 1:2. http://www.revistapolis.cl.

Foley, Michael W. 1996. "Laying the Groundwork: The Struggle for Civil Society in El Salvador." *Journal of Interamerican Studies and World Affairs* 38 (1): 67–104.

Foley, Michael W., and Bob Edwards. 1996. "The Paradox of Civil Society." *Journal of Democracy* 7:38–52.

Franceschet, Susan. 2003. "'State feminism' and Women's Movements: The Impact of Chile's Servicio Nacional de la Mujer on Women's Activism." *Latin American Research Review* 38 (1): 9–40.

Fraschini, Mariano. n.d. "El movimiento feminista ante las políticas neoliberales de los '90." *Agenda de las Mujeres (El portal de las mujeres argentinas, iberoamericanas y del MERCOSUR)*. http://www.agendadelasmujeres.com.ar.

Fraser, Nicholas, and Marysa Navarro. 1980. *Evita: The Real Lives of Eva Perón*. London: André Deutsch.

Freeman, Sue J. M., Susan C. Bourque, and Christine M. Shelton, eds. 2001. *Women on Power: Leadership Redefined*. Boston: Northeastern University Press.

Friedman, Elisabeth J. 2005. "The Reality of Virtual Reality: The Internet and Gender Equality Advocacy in Latin America." *Latin American Politics and Society* 47 (3): 1–34.

———. 2009. "Gender, Sexuality and the Latin American Left: Testing the Transformation." *Third World Quarterly* 30 (2): 415–433.

———. Forthcoming. "Seeking Rights from the Left: Gender and Sexuality in Latin America." In *Rethinking Global Women's Movements*, ed. Amrita Basu. Boulder, CO: Westview Press.

Fuller, Norma. 2003. "Work and Masculinity among Peruvian Urban Men." Paper presented in DAW with ILO, Brasília, Brazil, October. http://www.un.org/womenwatch/daw/egm/men-boys2003/EP9-Fuller.pdf.

Gailey, Christine. 1988. "Evolutionary Perspectives on Gender Hierarchy." In *Analyzing Gender*, ed. B. Hess and M. Ferree, 32–67. London: Sage.

García-Guadilla, María Pilar, and Carlos Peréz. 2002. "Democracy, Decentralization, and Clientelism: New Relationships and Old Practices." *Latin American Perspectives* 29 (5): 90–109.

Gaviola, Edda, Lorella Lopresti, and Claudia Rojas. 1988. *Nuestra Historia de Mujeres*. Santiago: Ediciones La Morada.

Gaviola, Edda, Eliana Largo, and Sandra Palestro. 1992. "Si la mujer no está, la democracia no va." *Revista Proposiciones* 28:79–85.

Geiger, Susan. 1990. "What's So Feminist About Women's Oral Histories?" *Journal of Women's History* 2 (Spring): 169–182.

Gould, Jeffrey L., and Aldo Lauria-Santiago. 2004. "'They Call Us Thieves and Steal Our Wage': Toward a Reinterpretation of the Salvadoran Rural Mobilization, 1929–1931." *Hispanic American Historical Review* 84 (2): 191–237.

Gramsci, Antonio. 2000. *The Antonio Gramsci Reader: Selected Writings 1916–1935*. Ed. David Forgacs. New York: New York University Press.

Growth and Equity through Micro-Enterprise Investments and Institutions (GEMINI). 1991. "Ecuador Micro-Enterprise Sector Assessment: Key Characteristics of the Micro-enterprise Sector." *GEMINI* 12. A book-length manuscript.

Gutiérrez Castañeda, Griselda. 2001. "El ejercicio de la ciudadanía de las mujeres y su contribución a la democracia." *Revista Debate Feminista* 23:125–137.

Guy, Donna. 1981. "Women, Peonage, and Industrialization: Argentina, 1810–1914." *Latin American Research Review* 16:65–89.

———. 1988. "White Slavery, Public Health, and the Socialist Position on Legalized Prostitution in Argentina, 1913–1936." *Latin American Research Review* 23:60–80.

Hall, Budd L. 2001. "A Personal Reflection on Nita Barrow and the International Council for Adult Education." In *Stronger, Surer, Bolder Ruth Nita Barrow: Social Change and International Development*, ed. E. Barriteau and A. Colbey, 177–187. Kingston, Jamaica: University of West Indies Press.

Harding, Sandra. 1987. *Feminism and Methodology: Social Science Issues*. Bloomington: Indiana University Press.

Hartnell, Caroline, and Kavita Ramdas. 2004. "Focus on . . . Investing in Women: Kavita Ramdas Interview." *Alliance* 9. http://www.allavida.org/alliance/scpo4b .html.

Heckathorn, Douglas D. 1997. "Respondent-Driven Sampling: A New Approach to the Study of Hidden Populations." *Social Problems* 44 (2): 174–199.

Heinrich, V. Finn, ed. 2007. *CIVICUS Global Survey of the State of Civil Society*. Vol. 1, *Country Profiles Civil Society Index Project 2003–2006 Phase*. Bloomfield, CT: Kumarian Press.

Herrera, Morena S., Blanca M. Benavides, Christine Hopkins Damon, Flora Blandón de Grajeda, FUNDE; Ana L. Ugarte, Rubidia Martínez, Laura Romero, Colectivo Feminista para el Desarrollo Local; Olga L. Rodríguez, Las Dignas; Nancy Orellana, Candelaria Navas, IMU; Silvia Matus, Melisa Oliva, Las Mélidas; Jeannette Urquilla, Ledy Moreno, Vilma Vaquerano, Jorge Vargas. 2008. *Movimiento de Mujeres en El Salvador 1995–2006: Estrategias y miradas desde el feminismo*. San Salvador: FUNDE.

Herrera, Morena S. 2008. "Capítulo II: Marco de referencia: Movimiento de Mujeres en El Salvador 2005–2006: Estrategias y miradas feministas." In *Movimiento de Mujeres en El Salvador 1995–2006: Estrategias y miradas desde el feminismo*, 27–60. San Salvador: FUNDE.

Herrera, Morena S., Blanca M. Benavides, Christine Hopkins Damon, and Flora Blandón de Grajeda. 2008. "Capítulo V: Análisis de las estrategias multitemáticas del Movimiento de Mujeres y feministas." In *Movimiento de Mujeres en El Salvador 1995–2006: Estrategias y miradas desde el feminismo*, 177–235. San Salvador: FUNDE.

Hirsch, Silvia Maria. 2004. "Solidarity and Civic Participation: The Politics of a Soup Kitchen in Buenos Aires." Paper presented at the Latin American Studies Association XXV International Congress: Los Angeles, October 2004.

Hitt, Jack. 2006. "Pro-Life Nation." *New York Times*, April 9.

Hodgkinson, Virginia A., and Michael W. Foley, eds. 2003. *The Civil Society Reader.* Hanover: University Press of New England.

Hopkins Damon, Christine. 2008. "Capítulo III: Contexto." In *Movimiento de Mujeres en El Salvador 1995–2006: Estrategias y miradas desde el feminismo,* 61–83. San Salvador: FUNDE.

Htun, Mala. 1997. *Moving into Power: Expanding Women's Opportunities for Leadership in Latin America and the Caribbean (a Study on the Status of Women's Leadership).* Washington, DC: Inter-American Development Bank.

———. 1998. *Women's Political Participation, Representation, and Leadership in Latin America.* Boston: Weatherhead Center for International Affairs at Harvard University.

———. 2003. *Sex and the State: Abortion, Divorce, and the Family under Latin American Dictatorships and Democracies.* Cambridge: Cambridge University Press.

Huenchuán Navarro, Sandra. 1995. "Mujeres indígenas en la Araucanía: Huellas demográficas y de sus condiciones de vida." *Fundación Rehue.* http://www.xs4all .nl/~rehue/art/huen1.html.

Huitraqueo Mena, Eliana. 2007. "Las mujeres mapuche y su participación en escenarios organizativos: El caso de la IX región, Chile." In *Mujeres Indígenas, Territorialidad y Biodiversidad en el Contexto Latinoamericano,* ed. L. M. Donato, E. M. Escobar, P. Escobar, A. Pazmiño, and A. Ulloa, 63–78. Bogotá: Universidad Nacional de Colombia.

Instituto Nacional de Estadística y Censos. INDEC. 2001. *Censo Nacional de Población, Hogares y Viviendas 2001.* Buenos Aires: Instituto Geográfico Militar. http://www .indec.gov.ar/.

Instituto Salvadoreño para el Desarrollo de la Mujer (ISDEMU). 2005. *Política nacional de la mujer.* San Salvador: ISDEMU. http://www.isdemu.gob.sv/documentos/ PNM%20PA2005–2009.pdf.

Inter-American Development Bank (IADB). 1995. *Women in the Americas: Bridging the Gender Gap.* Washington, DC: IADB.

Irarrázaval, Ignacio, Eileen Hairel, S. Wojciech Sokolowski, and Lester Salamon. 2006. *Comparative Nonprofit Sector Project Chile.* Santiago: Johns Hopkins University / UNDP / FOCUS Estudios y Consultorias.

James, Daniel. 2000. *Doña María's Story: Life History, Memory, and Political Identity.* Durham, NC: Duke University Press.

Jaquette, Jane S., ed. 1994. *The Women's Movement in Latin America: Participation and Democracy.* Boulder, CO: Westview Press.

Jara, Paola, Eliana Largo, and Luis Lobos. 2003. *Mujer mapuche y desarrollo: Miradas y huellas de cambio.* Temuco: Pehuén Editores.

Jelin, Elizabeth, ed. 1990. *Women and Social Change in Latin America.* London: Zed Books.

John, Mary. 1988. "Postcolonial Feminists in the Western Intellectual Field: Anthropologists and Native Informants?" *Inscriptions* 5:49–73.

Kampwirth, Karen. 2004. *Feminism and the Legacy of Revolution: Nicaragua, El Salvador, and Chiapas.* Athens, OH: Ohio University Press.

Klubock, Thomas. 1992. "Sexualidad y proletarización en la mina El Teniente." *Revista Proposiciones* 21:45–54.

LaFeber, Walter. 1984. *Inevitable Revolutions: The United States in Central America.* New York: W. W. Norton and Co.

Laudano, Claudia, and Silvia Chejter. 2002. "Capitulo I: Piqueteras." *Revista Travesías* 11:5–39.

Lavrin, Asunción. 1995. *Women, Feminism, and Social Change in Argentina, Chile, and Uruguay 1890–1940.* Lincoln: University of Nebraska Press.

Lernoux, Penny. 1980. *Cry of the People: The Struggle for Human Rights in Latin America— The Catholic Church in Conflict with U.S. Policy.* New York: Penguin Books.

Lind, Amy. 1992. "Power, Gender, and Development: Popular Women's Organizations and the Politics of Needs in Ecuador." In *The Making of Social Movements in Latin America: Identity, Strategy, and Democracy*, ed. Arturo Escobar and Sonia E. Alvarez, 134–149. Boulder, CO: Westview.

Lorber, Judith. 1994. *Paradoxes of Gender.* New Haven, CT: Yale University Press.

Luciak, Ilja A. 1998. "Gender Equality and Electoral Politics on the Left: A Comparison of El Salvador and Nicaragua." *Journal of Interamerican Studies and World Affairs* 40 (1): 39–66.

Luna, Elba, and Alejandra Morales. 1998. "El fortalecimiento institucional y los desafíos del desarrollo." In *Con-Juntos: Sociedad Civil en Argentina*, 242–253. Buenos Aires: EDILAB.

Luna, E., N. Sanchís, A. Cousouschi, and M. Muro de Nadal. 1999. "Comisión ad hoc para el seguimiento del plan de acción de la IV conferencia mundial sobre la mujer." In *Unidas: Directorio de Organizaciones de Mujeres*, 9–15. Buenos Aires: Gama Producción Gráfica.

Madison, James. 2003. "The Federalist, No. 10." In *The Civil Society Reader*, ed. Virginia A. Hodgkinson and Michael W. Foley," 70–75. Lebanon, NH: University Press of New England.

Mallon, Florencia E. 2005. *Courage Tastes of Blood: The Mapuche Community of Nicolás Ailío and the Chilean State, 1906–2001.* Durham, NC: Duke University Press.

Mariman, José A. 1997. "Movimiento mapuche y propuestas de autonomía en la década post dictadura." http://www.mapuche.info/mapuint/jmar4a.htm.

Mariman Quemenado, Pablo. 1998. "Elementos de historia mapuche." *Fundación Rehue.* http://www.xs4all.nl/~rehue/art/mariman.html.

Marin, Llanca. 2005. "Contra el patriarcado occidental: La matria mapuche." *Enlace Mapuche Internacional.* http://www.mapuche-nation.org/espanol/html/articulos/art-77.htm.

Martins Costa, Delaine, and Gleisi Heisler Neves. 1996. "Feminism and Institutional Development: Women's NGOs in Brazil and Peru." In *Women's Leadership in a Changing World: Reflecting on Experience in Latin America and the Caribbean*, 44–61. New York: UNIFEM.

Marx, Karl. 2003. From "On the Jewish Question." In *The Civil Society Reader*, ed. Virginia A. Hodgkinson and Michael W. Foley, 96–112. Lebanon, NH: University Press of New England.

Mayoux, Linda. 2001. "Tackling the Down Side: Social Capital, Women's Empowerment and Micro-Finance in Cameroon." *Development and Change* 32:435–464.

McIlwaine, Cathy. 1998a. "Civil Society and Development Geography." *Progress in Human Geography* 22:415–424.

———. 1998b. "Contesting Civil Society: Reflections from El Salvador." *Third World Quarterly* 19:651–672.

Mercer, Marilyn. 1998. "Feminism in Argentina." http://www.cddc.vt.edu/feminism/arg.html.

Ministerio del Interior (Chile). 1991. "Informe de la Comisión Nacional de Verdad y Reconciliación (Informe Rettig)." http://www.ddhh.gov.cl/ddhh_rettig.html.

———. 2004. "Informe de la Comisión Nacional sobre Prisión Política y Tortura (Informe Valech)." http://www.comisiontortura.cl/index.html.

Mitlin, Diana. 2000. "Civil Society and Urban Poverty: Overview of Stage One City Case Studies." http://www.idd.bham.ac.uk/research/Projects/urban-governance/resource_papers/theme_papers/6_urbenvironment.pdf.

Molyneux, Maxine. 1985. "Mobilization without Emancipation? Women's Interests, the State, and Revolution in Nicaragua." *Feminist Studies* 11 (2): 227–254.

———. 1986. "No God, No Boss, No Husband: Anarchist Feminism in Nineteenth-Century Argentina." *Latin American Perspectives* 13:119–145.

Montesino, Sonia. 1992. "Presencia y ausencia: Género y mestizaje en Chile." *Revista proposiciones* 21: 18–19.

Montgomery, Tommie Sue. 1995. *Revolution in El Salvador: From Civil Strife to Civil Peace.* San Francisco: Westview Press.

Moodie, Ellen. 2006. "Microbus Crashes and Coca Cola Cash: The Value of Death in 'Free-Market' El Salvador." *American Ethnologist* 33 (1): 63–80.

Moreno, Sandra. 2006. *Soy feminista, ¡Y qué!* San Salvador: Algier's Impresores.

Morgan, Betsy, and Serena Gosgrove [*sic*]. 1994. "Seizing History in El Salvador." *On the Issues* (Winter): 28–35.

Morgan, Robin. 1989. *The Demon Lover: On the Sexuality of Terrorism.* New York: Norton.

Morrison, Andrew, Mary Ellsberg, and Sarah Bott. 2004. "Addressing Gender-Based Violence in the Latin American and Caribbean Region: A Critical Review of Interventions." *World Bank Policy Research Working Paper 3438.*

Moser, Caroline O. N. 1993. *Gender Planning and Development: Theory, Practice and Training.* New York: Routledge.

Moya-Raggio, Eliana. 1984. "'Arpilleras': Chilean Culture of Resistance." *Feminist Studies* 10 (2): 277–290.

Murray, Kevin. 1997. *El Salvador: Peace on Trial.* London: Oxfam.

Naciones Unidas. 2007. *De la locura a la esperanza: La guerra de 12 años en El Salvador / Informe de la Comisión de la Verdad 1992–1993.* San Salvador: Editorial Arcoiris.

Narayan, Kirin. 1993. "How Native Is a 'Native' Anthropologist?" *American Anthropologist* 95:671–686.

Nash, June, and Helen Safa, eds. 1985. *Women and Change in Latin America.* New York: Bergin and Garvey.

National Security Archive. 2004. "Electronic Briefing Book No. 110." http://www.gwu.edu/~nsarchiv/NSAEBB/NSAEBB110/.

Odendahl, Teresa, and Michael O'Neill. 1994. *Women and Power in the Nonprofit Sector*. San Francisco: Jossey-Bass.

Paine, Thomas. 2003. From *Rights of Man*. In *The Civil Society Reader*, ed. Virginia A. Hodgkinson and Michael W. Foley, 63–69. Lebanon, NH: University Press of New England.

Painemal, America Millaray. 2005. "El velo de la mujer mapuche." *Boletín IFP Fundación Equitas* 12. http://boletin.fundacionequitas.org/12/12.4.htm.

Painemal, A. Millaray, and Sara MacFall. 2000. "La resistencia cultural . . . Ser mujer mapuche en el Chile del 2000." *Revista Lola Press* 1. http://www.lolapress.org/elec1/artspanish/ pain_s.htm.

Panfichi, Aldo. 1999. "Andean and Southern Cone Report: Civil Society and Democratic Governance in South America (Document for Discussion)." http://nt1.ids .ac.uk/ids/civsoc/docs/southcone.doc. (Published in 2003 as *Sociedad Civil, Esfera Pública y Democracia en América Latina: Andes y Cono Sur* [Mexico City: Fondo de Cultura Económico]).

Pardo, Adolfo. 1995. "Historia de la mujer en Chile: La conquista de los derechos políticos (1900–1952)." *Crítica.cl (Revista Digital de Ensayos Críticos e Historia del Arte)*. http://www.critica.cl/html/pardo_01.html.

Peruzzotti, Enrique. 2002. *Civic Engagement in Argentina: From the Human Rights Movement to the "Cacerolazos."* Washington, DC: Woodrow Wilson International Center for Scholars. http://wwics.si.edu/news/docs/perrozutti.pdf.

Pite, Rebekah. 2002. "Breaking the Waves: Centering a History of Argentine Feminisms." Paper presented at the Third Wave Feminism Conference at Purdue University, West Lafayette, IN, April 7, 2002.

Pohlmann, Lisa. 1995. "Ambivalence about Leadership in Women's Organizations: A Look at Bangladesh." *IDS Bulletin* 26:117–124.

Popkin, Margaret. 2004. "The Salvadoran Truth Commission and the Search for Justice." *Criminal Law Forum* 15:105–124.

Power, Margaret. 2002. *Right-Wing Women in Chile: Feminine Power and the Struggle against Allende 1964–1973*. University Park: Pennsylvania State University Press.

——. 2004. "More Than Mere Pawns: Right-Wing Women in Chile." *Journal of Women's History* 16 (3): 138–151.

Pozzi, Pablo. 2000. "Popular Upheaval and Capitalist Transformation in Argentina." *Latin American Perspectives* 27:63–87.

Primer Encuentro de Mujeres Sindicalistas Bonaerenses (Organizado por el Instituto de la Mujer de la Confederación General del Trabajo). 1997. *Revista CNM* 4:42–43.

Quinto Encuentro Feminista Nacional. 2000. "Zita Montes de Oca." Publication available in the Centro de Documentación Subsecretaría de la Mujer, Buenos Aires.

Rao, Aruna, Rieky Stuart, and David Kelleher. 1999. *Gender at Work: Organizational Change for Equality*. West Hartford, CT: Kumarian Press.

Ready, Kelley. 1994. "It's a Hard Life: Women in El Salvador's Economic History." In *Hear My Testimony: María Teresa Tula Human Rights Activist of El Salvador*, by María Teresa Tula, 187–200. Trans. and ed. Lynn Stephen. Boston: South End Press.

Ready, Kelley, Lynn Stephen, and Serena Cosgrove. 2001. "Women's Organizations in El Salvador: History, Accomplishments, and International Support." In *Women and Civil War: Impact, Organizations, and Action*, ed. Krishna Kumar, 183–204. Boulder, CO: Lynne Rienner Publishers.

Rebouças, Lidia. 2008. "A rede das mulheres esquecidas." *Epoca Negócios*. http://epocanegocios.globo.com/Revista/Epocanegocios/0,,EDG84175–8379–18,00-A+REDE+DAS+MULHERES+ESQUECIDAS.html.

Red de Mujeres Rurales de América Latina y el Caribe (Red LAC). 2007. *Una historia muy linda: Perpetuando la Red LAC*. Recife, Brazil: Red LAC.

Reuque Paillalef, Rosa I. 2002. *When a Flower Is Reborn: The Life and Times of a Mapuche Feminist*. Ed. and trans. Florencia Mallon. Durham, NC: Duke University Press.

Reinharz, Shulamit. 1992. *Feminist Methods in Social Research*. New York: Oxford University Press.

Richards, Patricia. 2004. *Pobladoras, Indígenas and the State: Conflicts over Women's Rights in Chile*. New Brunswick, NJ: Rutgers University Press.

Riesco, Manuel. 1998. "Chile, 25 años después." *CENDA (Centro De Estudios Nacionales de Desarrollo Alternativo)*. http://www.cenda.cep.cl.

Rios Tobar, Marcela. n.d. "Paradoxes of an Unfinished Transition: Chilean Feminism(s) in the Nineties." *Archivo Chile Historio Politico Social—Movimiento Popular*. http://www.archivochile.com/Mov_sociales/mov_mujeres/MSmovmujeres0026.pdf.

Rodríguez, Ileana. 1996. *Women, Guerillas, and Love: Understanding War in Central America*. Trans. Ileana Rodríguez with Robert Carr. Minneapolis: University of Minnesota Press.

Rodríguez, María Teresa. 1994. "La relación entre movimiento social y democracia desde una perspectiva de género." In *La mitad del país: La mujer en la Argentina*, 417–429. Buenos Aires: Centro Editor de América Latina.

Rodríguez, Victoria E. 2003. *Women in Contemporary Mexican Politics*. Austin: University of Texas Press.

Rodríguez Alvarez, Olga L. (investigator) and América Romualdo (coordinator). 2008. "Capítulo VI: Estrategias para la erradicación de la violencia contra las mujeres 1995–2006." In *Movimiento de mujeres en El Salvador 1995–2006: Estrategias y miradas desde el feminismo*, 237–349. San Salvador: FUNDE.

Roitter, Mario, Regina List, and Lester Salomon. 1999. "Argentina." In *Global Civil Society: Dimensions of the Nonprofit Sector*, 373–392. Baltimore, MD: Johns Hopkins Center for Civil Society Studies.

Roseberry, William. 1994. "Hegemony and the Language of Contention." In *Everyday Forms of State Formation*, ed. Gilbert M. Joseph and Daniel Nugent, 355–366. Durham, NC: Duke University Press.

Rosenblatt, Karin Alejandra. 2000. "Domesticating Men: State Building and Class Compromiso in Popular-Front Chile." In *Hidden Histories of Gender and the State in Latin America*, ed. Elizabeth Dore and Maxine Molyneux, 262–290. Durham, NC: Duke University Press.

Rotondi, G., A. Soldevilla, A. Domínguez, and M. Rodigou. 1991. "¿Qué nos habla en esta realidad de un movimiento de mujeres en la Argentina?" In

Nuestro movimiento, expresión de una lucha, ed. Di Pascuales, 7–15. Córdoba, Argentina: n.p.

Rowlands, Jo. 1997. *Questioning Empowerment: Working with Women in Honduras.* Oxford: Oxfam.

Ruiz, Olga, Sandra Solano, and Claudia Zapata. 1998. "Redes de mujeres pobladoras de la comuna de San Joaquín: Participación y ciudadanía emergente." *Revista Proposiciones* 28:1–13.

Ruiz Abril, Maria Elena. 2003. "Challenges and Opportunities for Gender Equality in Latin America and the Caribbean." *World Bank Regional Gender Review.* http://wblnoo18.worldbank.org/LAC/LAC.nsf/ECADocByUnid/98CC1A5B56B2733 985256CDF006DF094?Opendocument.

Ruiz Rodríguez, Carlos. 2005. "El pueblo mapuche y el gobierno de la Unidad Popular." *Espacio virtual Chile Vive: Una página abierta a las utopías.* http://www .chilevive.cl.

Sácnz de Tejada, Ricardo. 2007. *Revolucionarios en tiempos de paz: Rompimientos y recomposición en las izquierdas de Guatemala y El Salvador.* Guatemala: FLACSO.

Safa, Helen. 1995. *The Myth of the Male Breadwinner: Women and Industrialization in the Caribbean.* Boulder, CO: Westview Press.

Salamon, Lester M. 1994. "The Rise of the Nonprofit Sector." *Foreign Affairs* 73: 109–122.

Salamon, Lester M., S. Wojciech Sokolowski, and Associates. 2004. *Global Civil Society: Dimensions of the Nonprofit Sector.* Vol. 2. Bloomfield: Kumarian Press.

Salazar, Gabriel. 1992. "La mujer de 'bajo pueblo' en Chile: Bosquejo histórico." *Revista Proposiciones* 21:64–78.

———. n.d. "Reflexiones sobre el Voluntariado en Chile." *Universidad Academia de Humanismo Cristiano.* http://www.piie.cl/documentos/documento/GABRIEL SALAZAR_seminario_uahc.pdf.

Sanford, Victoria. 2001. "From I, Rigoberta to the Commissioning of Truth: Maya Women and the Reshaping of Guatemalan History." *Cultural Critique* 47 (Winter): 16–53.

Schamis, Hector E. 1991. "Reconceptualizing Latin American Authoritarianism in the 1970s: From Bureaucratic-Authoritarianism to Neoconservatism." *Comparative Politics* 23 (2): 201–220.

Schrading, Roger. 1990. *The Repopulation Movement in El Salvador.* New York: Project Counselling Service for Latin American Refugees.

Scott, James. 1985. *Weapons of the Weak.* New Haven, CT: Yale.

Shayne, Julie. 2004. *The Revolution Question: Feminisms in El Salvador, Chile, and Cuba.* New Brunswick, NJ: Rutgers University Press.

———. 2009. *They Used to Call Us Witches: Chilean Exiles, Culture, and Feminism.* Lanham, MD: Lexington Books.

Silber, Irina Carlota. 2004. "Mothers/Fighters/Citizens: Violence and Disillusionment in Post-War El Salvador." *Gender and History* 16 (3): 561–587.

———. 2007. "Local Capacity Building in 'Dysfunctional' Times: Internationals, Revolutionaries, and Activism in Postwar El Salvador." *Women's Studies Quarterly* 35 (3/4): 167–183.

Simon, Laurence R., and James C. Stephens Jr. 1982. *El Salvador Land Reform 1980–1981: Impact Audit*. With supplement by Martin Diskin. Boston: Oxfam America.

Sobrado-Chaves, Miguel, and Richard Stoller. 2002. "Organizational Empowerment versus Clientelism." *Latin American Perspectives* 29 (5): 7–19.

Sobrino, Jon. 1989. *Monseñor Romero*. San Salvador: UCA Editores.

Spelman, Elizabeth V. 1988. *Inessential Woman: Problems of Exclusion in Feminist Thought*. Boston: Beacon Press.

Stephen, Lynn. 1995. Women's Rights Are Human Rights: The Merging of Feminine and Feminist Interests among El Salvador's Mothers of the Disappeared (CO-MADRES). *American Ethnologist* 22 (4): 807–827.

————. 1997. *Women and Social Movements in Latin America: Power from Below*. Austin: University of Texas Press.

Svampa, Marisella, and Sebastian Pereyra. 2003. "Las ambivalencias del protagonismo femenino: Entre el asistencialismo y la politización." In *Entre la ruta y el barrio*, 160–165. Buenos Aires: Editorial Biblos.

Sweetman, Caroline, ed. 2001. *Women and Leadership*. Oxford: Oxfam Publishing.

Tallarico, Valeria Mariana. 1998. "Mujer." In *Con-Juntos: Sociedad civil en Argentina*, 220–235. Buenos Aires: EDILAB.

Tapia Ladino, Marcela. 1994. "Organizaciones de mujeres en Iquique, Chile (1949–1973): Ciudadanas, damas caritativas y mujeres populares." Paper presented at the XI Jornadas de Historia Regional de Chile, Departamento de Ciencias Históricas y Sociales de la Universidad Arturo Prat. http://www.udec.cl/rhistoria/resumen%20ponencias.doc.

"Tercer Sector." 1999. In *Mujeres en Argentina*, 97–99. Buenos Aires: Subsecretaría de la Mujer.

Thompson, A. 1994. "¿Qué es el tercer sector en Argentina? Dimensión, alcance y valor agregado de las organizaciones privadas sin fines de lucro." *CEDES*. http://www.cedes.org/informacion/ci/publicaciones/doc_c.html.

Thompson, A., and M. A. Campetella. 1995. "El tercer sector en la historia Argentina." *CEDES*. http://www.cedes.org/informacion/ci/ publicaciones/doc_c.html.

Tiano, Susan. 1986. "Authoritarianism and Political Culture in Argentina and Chile in the mid 1960s." *Latin American Research Review* 21 (1): 73–98.

Townsend, Janet, Emma Zapata, Jo Rowlands, Pilar Alberti, and Marta Mercado. 2000. *Women and Power: Fighting Patriarchies and Poverty*. London: Zed Books.

Tula, María Teresa. 1984. *Hear My Testimony: Human Rights Activist of El Salvador*. Ed. and trans. Lynn Stephen. Boston: South End Press.

Ulloa, Astrid. 2007. "Introducción: Mujeres indígenas: Dilemas de género y etnicidad en los escenarios latinoamericanos." In *Mujeres Indígenas, Territorialidad y Biodiversidad en el Contexto Latinoamericano*, ed. L. M. Donato, E. M. Escobar, P. Escobar, A. Pazmiño, and A. Ulloa, 17–33. Bogotá: Universidad Nacional de Colombia.

UNIFEM. n.d. "Resistencias: Testimonios de Cinco Mujeres desde Distintos Ámbitos de Participación." In *Argentina: Crisis y resistencias: Voces de mujeres*, 15–28. Buenos Aires: Paz Producciones.United Nations Children's Fund (UNICEF). 2006. *The State of the World's Children 2007 Women and Children: The Double Dividend of Gender Equality*. New York: UNICEF.

U.S. Department of State. 2008. *El Salvador country specific information: Crime.* http://travel.state.gov/travel/cis_pa_tw/cis/cis_1109.html#crime.

Valdés, Teresa, Ana Maria Muñoz, and Alina Donoso, eds. 2005. "1995–2003: Have Women Progressed? Latin American Index of Fulfilled Commitment." New York: UNIFEM.

Valdés, Teresa, and Marisa Weinstein. 1993. *Mujeres que sueñan: Las organizaciones de pobladoras en Chile 1973–1989.* Santiago: FLACSO.

Vázquez, Norma, Cristina Ibáñez, and Clara Murguialday. 1996. *Mujeres~Montaña: Vivencias de guerrilleras y colaboradoras del FMLN.* Madrid: horas y HORAS.

Vianello, Mino, and Gwen Moore, eds. 2000. *Gendering Elites: Economic and Political Leadership in 27 Industrialized Societies.* New York: St. Martin's Press.

Videla de Real, Paula. 1999. "El conflicto mapuche y su impacto en la seguridad nacional." *Centro de Estudios e Investigaciones Militares de Chile.* http://www.cesim.cl.

Viveros Felipe. n.d. "Estado y legalidad: El peso de la noche en la sociedad civil chilena." *Biblioteca del Congreso Nacional de Chile.* http://www.bcn.cl/carpeta_temas/ temas_portada.2005–10–25.4785762907/area_2.2005–10–25.2408148143.

Wachs Book, Esther. 2000. *Why the Best Man for the Job Is a Woman.* New York: Harper-Collins.

Waylen, Georgina. 1994. "Women and Democratization: Conceptualizing Gender Relations in Transition Politics." *World Politics* 46 (3): 327–354.

Williams, Brackette F. 1996. "Skinfolk, Not Kinfolk: Comparative Reflections on the Identity of Participant-Observation in Two Field Situations." In *Feminist Dilemmas in Fieldwork*, ed. Diane L. Wolf, 72–95. Boulder, CO: Westview Press.

Wills, Garry. 1994. *Certain Trumpets: The Call of Leaders.* New York: Simon and Schuster.

Wilson, Marie C. 2004. *Closing the Leadership Gap: Why Women Can and Must Help Run the World.* New York: Penguin Group.

Wolf, Diane, ed. 1996. *Feminist Dilemmas in Fieldwork.* Boulder, CO: Westview Press.

Wolf, Margery. 1992. *A Thrice-Told Tale: Feminism, Postmodernism, and Ethnographic Responsibility.* Palo Alto, CA: Stanford University Press.

World Bank. 2007. *Latin America and the Caribbean—Global Monitoring Report 2007: Confronting the Challenges of Gender Equality and Fragile States.* http://web.worldbank.org/WBSITE/EXTERNAL/EXTDEC/EXTGLOBALMONITOR/EXTGLOMONREP2007/0,,contentMDK:21256825~menuPK:3413287~pagePK:64218950~piPK:64218883~theSitePK:3413261,00.html.

World Health Organization. 2007. *Preventing Unsafe Abortion: Magnitude of the Problem.* http://www.who.int/reproductive-health/unsafe_abortion/map.html.

Ynoub, Roxana Cecilia. 1998. "Analysis of Services Targeting Family Violence against Women in Greater Metropolitan Buenos Aires, Argentina." *Cadernos: Saúde Pública* 14 (1): 71–83. http://www.scielosp.org/scielo.php?pid=°0102-311X 1998000100015&script=sci_abstract.

INDEX

Ad Mapu, 119
Agency of Local Economic Development (ADEL), 156
Alexander, Jeffrey C., 16
Allende, Salvador, 28, 31, 69–72
Alliance for Progress, 81
Almeida, Maria Vanete, 189–190
alternative tourism, 150
Alvarez, Sonia, 189, 190
Alwyn, Patricio, 73
Amat, Lina, 104
Amuedo, Rosa Nair, 42, 60–61, 92, 98
ANAMURI (National Association of Rural and Indigenous Women), 122, 125, 129, 131, 140
ANDRYSAS (National Association of Salvadoran Councilwomen and Women Mayors), 1, 2–3, 175–177, 182, 187, 190
Araujo, Arturo, 77
Argentina: anarchism in, 51–52; anarchist feminism in, 52–53, 115; anti-abortion laws in, 4; authoritarian rule in, 27–28, 30–31, 32; Catholic Church in, 29; *caudillos* in, 48; centralization of, 49; charity activities/efforts, 43, 45, 47–48, 50; Charity Society in, 50, 55; civil war in, 48–49; clientelism in, 55; cottage industries in, 49–50; democracy, return to, 90; dirty war (1976–1983) in, 8, 28, 59–62; disappeared children, 2; disappeared in, 28, 42, 43, 57–58, 59–60; economic modernization in, 49–50; educational system in, 51; European immigration to, 50, 51, 54; exile of activists, 62; female convicts in, 48; gender-based violence in, 101–104; Grandmothers of Plaza de Mayo, 33, 61; immigrant rights in, 51; independence from Spain, 48; inflation in, 96; legal status of women in, 53; Madres de Plaza de Mayo, 2, 31, 33, 59–61, 88, 94, 97, 98, 190; Madres de Plaza de Mayo–Línea Fundadora (Founding Line), 61; Mothers and Grandmothers of Plaza de Mayo, 33;

organizations of interviewees, 199–200; Peronismo in, 55–56; Peronist party in, 4, 30–31, 56–58; Peronist Women's Party in, 54–55; political representation gender inequality, 4; poverty in, 90, 95; privatization in, 90; return of Perón, effects of, 58–59; size/population density, 9; socialism in, 51–52; socialist feminists in, 53; Socialist Party in, 53; Sociedad de Fomento in, 112; standard of living in, 9; suffrage, females, 45–46, 54; suffrage, males, 51; unemployment in, 4, 95, 96, 109–110; union organizing in, 54, 56, 57–58; villa miseria in, 95, 206n6; wage inequality in, 4, 54.
See also Argentina, civil society in; Argentina, civil society organizations; disappeared; neoliberal reforms; Perón, Eva; Perón, Juan
Argentina, civil society in: from colonial–early years of republic, 7, 46–49; from early republic–consolidated state, 49–53; factors in growth of, 95–96; from Peronismo–dirty war, 54–62; at present time, 92–96
Argentina, civil society organizations in: and cartoneros movement, 113–114; and community child care, 111; CSOs, double role of, 90–91; and economic crisis, 109–115; elite women in, 104; fears experienced by women leaders, 92; funding of, 93, 94; gender and leadership, 96–104, 110–111, 114; gender of managers and directors, 94; growth in, 33; identity crisis for men, 112–113; low-income women in, 108–109; middle-class women in, 104–107; motivation for women leaders, 91–92; National Women's Meeting, 91, 108–109; number/distribution of, 93; piqueteros movement, 109–111; *porteña* women leaders, 105, 108; re-emergence of, 90; working-class women in, 108–109

Aristotle, 16
arpilleristas (craftswomen), 73
arranged marriage, 144–145
Avila, Rodrigo, 171
AVINA, 36–37, 186
Aylwin, Patricio, 28

Bachelet, Michelle, 4, 89, 125–126
Bacigalupo, Ana M., 127
Baldez, Lisa, 123
Barrow, Nita, 8, 25–26, 34
Benavides, Blanca Mirna, 86–87, 155, 157, 171, 180, 182
Bengoa, José, 42–43
Binford, Leigh, 83, 85
Bonilla, Blanca Flor, 164–165, 168, 169, 170–171, 172, 183
Borquez, Nelly, 107, 109, 112, 188
Bourque, Susan C., 24, 34
Brodkin Sacks, Karen, 35
Bush, George, Sr., 83
business sector, overlap with civil society, 20

cacerolazos, 96
Caniguan, Jaqueline, 142–146, 153–154
Capeling-Alakija, Sharon, 25
cartoneros (recyclers), 96, 113–114
Casaurang, Susy, 98
Castro, Fidel, 70, 81
Catholic Church: in Argentina, 29; in Chile, 29, 72–73; in El Salvador, 29, 80, 81–82, 87–88, 159
Catrileo, Petronila, I, 117, 136–139, 153–154, 188
caudillos, 48
Center for Legal and Social Studies (CELS), 33
Charity Society, in Argentina, 50, 55
Chile: agriculture in, 70, 139; Allende government in, 69–71; ANAMURI, 122, 125, 129, 131, 140; anti-abortion laws in, 4; arpilleristas (craftswomen), 73; authoritarian rule in, 27–28, 30, 31, 32–33; birth control access, 4; campesino sector, 64; Catholic Church in, 29, 72–73; Chileanization, 64, 66–67, 142–143; Christian Democrats, 133; and CIA, 70–71; CONADI in, 74; Constituent Assembly of Workers and Intellectuals, 68, 69; democratization of, 123, 124–125; disappearance of Allende supporters, 72; economic boom in textiles/clothing, 67; education access, 69; elites, 67–68; elite women in, 45; employment/income gender inequality, 4; ethnic blindness of Chileans, 127; exiled Chileans, 123; exile of Allende supporters, 72; feminists/activists on

working for state, 24–25; femocrats in, 124; forestry in, 138–139; gender roles, 68, 70; health care access, 69; independence from Spain, 66; Indigenous Law of, 130; indigenous women during Spanish Conquest, 62–63; mestizos, 63, 64; National Corporation for Indigenous Development (CONADI) in, 74; National Food Workers Assembly, 68; nationalization in, 70; National Women's Service (SERNAM) in, 25, 74, 125–126, 187; organizational efforts for justice, 67–69, 88; organizations of interviewees, 200–201; Pinochet coup and dictatorship, 8, 71–72; pobladores in, 31, 124; political representation gender inequality, 4–5; Popular-Front leftist coalitions, 69; poverty in, 73; ranchos, 66; SERNAM, 25, 74, 125–126, 187; size/population density, 9; solidarity among poor women, 63; solidarity movement in exile, women in, 114; standard of living in, 9; suffrage, female, 69; torture in, 71; unlawful detention in, 71; and U.S., 70–71; volunteerism level in, 121; women's movement, 122–125; working-class/poor women activism, 7. See also Chile, civil society in; Mapuche people
Chile, civil society in, 120–126; closing of civil society organizations, 72; CONADI, 118–119, 122, 130, 135, 138; growth of organizations in, 33–34; mixed-gender organizations, 119; National Corporation for Indigenous Development (CONADI) 118–119, 122, 130, 135, 138; National Service for Women (SERNAM), 120; need for new leadership models, 117–118; reasons for extensive organizing, 62–74; SERNAM, 120
Chileanization, 64, 66–67, 129, 142–143
Ching, Erik, 79–80
Christian Base Communities, 29, 90, 91
Christian Democrats, Chile, 133
Chuchryk, Patricia, 15, 32
Citizen Participation (Participación Ciudadana), 33
Citizen Power (Poder Ciudadano), 33
Citizens in Action (Ciudadanos en Accion), 33
civic culture, 27–34
civil society, 6–7; defining, 15–16, 21–22; liberal approach to, 18, 19–20; and other sectors of society, 20, 21; and political parties, 20; present-day interpretation, 18; revolutionary approach to, 18–20; roots of, 16–17

civil society organization (CSO), overview of women leaders, 1–2, 7
Clendinnen, Inga, 42, 43
clientelism, 27, 55
Coalition of Women for Democracy, 122–123
Collins, Patricia Hill, 127
colonial law, on legal status of women, 46–47
CO-MADRES, El Salvador, 11
community theater, Mapuche, 151–153
CONADI, 118–119, 122, 130, 135, 138
Concertación, 4
Conscience (Conciencia), 33
consciousness raising, 35–36
convents/nuns, in colonial times, 47
cottage industries, in Argentina, 49–50
culture of resistance, 32

De la Maza, Gonzalo, 33–34, 121
democratization: in Argentina, 90; in Chile, 123, 124–125; civil society role in, 16
de Tocqueville, Alexis, 17–18
dictadura (dictatorship), 28
Dignas (Women for Dignity and Life), 161, 164, 175, 182
dirty war (1976–1983), in Argentina, 8, 28, 59–62
disappear, definition of, 204n6. *See also* disappeared
disappeared, 30; Allende supporters, 72; from Argentina, 28, 42, 43, 57–58, 59–60; children from Argentina, 2; from Chile, 72; from El Salvador, 11, 78, 82, 83; and FEDEFAM, 189; and Madres de Plaza de Mayo, 2, 31, 33, 59–61, 88, 94, 97, 98, 190; and Madres de Plaza de Mayo–Línea Fundadora (Founding Line), 61; and Grandmothers of Plaza de Mayo, 33; women, 25
discrimination: gendered, 3, 11, 86–87, 119; against Mapuche, 118, 119, 147
domestic violence, 5–6, 20, 37, 189, 193; in Argentina, 45, 69, 100, 101–104, 107; in El Salvador, 163, 167–168, 170, 175
Durate, Napoleon, 83

Ecclesiastical Base Communities, 29
education: access in Chile, 69; in Argentina, 51; gender inequality in, 3; Mapuche, 134–135, 137; role in income generation, 51
Edwards, Michael, 16, 18, 22
El Mozote massacre, 84–85
El Salvador: agricultural system in, 76, 77; ANDRYSAS, 1, 2–3, 175–177, 182, 187, 190; anti-abortion laws in, 4; Araujo presidency, 77; ARENA, 155, 173, 174, 175; authoritarian rule in, 27–28, 30, 33; birth control access, 4; Catholic Church in, 29, 80, 81–82, 87–88, 159; civil war, women during, 83–84; civil war in, 8, 80–86; class relations, 182–183; CO-MADRES, 11; Communist Party in, 78, 167; coup by Martínez, 77–78; differences from Argentina, 74; differences from/similarities to Chile, 74–75; Dignas, 161, 164, 175, 182; disappeared persons, 78, 82; dual standard for women, 87–88; Duarte election, 83; economic model, 166–168; elites in, 166–165; El Mozote massacre, 84–85; emergence of feminism in, 45; emigration, 156; employment/income gender inequality, 4; encounter with Spanish, 75–76; exiled persons, 78; feminists/activists on working for state, 25; FMLN, 30, 31, 82–83, 84, 85–86, 155, 159, 173, 175; FMLN, women in, 85, 88, 173, 174; Fraternity of Salvadoran Women, 80; gender and leadership in, 179–184; gender and politics in, 171–179; gender discrimination in, 86–87; hacienda system in, 76, 77; high levels of violence in, 168–171; human rights violations in, 166; independence from Spain, 76–77; Inter-American Women's Commission in, 77; ISDEMU, 161, 162; labor force participation by women, 87–88; *ladino* identity in, 77; La Matanza (the Slaughter) in, 78–80; land issues in, 76, 81; leadership styles, 180–182; Mélidas, 160–161, 164; *mestizaje* in, 77; National Platform of Salvadoran Women, 174–175; National Policy for Women, 161, 175; organizations of interviewees, 201–202; Peace Accords, 28, 34, 155, 158; Peace Accords, limitations of, 164–168; political representation gender inequality, 4; poverty in, 156; Reconstruction in, 34; repression of indigenous people in, 78–80; role of women in society, 156–158; safe sex/birth control, 183–184; Salvadoran women's movement, 162–164; security industry-state connection, 170–171; service provisioning in, 162; size/ population density, 9; standard of living in, 9; suffrage, female, 77; *tendencias* (FMLN groups), 82; torture in, 82, 85; and United States, 80, 81, 83, 86; violence against women in, 170; voting patterns, 174; wartime violence in, 169–170; watchdogs in, 162; working-class/poor women activism, 7. *See also* El Salvador, civil society in

El Salvador, civil society in: growth of organizations, 34; impact of civil war on, 80–87; political autonomy of organizations, 159–161; reasons for extensive organizing, 74–87; re-emergence of, 83; role of civil society in, 158–162; and "shrinking state," 161–162; from Spanish conquest-worker/peasant insurrection, 75–80
employment/income gender inequality, 4
empowerment of women, concept of, 203n2
Enslin, Elizabeth, 106
Erkut, Sumru, 23, 26
Etchart, Nicole, 118
Eva Perón Foundation, 55

Farabundo Martí National Liberation Front (FMLN), 28, 30, 31, 82–83, 84, 85–86, 155, 159, 175; women in, 85, 88, 173, 174
Federation of Community Childcare Centers of La Matanza, 111
Feijoó, María del Carmen, 94, 115–116
female convicts, in Argentina, 48
feminist/feminine dichotomy, 10, 11–12
feminists: in Argentina, 52–53, 115; in Chile, 123–126; in El Salvador, 25, 45
feminist social science, methodologies and dilemmas, 35–37
femocrats, 25, 124
Ferguson, Adam, 17
first wave feminism, 206n29
Flores, Rosibel, 87, 160–161, 179
Foley, Michael, 16, 158, 159
Fourth World Conference on Women (Beijing), 6
Freeman, Sue J. M., 24, 34
Fridman, Viviana, 99, 100, 113
Friedman, Elisabeth, 114, 172
Fuller, Norma, 113
Funes, Mauricio, 33

Galeano, Norma, 110, 188
gaze (mirada), 95, 131
gender: definition of, 13–14; empowerment workshops, 3; hierarchies, 14, 24; and leadership styles, 23–24; stereotypes, 6, 97–98
gendered expectations, 6
gender perspective, 14
Gramsci, Antonio, 17
Grandmothers of Plaza de Mayo, 33 Grandmothers
Grierson, Cecilia, 53
Guirola, Alba América, 170
Guy, Donna, 42

hacienda system, in El Salvador, 76
Hernández Martínez, Maximiliano, 77–78

Herrera, Morena, 85, 170, 171, 178, 179, 180–181, 183, 184
homicide rates, 33, 155, 168–169
homogenizing difference, 13
Hopkins Damon, Christine, 172
Htun, Mala, 5, 203n3
Huelche, Irene, 146–150, 153–154

income generation, and women, 187–188; in Argentina, 104, 112, 113–114; changes in Brazil, 49; in Chile, 73, 121, 136, 154; in El Salvador, 88, 156, 157, 163; gender inequality in, 186–187; in informal sector, 4, 113–114, 187–188; Mapuche, in Chile, 136, 154; by organizations, 34, 121, 136, 163; role in triple workday, 5, 11; role of education in, 51
institucionalizadas, 25
ISDEMU (Salvadoran Institute for the Development of Women), 161, 162

Jamargo, Magdalena, 1, 57–58
Jaquette, Jane S., 30
Jara, Pati (Patricia), 118, 119
Jiménez, Cata, 58, 101–102, 104
Johns Hopkins Center for Civil Society Studies, 94, 120–122
Justo, Alicia, 53

Kennedy, John F., 81
Kirschner, Cristina, 4, 89
Kissinger, Henry, 71

LaFeber, Walter, 81
La Matanza (the Slaughter), 44, 78–80
land issues: in El Salvador, 76, 81; and Mapuche people, 66–67, 138–139
Latin American and Caribbean Committee for the Defense of Women's Rights (CLADEM), 190
Latin American and Caribbean Feminist Meetings, 190
Latin American Federation of Associations for Relatives of the Detained-Disappeared (FEDEFAM), 189
Latin American Index of Fulfilled Commitment, 5
Laub, Claudia, 100, 109
Lauria-Santiago, Aldo, 42
leadership: consensus-building model, 26–27; definition of, 23; feminists on, 24–25; power of, 25–26; stereotypes of, 24, 34–35; styles of, 23; styles of male, 99–100; styles of women, 99, 100
leadership roles: of elite women, 7; impetus for women to assume, 7–8; of women, vis-à-vis state, 24–25
liberal approach, to civil society, 18, 19–20

Lorber, Judith, 14
Lorde, Audre, 24, 25
Luciak, Ilja A., 173, 175

machi, 65, 132, 133, 135, 155
machitun (religious ceremony), 132
Madison, James, 17
Madres de Plaza de Mayo, 2, 31, 33, 59–61, 88, 94, 97, 98, 190
Madres de Plaza de Mayo–Línea Fundadora (Founding Line): Argentina, 61
Magaña, Virginia, 1, 156, 172, 174, 176–177
Mallon, Florencia, 133, 134, 208n2
Malvinas Islands, 88
Manterola, Marta, 95, 113
Mapuche civil society: alternative tourism, 150; Amalia Quilapi, 139–142; ANAMURI, 125, 131, 140; arranged marriages, 144–145; *autonomas*, 126; Chileanization, 64, 66–67, 129, 142–143; Coalition of Women for Democracy, 122–123; community theater, 151–153; conclusions, 153–154; definition of civil society, 120; discrimination, 147; education, 134–135, 137; funding for civil society, 121–122; gender relations, 145–146; gender roles, 135, 138, 140–141, 143–144, 147–148, 152–153; *institucionalizadas*, 126; Irene Huelche, 146–150; Jaqueline Caniguan, 142–146; Julia Matamala, 150–153; land issues, 138–139; language issues, 149; mixed gender organizations, 137, 146; new models for new Chile, 153–154; NGO-ization, 125; paid employment in civil society, 121; Petronila Catrileo, 1, 117, 136–139, 153–154, 188; REMOS, 125; SERNAM, 122, 125–126; Silvia Nain Catrilelbún, 134–136, 153–154; Women for Life, 122–123; women's activism and leadership, 127–133; Women's Initiative Group, 125; work ethic, 141–142
Mapuche Cultural Centers (Centros Culturales Mapuches), 119
Mapuche people, 65–66; adaptation by, 129–130; Ad Mapu, 130; chiefs (*lonkos*), 65; cholera epidemic, 67; cultural centers, 130–131; discrimination against, 118; family lineages (*lofs*), 64–65, 67; gender discrimination, 119; identity issues, 129, 130, 208n2; indigenous religious beliefs, 65; land issues, 66–67; language of, 132, 135; *machi*, 65, 132–133, 135–136, 155; *machitun* (religious ceremony), 132; marriage practices, 130, 143–146, 151–152; military campaigns against Mapuche, 66–67; movement by, 33–34,

39; *ngillatun*, 130, 132, 135–136, 138, 140; organizational efforts for justice, 68; polygamy among, 65, 130, 143; *ranchos*, 67; Rayen Voygue, 2, 131, 134, 135–136, 137, 140, 190, 191; Reche people, 64–65; *reducciones*, 66–67, 129; and sexism, 131; and Spanish colonizers, 64–67; typhoid fever, 65; women leaders, 117; women's activism/leadership, 127–133. *See also* Mapuche civil society study
maquilas (assembly plants), 4
Mármol, Miguel, 78
marriage: arranged, 143–146, 151–152; polygamy among Mapuche, 65, 130, 143
Martí, Agustín Farabundo, 78
Martínez, María Rosa, 99, 100
Marx, Karl, 17
Matamala, Julia, 150–154
Matamoro, Victoria, 62, 95, 96–97, 98–99, 108
McIlwaine, Cathy, 20, 21, 165, 169
Mélidas (Association of the Movement of Women Mélida Anaya Montes), 160–161, 164
mestizos, 46
Molyneux, Maxine, 10–11, 52
mono-cropping, 76, 139
Monterrosa, Celina, 165, 171, 174
Moodie, Ellen, 168, 195
Moser, Caroline, 13–14
Moya, Rita, 118, 185

Nain Catrilelbún, Silvia, 134–136, 153–154
Narayan, Kirin, 36
National Association of Salvadoran Councilwomen and Women Mayors (ANDRYSAS), 1, 2–3, 175–177, 182, 187, 190
National Association of Rural and Indigenous Women (ANAMURI), 122, 125, 129, 131, 140
National Coordinator against Police and Institutional Repression (CORREPI), 33
National Corporation for Indigenous Development (CONADI), 118–119, 122, 130, 135, 138
Nationalist Republican Alliance (ARENA), 155, 173, 174, 175
National Platform of Salvadoran Women, 174–175
National Policy for Women, in El Salvador, 161, 175
neoliberal reform and structural adjustment policies, 3, 90, 109, 205n20
Network of Rural Women in Latin America and the Caribbean (Red LAC), 189
ngillatun (religious ceremony), 130, 132, 135–136, 138, 140

NGO-ization, 125
Nixon, Richard, 71

Olaechea, Carmen, 95, 97–98, 105–107
Orellana, Blanquita, 157, 177

Paine, Thomas, 17
Painemal, A. Millaray, 131, 146
patria potestad (legal rights over minor
    children), 53
Peace Accords, 28, 34, 155, 158, 164–168
Perón, Isabelita de, 59
Perón, Juan, 30–31; coup against, 57;
    criticism of, 56–57; effects of exile of
    from Argentina, 57–58; effects of
    return to Argentina, 58–59; grants
    suffrage for women, 45–46, 54;
    popularity of, 56
Perón, María Eva "Evita," 30–31, 54–56
Peronist party, 4, 30–31, 56–58
Peronist Women's Party, 54–55
Peru, masculinity/work association
    in, 113
Pinochet, Augusto, 8, 28, 44
piqueteros movement, 96, 109–111
policy implications: in Brazil, 189; in
    Guatemala, 189; for organizations
    committed to gender equity, 190–193;
    trends among Argentina/Chile/
    El Salvador, 186–188
political citizenship, 204n5–205n5
political parties, and civil society, 20
polygamy, among Mapuche, 65, 130,
    143
poverty: in Argentina, 90, 95; in Chile, 73;
    in El Salvador, 156; gender inequality
    in, 3
Pozzi, Pablo, 110
practical vs. strategic gender interests, 10
Process for National Reorganization
    (el proceso), 59
public/private dichotomy, 10, 12–13

Quilapi, Amalia, 139–142, 153–154
Quilapi, Dominica, 139–141
Quilapi, Luis, 139–142, 153
Quiles, Gilda, 95, 100, 101, 102–103, 104

Ramos Mejía, Josefa, 48
Rayen Voygue Association of Women
    Farmers and Craftswomen, 2, 131, 134,
    135–136, 137, 140, 190, 191
Ready, Kelley, 85
Reche people, 64–65
reducciones (reservations), for Mapuche,
    66–67, 129
reproductive health: abortion, 4, 5; birth
    control access, 4; gender inequality in,
    5; safe sex/birth control, 183–184

research: methodology of present study,
    37–39; power relations during, 36;
    researcher-participant relationship,
    106; topics for further study, 193–196
Reuque Paillalef, Rosa Isolde, 119, 133,
    134
revolutionary approach, to civil society,
    18–20
Richards, Patricia, 123, 128–129, 130–131,
    205n20
Rios Tobar, Marcela, 34
Rivadavia, Bernardino, 50
Rodríguez, Francisca, 122
Roitter, Mario, 94
Roldán, María, 56
Romero, Oscar, 29, 82
Rosales, Angela, 178, 179, 183, 184
Rouco, Juana, 53
ruka (traditional Mapuche house), 66,
    139, 150

Saavedra, Cornelio, 66, 142
Salamon, Lester M., 22
Salazar, Gabriel, 63
Salvadoran Institute for the Development
    of Women (ISDEMU), 161, 162
Sanford, Victoria, 189
Sarmiento, Domingo, 51
Schiffrin, María Laura, 100, 101
Schmidheiny, Stephan, 186
Scott, James, 32
Second Vatican Council (1962–1965),
    28–29
second wave feminism, 86, 206n29
self-governing private organizations, 22
Shayne, Julie, 114
Shelton, Christine M., 24
Silber, Irina Carlota (Lotti), 167–168, 169,
    195
Sobrino, Jon, 82
social citizenship, 95, 204n5–205n5
social class, 44–45
social movements, defining, 203n3
Spain, independence from, 48, 66,
    76–77
standard of living, 9
Stephen, Lynn, 7, 12–13, 15, 38, 81, 85,
    188–189
stereotypes: gender, 6, 97–98; leadership,
    24, 34–35
strategic vs. practical gender interests,
    10–11; discrimination, 11; domestic
    violence, 5–6, 11; gendered division of
    labor, 11; gender roles, 11
suffrage, by country, 44

technical training, 3
third wave feminism, 206n29
Thompson, Andres, 55, 94

Tilley, Virginia, 79–80
triple burden/workday, 5, 10, 11

union organizing, 54, 56, 57–58
United Nations Development Fund for
    Women (UNIFEM), 25
United Nations Truth Commission, 166
U.S. Agency for International
    Development (USAID), 81

villa miseria, 95, 206n6
violence: domestic, 5–6, 20, 37, 189, 193;
    domestic, in Argentina, 45, 69, 100,
    101–104, 107; domestic, in El Salvador,
    163, 167–168, 170, 175; high levels, in

El Salvador, 168–171; state, 2, 89;
    wartime, in El Salvador, 169–170

wages, gender inequality in, 5
Wills, Gary, 23
winkas, 142, 151, 208n5
woman, defining, 14–15, 206n29
Women's Decade, 6
Women's Voice (La Voz de la Mujer),
    43, 52

Yafluayin Women's Association,
    68

Zetino, Santos, 75–76, 79

ABOUT THE AUTHOR

SERENA COSGROVE has spent the past twenty years working in the field of international development throughout Latin America. In the 1980s she monitored human rights in Nicaragua and El Salvador. In the 1990s she earned a master's degree in social anthropology and a doctorate in sociology at Northeastern University, where she studied the impact of microcredit lending on women clients and the nongovernmental organizations serving them in El Salvador. From 1998 until 2009, she worked for the AVINA Foundation, helping them to promote knowledge flow between staff and partners, as well as between partners across the Americas. Currently Serena is an assistant professor in the humanities at Seattle University, where she teaches courses on global poverty, leadership, and Latin America.

Breinigsville, PA USA
20 July 2010
242149BV00002B/2/P